BRIDGES
Over the
Brazos

BRIDGES
Over the
Brazos

JON McCONAL

TCU PRESS ❖ FORT WORTH, TEXAS

❖   ❖   ❖

In memory
of my son, Patrick,
who loved writing
as much as I do.

To Dr. Ferol Robinson,
who fired my ambition
to become a writer.

❖   ❖   ❖

Library of Congress Cataloging-in-Publication Data

McConal, Jon, 1937-
  Bridges over the Brazos / Jon McConal.
    p. cm.
  Includes bibliographical references.
  ISBN 0-87565-312-X (trade paper : alk. paper)
  1. Bridges--Texas--Brazos River. 2. Bridges--Texas--Brazos River--
Pictorial works. 3. Brazos River Region (Tex.)--History, Local. 4. Brazos
River Region (Tex.)--Biography. 5. Brazos River Region (Tex.)--
Description and travel. 6. McConal, Jon, 1937---Travel--Texas--Brazos
River. I. Title.
  TG24.T4M33 2005
  388.1'32'09764--dc22
                                            2005010870

Lines from "On The River" from THE COLLECTED POEMS OF LANGSTON HUGHES
by Langston Hughes, copyright © 1994 by The Estate of Langston Hughes. Used by permission of Alfred A. Knopf, a division of Random House, Inc.

Jacket photo: The Tin Top Bridge in southern Parker County collapsed in 1980, after
being ripped from its cables by the flooding waters of the Brazos River. Many harrowing
stories are told about crossing the old suspension bridge, built in the early 1900s. Photo
by Byron Scott, courtesy David Scott.

Cover and text design by Bill Maize; Duo Design Group
Printed in Canada

Table of Contents

List of Illustrations

Foreword

❖   ❖   ❖

I'VE KNOWN RIVERS:

I've known rivers ancient as the world and older than the flow
of human Blood in human veins;
My soul has grown deep like the rivers.

LANGSTON HUGHES, 1926

❖   ❖   ❖

*A*s long as man has known rivers, he has longed to explore, navigate, and cross them. The rivers have been man's connection to the Creator and to the rest of creation. Their banks have been the fertile soil that became the breeding grounds for sometimes desperate, often struggling, and occasionally very vibrant communities.

But, the bridge—that man-made span across the river—would become the ultimate connector, tying bank to bank, community to community, people to people.

It didn't surprise me that my friend and colleague, Jon McConal, shared my fascination for rivers and bridges, because my fellow writer has always been an explorer, navigator, and connector. Through his own exploration of places and people he has come to know and because he possesses the most sensitive writer's mind and heart, he naturally became a chronicler of events, a writer who vividly documents the past, and a brilliant storyteller of lives. In many ways, he has been a bridge builder, but that's a foreword for another book.

Great bridges of this country and of the world are a testament to the human imagination and ingenuity. I continue to marvel at their designs—

engineering feats that will stand the test of time—as well as their obvious strength, complexity, beauty, and sheer practical application.

Whether the Golden Gate on the West Coast, the Ambassador in Michigan/Canada, or the Brooklyn in New York, these monuments demand our attention and our respect. But there are thousands of bridges and trestles across this country, spanning noble rivers and lesser streams, which also speak with a quiet eloquence and wonderment.

Jon naturally focused on our native state and that major artery that flows through the very heart of Texas, the Brazos, originally named Brazos de Dios (the Arms of God). He long ago left his first footprints along the banks of the Lone Star State's third-largest river, and few people know the territory around it better than he does. Jon has explored its more than nine hundred miles, and he is quite familiar with the land through which it meanders, the plants and animals that depend on it, and the people who all but worship it.

Yes, Jon knows the Brazos well, and he knows its bridges and people surrounding its levees. His book, *Bridges Over the Brazos*, is a timely documentation of those timeless structures that have amazed Texans for generations. Those bridges he has known since childhood, those wonders he has beheld all his life, take on new meaning and greater significance as he reflects on their creation, their purpose, and most of all the people they serve.

This writer and bridge builder takes a close look at some of Texas' unique and functional bridges and gives the reader a heartwarming glimpse of the spirited individuals and diverse communities existing in their shadows. *Bridges Over the Brazos* is a book that most definitely will connect with the reader.

Bob Ray Sanders
Fort Worth
2004

Preface

The Brazos River's 923-mile spiral from the Texas Panhandle to where it empties into the Gulf of Mexico at Freeport has furnished delightful material for writers since the first settlers came to the state. No one has captured the magic or personality of the river like John Graves did in his wonderful book, *Goodbye to a River*. Several more books have been penned about this river, which according to the *Texas Almanac*, is the largest river between the Rio Grande and the Red River and is third in size of all Texas rivers. Other facts from the *Texas Almanac* about the Brazos say that it crosses most of the main regions of Texas. Those include the High Plains, West Texas Lower Rolling Plains, Western Cross Timbers, Grand Prairie, and Gulf Coastal Plain. The Brazos has a drainage area of nearly 43,000 square miles, and its annual runoff at places along its lower channel exceeds five million acre-feet.

My fascination with the Brazos came from having spent many hours hiking along its banks and camping out on its sandbars. That led to my discovering the bridges that have been built across the river. These bridges, functional and crucial parts of communities, have become landmarks, often used by people when giving directions. A common directive for finding someone's house goes, "Well, I live four and a half miles west of the Brazos Bridge." Bridges are also used in emphasizing nature's dangers from flooding, when people say things like, "Once the water gits up to within a foot of the Brazos Bridge, you'd better pack yore stuff and git out of there."

The millions of gallons of water that flow in the Brazos beneath the bridges find many uses. Twenty-six percent of the water goes for toilet flushing. Every time somebody cleans a chicken along the Brazos, he uses 11.6 gallons of water. Those facts came from the Brazos River Authority.

Eddie Lane of Granbury, a friend, also has a longtime interest in the Brazos and its bridges. He has spent many hours canoeing and camping on the river, and he retraced the canoe Graves' journey so eloquently described in *Goodbye to a River*. "Those trips, plus studying Texas maps and tracing the route of the Brazos from its headwaters to its mouth, made me aware of how important the bridges over the river were to the development of the state," said Lane. "I would bet that better than half of us Texans live within a day's drive of the river. Our early well-being and commercial success depended on the river and a way to cross it." Lane suggested that we follow the Brazos from its beginning to its end and write about its bridges. That suggestion came in 1993 when I still worked for the *Fort Worth Star-Telegram*. The editors did not approve of my proposal for such a project. But, I felt it was a good idea, and when I retired, I talked to Lane again and asked if he were still interested in looking at the bridges. His eyes brightened and he said immediately, "Let's do it."

And so began our journey, and what a journey this has been. In driving more than 4,000 miles to look at sixty-two bridges, we have met many interesting people who live near these bridges—like the elderly man who resides in Jerry's Quarters near Washington-on-the-Brazos and says proof of God can be found by just listening to the wind as it fans the trees along the Brazos River and sends its echoes through bridge structures.

We also heard many stories about the early bridges and saw photographs of some of those structures that resembled Rube Goldberg creations, such as the pontoon contraption once used as a railroad bridge near Richmond. We saw a private bridge made from oil-field pipe and used by a rancher in Stephens County. He drives herds of cattle or hauls cattle and horses packed in a trailer pulled by a pickup truck over this bridge.

Lane and I traveled together to look at most of these bridges. John Tushim, another close friend, accompanied me to look at the first structures north of Abilene. All of us agreed early in this venture that it was important to pinpoint the exact location of the bridges. So the reader will find these locations plus statistical information about each bridge in the final chapter.

But, this is not an engineer's report on the bridges. This is a story of two men with a love of the outdoors, the Brazos River, and the people they met during their journey. I have written about the bridges in the sequence that we visited them. That means that I have started with the bridge in Knox County where we began our adventure. From there, we followed the Brazos until it emptied into the Gulf of Mexico, and I wrote about each bridge. I would also point out that we looked at bridges that crossed over the Brazos and its three upper forks – the Double Mountain Fork, the Salt Fork, and the Clear Fork of the Brazos. These three upper forks are separate rivers from the Brazos that begins where the Double Mountain and Salt Forks flow together in Stonewall County. The Clear Fork joins this main stream in Young County just above Possum Kingdom Lake.

Eddie Lane drew the original maps by hand. Bill Maize of DuoDesign later refined them by computer. They show the specific location of each bridge over the Brazos from the Panhandle to Freeport and may be helpful to others who want to look for the bridges. In my research for this book, I did not find any agency, including the Brazos River Authority and the Texas Department of Transportation, that had anything comparable to these.

I had originally thought about starting each chapter with a short poem about bridges or the river, but one night while Eddie and I were camped at Stephen F. Austin State Park near Richmond, the idea for the short story, "An Episode of Bridges," came to me. A loud thunderstorm that sounded like an elephant stumbling against some giant brass bells had started. Rain began rocketing onto the tin roof of our screen shelter. I got my notebook and began writing the story about a youngster finding true love beneath a bridge over the Brazos River. I have used portions of the story to begin each chapter.

This has been a great experience for many reasons. I have been able to see many of the old-style bridges still in use across the Brazos. The people living near these have told some delightful stories. I hope many of you find

Eddie Lane, left, who accompanied author Jon McConal, right, on trips to look at the sixty-two bridges over the Brazos River.

time to take day trips to visit these bridges and talk to these people. Because of that possibility and in case you might get hungry, I have mentioned some down-home restaurants we found. Don't be surprised if you see Eddie and me sitting at a counter in one of these cafés or standing in the shade of one of the bridges. He's the one wearing jeans, black suspenders, and looks like an old-time lawman. I'm the short guy with the beard.

CHAPTER ONE

Knox County Bridge

❖   ❖   ❖

He had discovered the bridge after years of unhappiness. His
father was a tough man. He dealt that toughness out in liberal por-
tions to his son. Then the boy had found the bridge over the Brazos
River. It became his safe place. But really he used the bridge as a
place to play his harmonica.

He found solace there as he played songs like "That Old Time
Religion" and "I'll Fly Away." The rafters of the bridge, built in the
early 1930s, caught his notes and amplified them. The cars and
trucks passing overhead made booming echoes that sounded like a
bass horn.

Aw, yeah, the bridge was a good place. He was twelve.

❖   ❖   ❖

We left Granbury early one morning and began our first day of bridge
looking. As we drove west, ribbons of gray clouds rolled across the sky. The
recent rains had made the pastures that were aching for moisture a brilliant
green as if giant buckets of green paint had been spilled on them. We
headed north on Highway 277 and passed a scrap yard of old oil-well
pumps lined up along the highway. They looked like aging, skinny-headed
horses standing at feed troughs. We passed through Hawley and then Anson
with its beautiful red sandstone courthouse. We drove past cotton fields
thick with growth. Near one of the fields stood a farmhouse with several

hog feeders placed in its yard. Contented hogs lay in the red clay, which was now mud. I wondered if these hogs were related to the ones that the Spanish explorer Hernando de Soto had brought with him from Cuba. A rancher told me that descendants of those early hogs had escaped and now large feral herds roam in much of the Texas ranching country.

De Soto had been but one of many early explorers who had crossed the Brazos River during their southwest wanderings. Other of those early adventurers included Father Gaspar Jose de Solis, Frenchman Pierre de Pages, Athanase de Mezieres, Pedro Vial, and Coronado Luys de Moscoso. These adventurers had several names for the Brazos. They called it the Colorado, which in Indian meant red, William C. Foster noted in his book *Spanish Expeditions into Texas: 1689-1768*. That name may have come from the fact that the tributaries of the Brazos have their headwaters on the High Plains Plateau in the Texas Panhandle. As a result as explained by Darwin Spearing in his book, *Roadside Geology of Texas*, the Brazos frequently flows red-brown from the red-colored sediment it picks up as it winds across the Permian red beds in the state's northwestern country.

Certainly, the early explorers would have loved having bridges or cross-ings of the river to ease their travels. That finally happened in 1716 when Jose Domingo Ramon forged a road across Texas. Ramon, who was sent to Texas with supplies to open a chain of missions, crossed the Brazos about five miles west of the town of Hearne. He named the crossing that was near the Little River and the Brazos River, Brazos de Dios. It became the principal place to cross the stream for most of the eighteenth century. In his book, *Old Texas Trails*, J.W. Williams said the early Spanish explorers chose the name Brazos de Dios as a way of thanking God for dividing the Brazos into two branches so it could be more easily crossed.

Ramon thanked the Indians for showing him the crossing by serving them barbecued goat and beef. The tables were probably also filled with wild fruit, as reports said the two rivers were separated by about four miles of thick mulberries, pecans, sycamores, cottonwood, grapevines, and wild plums. Ramon also reportedly shot several alligators that the natives feared as they swam in the river.

Those early-day crossings could be difficult. Williams tells about one made by James B. Leach who led a wagon train across Texas in 1857. He crossed the Brazos River near Fort Belknap in Young County, hiring a man who owned a yoke of oxen to pull his wagons across the river. Leach wrote in his diary:

> This plan saved the mule trains much severe labor and straining, the bottoms of the Brazos being of a quicksand nature, and left them in much better plight for the prosecution of the long and tedious journey before them. All of the work necessary to be done being completed and all of the arrangements made for departure, the work of crossing of the wagons was commenced at 10 A.M. and at 3 P.M. the entire train was over the river.

Our arrival at Stamford interrupted my thoughts of those early-day adventures. We headed for Highway 6, a road that stretches on and on so far into the distance that objects on its horizons look out of focus. John Tushim, my driving partner commented on the road.

"Boy, a man could become dizzy if he looked at this stretch of road for very long."

Eventually, Rule, population 698, rolled into our vision with such businesses as an antiques and collectibles store that had an old washing machine sitting out front. The machine featured hand rollers that mashed water out of the wash. Closed signs hung from a drug store, a café, and an ancient filling station. A trailer loaded with aging hay sat beneath the station's old-fashioned overhang. We drove past the Tower Drive Inn Theater that had a "for sale" sign nailed onto its front. The theater reminded me of a story

I wrote one time about a man who lived in this country and owned a drive-in. He started showing X-rated films when business began falling off. "I would get people coming to the movies with paper sacks over their heads," he said. "When they bought their tickets, I recognized them by their voices. I never let on I did. But those people coming to those X-rated movies kept me from going bankrupt."

We passed home gardens with heavy black-eyed peas and tomato vines crawling on vine holders. We saw fencerows where tumbleweeds had lodged in the wires and had not been pulled away. In about two years the sand will bury these fencerows.

"See those, John," I said pointing to what looked like huge drifts of sand. "If you dug beneath those, you would find a fence."

We never had that problem when I lived in West Texas. As a youngster, my job was to take a hoe, cut the tumbleweeds, wrench them from the wire and let them go tumbling across the countryside. Other farmers would burn the tumbleweeds from the fence. They turned this into a social event when they set fire to the weeds at night. That activity sometimes turned into chaos when the fire got out of control. I remembered that happening to a neighbor who had brought his girlfriend to the fencerow one night to watch the burning of the tumbleweeds. He had stationed his younger brother nearby with what he thought was an ample supply of water. When the younger brother saw the fire getting out of control and realized he did not have enough water, he ran out of reach of the flames. After about fifteen minutes, he exclaimed wisely, "Damn, Jimmy Lynn, you durn near burnt up a half mile of fence. I think if you'd taken Essie (the girlfriend) to the movie, it would have been cheaper."

We finally reached Knox City, population 1,219 – nearly a third of the population of the whole county of Knox and home of the seedless watermelon. We passed the Duck Walls Hometown Variety Store and the First Baptist Church that had a sign reading, "Exercise Daily with the

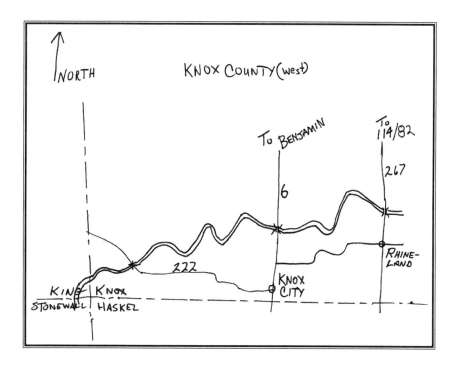

Lord." We went into Sue's, owned by Sue Shortes. The store has a tearoom and a nice collection of antiques, candles, gifts, jewelry, and furniture. Instantly friendly, she said she was born and reared here, graduated from Knox City High School and from Texas Tech at Lubbock. After college, she returned and ranched and farmed for some twenty years until tragedy hit her life.

"My husband and me and my twin girls were coming back from the rattlesnake roundup in Sweetwater, and we hit this pipe that had fallen off a trailer and been left in the highway. It killed him and one of my twins. That happened on March 10, 1991." Her voice got soft and her eyes became misty as she continued. "Yeah, it was terrible. I think about it every day," she said.

I told her we were there to look at what could be construed as the first or one of the first bridges on the Brazos as it begins its more than nine-hundred-mile run to the coast.

"My daddy's family – they were the Days – lived across the Brazos out there close to where the bridge is. They were so poor in those days, they would wade across it without any shoes on. They would ride across it to go get their groceries. That old river . . . oh, my gosh. There are so many memories out there," she said.

The bridge made things easier. She doesn't remember when it was built. But she does remember about that time her grandfather won some land in a card game one night. They later struck oil on that land and . . . no more walking across the river barefoot.

We said good-bye and stopped for lunch at Brenda Jo's at Knox City. The smells of fried chicken, chicken fried steak, and good home cooking enveloped us outside. The luncheon crowd wore mostly baseball caps and straw cowboy hats. They talked about how the recent rains were a gift from God.

"I won't have to say 'sir' to my banker so often now," laughed one rancher.

The food was delicious. I ate a fajita rollup loaded with tender broiled chicken, green peppers, tomatoes, onions, and lettuce. Brenda Larned talked as we ate. She has driven over the bridge for years. But as for special memories . . . well, she tells us about a bridge that really has some memories.

"We used to live in Wellington and my grandmother told me about a person who was kidnapped when Bonnie and Clyde came through there. This person was just a little girl and during a gun battle the police had with Bonnie and Clyde on that bridge, one of her fingers was shot off," she said. "Bridges are good for creating memories like that . . . memories you can hold onto."

A waitress had been listening. When she heard what we were doing, she said, "Gawd, you are writing about the bridges over the Brazos . . . how interesting. Wish I could go with you."

We made our farewells and headed for the bridge. A highway sign warned motorists to watch for wild hogs. Shortly after that we reached the bridge, a beautiful old steel girder type. A thick bed of prickly pears grew through part of the concrete footing. We found a tiny plaque that said the bridge was built in 1936 by the Texas Highway Department. Oran Speer was the contractor. Another sign said the bridge is fifteen feet and ten inches high. We later learned that few of the bridges contain any kind of plaque with statistical information.

We started walking across the bridge. Looking beneath us before the riverbanks began, we saw huge clumps of Johnson grass and salt cedars. We heard a cacophony of grasshoppers and locusts and discovered that locusts are always doing gigs here. Near the center of the bridge, we stopped and looked at the Brazos. The rains that had deluged this country had made the river run bank-full and had turned it into a giant swirl of red colors. The fast-flowing current ate more of the red clay from the banks. Masses of flotsam that looked like dirty red chunks of paint bobbed in the waters. The dirty waters reminded me of one day when I was a youngster and we had gone to Pecos to attend the rodeo. A man named Eugene went with us. Before he would ride in the grand entry, he said he needed to bathe. So my father took him to the Pecos River, which always ran red like the Brazos on this day. Eugene plunged in and washed himself for about five minutes. When he got out, little spirals of mud ran off his body.

"Boy, it feels good to get good and clean," he said.

We looked back along the riverbank. Nearby, an embankment had been used as a backdrop for target practice. I walked to its ragged edges and looked at the piles of empty shell casings. The remains of items used for targets lay in abundance. I kicked at broken beer bottles that I assumed had been tossed into the air and blasted with shotguns. There were also plastic milk cartons and empty coffee cans shredded with bullet holes. And, somebody had propped a target painted with the crude outline of a person against the embankment. Holes from a .22 caliber weapon riddled the target's head and groin area. A final bit of irony lay nearby in what once was a no trespassing sign, so riddled from bullets that it was hard to read the lettering.

The smell of moisture filled the trees and the weeds. I sucked in the smell like I was savoring one of the feasts cooking on the stove of my wife, Jane. I thought of the stories of this country that I had heard from Gerald White of Granbury, who was born near a tributary of the Brazos in Lamb County.

"The population never changes because ever time somebody is born, somebody leaves or dies," he said. He tells the story about a Louis Schrier, a blacksmith of German heritage who decided he would try to take a rowboat from Olton to Lubbock when a Brazos tributary known as Running Water Draw flooded. A man named Slim Ellis accompanied him.

"They picked up a cowboy along the way. And shortly after that they hit a tree in the middle of the stream and swamped the boat. They all were lucky because they grabbed hold of the tree and spent the night on some of its branches. Later, people called Schrier 'Columbus.' He would smile and say, 'Vell, it vas fun.'"

White also knows the dangers of the Brazos when it floods. The year of his birth, 1931, reminds him of that. "My father was drowned that same year in August. He ran his car off into a flooding Brazos and couldn't get out," said White.

As we headed for the second bridge on our trip, I looked at the Brazos and its colors like dried blood. It is a stream not to be taken lightly, a warning I heard many times before we reached the river's mouth on the coast.

CHAPTER TWO

Rhineland Bridge

❖   ❖   ❖

Actually, it was the music made by the Brazos that made him
want to learn to play some kind of instrument. The river's tunes were
wonderful. When the water was down, the softness of the stream's
echo reminded him of a youngster singing the soft part of a hymn. As
the channel enlarged either from local rains or water coming from
upstream, the river's voice became strong like an Italian soloist
booming his rendition of an opera.

Listening to those sounds made him decide that he would learn
how to play a musical instrument. So he went to see the Raleigh
family.

❖   ❖   ❖

We headed for Rhineland and bridge two on our list, passing through
country where Indian conscripts were used by Spanish explorers to mine
copper deposits along the Brazos. Ranching and farming were developed
here in the 1880s. I could picture some of the wagons used in those days
packed with supplies and headed for their destinations when they came
upon the Brazos, which had no bridge. I'm sure profanity flowed as strong
as the flooding river as the drovers and their helpers tried to coax their
wagons and goods across the river. I thought about what Randolph B. Marcy
said. Exploring northwest Texas along the Brazos in the 1800s, he found
plenty of game in the territory but said there was a scarcity of timber for

building. J. W. Williams said Marcy predicted that if people making a living from the land ever densely populated that country, a new industry would have to be started. That industry: the growing of timber to be used for building structures such as houses and bridges.

We breezed through Benjamin, population 264. Clothes hung on lines near a historical marker that said Pleasant C. Sams came to Texas in the 1860s from Arkansas. During the Civil War, he was left in charge of the family mills and was instructed by his father to give the entire flour output to widows of Confederates. In 1862 in Missouri, he sneaked through enemy lines to get his bride. He was successful in finding her and came back to Texas where he became a cattleman, businessman, and financial leader.

We continued on U.S. 82 through Knox County. It was still hard to believe the greenness of the country for this time of year when normally ovens of heat blister the land. In this country, the Brazos River begins what is considered one of the major drainage systems across Texas. "It heads in the high plateau country of the Panhandle and flows across the Caprock edge where its tributaries have cut magnificent canyons. The river then flows across the gypsum plains, red bed terrain, and rolling plains of North Central Texas before it crosses the limestone terrain of the Cross Timbers on its way southwest," writes Darwin Spearing in *Roadside Geology of Texas*.

As we drove, Tushim told of the most interesting bridge he had ever seen – the bridge over Antietam. During the Civil War, a thousand Confederates held the bridge from the attack of thousands of Union troops who thought they had to come across the bridge. The funny thing was, they could have gone a half-mile down the river, where there was a ford, and waded across. Such is the magic of bridges.

We had reached some flatland or bottomland. Our second bridge flashed in the distance. It is one of the newer bridges that are almost devoid of personality. The aches and moans have been eliminated from its roadway when traffic passes over. We walked across the bridge and looked upstream

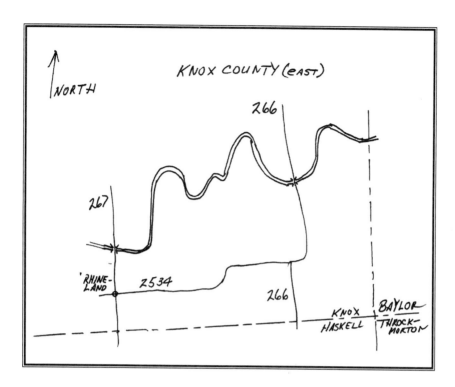

at what apparently are remainders of the bridge this one replaced. Some of the old rock formations still stand with looping cable lines that look like suspenders from an old man's pants. The Brazos whispered to us, carrying its secrets and the secrets of the old bridge down the river. Several head of cattle walked under the bridge. They stopped and looked at us, as though they were asking, "What do you crazy geezers want?"

We stopped at a nearby house to ask for information. Three pit bull dogs greeted us with roars which translated could mean you're not welcome here. We looked in the distance and saw a church in the tiny town of Rhineland. We drove there to try and find information about the bridge. That led us to realize that often when looking for the bridges, you make other interesting discoveries . . . people like Father Jeremy Myers, who stood in his front yard directing landscaping efforts. He has short, thick graying hair and is built like a college halfback.

"I'm a priest in Sherman but I was born and raised here," he said. "If you want some history of the bridge, let me give you a copy of what I wrote for our local history."

He invited us inside his house, built in 1905 and used as a parsonage. The sisters who taught in a Catholic school here lived in the two-story structure. Then it became vacant and remained so for five years.

"That's when I bought it and began refurbishing it," he said.

His efforts show. The house has beaded wood ceilings and wall paneling. The stairway has stunning hand-carved oak along the stairs.

"That's how the people who settled this community did things," he said. He picked up the thick book of the history of the community, *A Century of Faith*. It tells about the German immigrants coming here in wagons in the late 1800s from states that included Nebraska. "Many of these pioneers had been on the road for months when they finally crossed the Brazos River. Some of them had been traveling for years, not able to call any place home until they stepped onto the Knox County land," reads the book. The book describes the building of the magnificent St. Joseph's Cathedral. When a person looks at it, it's hard to believe that such a structure could be found in a tiny town like Rhineland, so far from any other city of size.

"We call it the Cathedral in the Cotton Patch," said Father Myers.

The community actually started building the structure in 1930. But because of the Depression and World War II, it was not finished until November 8, 1951. The more than 80,000 bricks used were handmade by church members. The rather crude machine that shaped the clay by a series of vices and steel blades, all hand powered, is propped against one of the outbuildings. I touched it and pulled one of the levers. It moved slowly. It's hard to believe that 80,000 bricks were handmade in this.

"They had determination in those days. Gosh, I admire that," said Tushim.

Father Myers smiled. "But you've come for information on the bridge," he said. "I wrote something about the bridge for our history. Let me let you read that."

So he handed me the book again. His treatise on the bridge is a philosophy about bridges in life.

To get here from there, you have to cross a bridge. It's a fact of life wherever you go. It begins at the beginning when a child is born. To get from the womb to the world, the child must cross the bridge of birth. Every major step after birth involves crossing a similar bridge. To cross from childhood to adulthood, one crosses the bridge of work. The bridge from being single to being a couple is marriage. And the way from this life to eternal life is across the bridge of death.

It is appropriate that a bridge lay to the north of Rhineland. There, where the Brazos River trails through the terrain, one crosses a bridge. We call it either the Rhineland Bridge, as if it belongs to us, or more often, we simply refer to it as "the bridge," as if there is not another one.

The earliest bridge was several miles up the river. No one seems to know why. A previous writer indicated it was there "for no good reason." Because it was upriver, many parish members who lived on the north side had to drive far out of their way in order to come to the Mass or to bring their small children to school. The thirteenth pastor of Rhineland, Father Boniface Spanke, saw to it that the bridge was moved to a more reasonable location, some two miles northwest of the church. This occurred in the early 1930s.

Another bridge would replace this early one, and it would be even closer to the seat of Rhineland. The Brazos helped in making this possible, busting at the seams in the late 1950s, and busting up the old bridge at the same time. The original beams can still be seen about a mile upriver from the present site. A sturdy steel-and-concrete bridge now lies across the Brazos.

Many memories can be found on that bridge, some good, some not so good. Many lives have been changed because they crossed over the structure. Even today, names from yesteryears are scribbled on the underside, indications of other people who once lived on this side of the Brazos. Mick Birkenfeld drives to the bridge each evening. So does Danny Myers. Maybe others do too. It is a simple ritual before turning in for the evening. They park their vehicles and walk to the edge of the river and take long looks in each direction. They are making sure that all is well in Rhineland.

"For those who have lived in Rhineland but have moved away, the bridge is even more important. It is the way back home, and, as such, it is both cherished and fondly remembered," said the priest.

We stood there for a minute after I had completed reading his thoughts on bridges. Then I asked:

"So do you think today's bridges have the character and personality that the old bridges did?"

"Absolutely not," he said. "Absolutely not. They are totally utilitarian."

I agreed. They serve their purpose well but evoke few memories.

We said our good-byes and went down river to search for the next bridge on our list.

CHAPTER THREE

Baylor County Bridge

❖   ❖   ❖

All of the Raleigh family members had been born with musical talent. The father and one of the sons played the fiddle. The other two sons and a daughter accompanied them on guitars and mandolins. Their music went deep into your soul, down where good feelings are stored like the vegetables canned and put on cellar shelves for future use.

Their fingers were strong and hard. But when they touched the necks of their instruments, their fingers danced lightly like ballerinas, making sounds like the sweet sounds made under the bridge. One night as he listened to them, he made a decision.

He was going to learn how to play the harmonica.

❖   ❖   ❖

We stayed on Highway 6 and went through Benjamin. When we hit Highway 82, we headed east for Seymour, going through the tiny town of Vera. I had a buddy who once was in love with a woman named Vera. They both had strong personalities and were quick to disagree with each other's viewpoint on practically anything. One day he told me about one of their arguments or disagreements, as she preferred to call them.

"You know, Vera is just like a pair of good boots that fit your feet perfectly. You can wear those suckers day after day and not even tell they are on your feet until one day you get a little wrinkle in your sock or maybe a tiny piece of wood or sticker inside them. Then they cause you o'billy hell in pain until you stop and take them off, shake out the sticker or smooth your socks. Same way with Vera," he said.

I wondered what happened to them. I don't know.

We passed several horses standing at rest in the field. They looked like they were almost leaning against each other. Call it "naptime." We went through Red Springs and on past another horse standing by itself out in the pasture. The animal, a buckskin color, looked absolutely beautiful. I wished I owned that buckskin. We passed a set of corrals made out of pipe and painted a wild orange color. What is the world coming to, I wondered . . . orange corrals. Maybe the rancher was like my dad. He needed to paint the corrals and got a good buy on some orange paint, so he painted them orange. We entered Baylor County, where the Comanche and Wichita tribes once roamed. They were removed in 1874-1875, about the same time the first settlers arrived.

We passed through Seymour, the county seat of Baylor County, that has a population of 3,185. The first settlers named their county after H.W. Baylor, an early-day surgeon who told wild stories about his medical practice while serving with the Texas Rangers. Not much stirring when we were there. I guessed they were preparing for that giant dove hunters' breakfast they have here every September. I'd like to come to that sometime. I imagine they serve biscuits and gravy, eggs and fried potatoes. I could make a meal from that. But, leave off the dove. I never did like those small birds that yield a clump of dark meat that might fill the toe end of a sock.

As we headed west of town on Highway 277, several doves sailed in front of us moments before we reached the third bridge on our list. Then I made a discovery. It was over the Salt Fork Brazos—which as I have already pointed out—is a different river from the Brazos. I had wondered about including those bridges in this book, but I remembered reading the 1919 publication *Gazetteer of Streams of Texas*. That publication had said the Brazos contained a "gazetteer of streams, lakes and ponds." The Brazos is one of the principal streams of the state; having the greatest discharge and being the longest of any stream in the state . . . the headwater areas, Clear Fork, Salt Fork, and Double Mountain Fork of Brazos River; the Double Mountain Fork and Salt Fork united in the southwest part of Stonewall County, about 470 miles above its mouth to form the main stream. So I figured, what the heck? Any bridge we came to, we would visit.

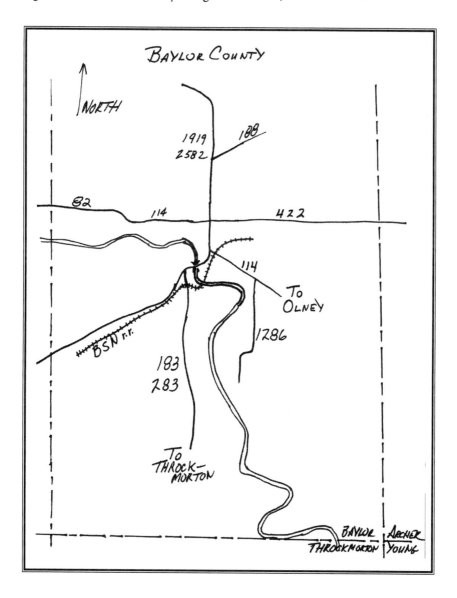

The bridge staring at us is a fairly new structure. It lacked the character of the older bridges. But with its four lanes, it functions quite well and area residents love it. They could care less about the lack of squeaking when they drive across the bridge, particularly if they are transporting a sick child with a possible burst eardrum or a ruptured appendix on a midnight run to the doctor. This bridge did have a locust choral group that hit the high notes from below the structure.

"ZZZZZZZZZZZZZZZZZZZZ," they went. Maybe they were singing this day in memory of that young Mexican couple some say the Brazos is named after. Julien Hyer tells that story in her book *Texas: The Land of Beginning Again: The Romance of the Brazos*. She says the couple was coming up from San Antonio when they suddenly came upon some Comanche warriors. The young man tried to outrun the Indians in the couple's wagon. He came to the Brazos, which was just beginning to flood. There were, of course, no bridges in those days, so he drove his team and wagon into the river. One of the warriors tried to follow but the flooding waters caught his horse and carried him downstream. By now the young couple was on the other side. The river had widened so much that the Indians abandoned their efforts to cross. So came the name, "El Rio de Los Brazos de Dios." I found a bit of irony that the Brazos was flooding this day.

Another story came to my mind from the novel by Lucia St. Clair Robson, *Ride the Wind*. According to her story, the Indians called the Brazos "*Tohopt Bah-e-homa*." That means blue river. In its upper reaches, the river flows with red sand and silt from ancient sediments beneath the Llano Estacado, materials originating in the ancient Rocky Mountains. The blue mud and clay at its mouth result from the gulf's water level, rising over many millennia, drawing the mouths of all Texas coastal rivers. The blue mud is characteristic of several rivers in the vicinity.

Well, on this day, the Brazos would be wrongly named. It should be called the River of Redness.

CHAPTER FOUR

Young County Bridge

❖　❖　❖

He saw the advertisement in one of the comic books. The company manufactured some kind of salve that supposedly cured everything from sunburn to wasp stings. They offered a long list of prizes including things such as bicycles and a .22 single shot rifle. They also offered a harmonica. You only had to sell twelve cans of the salve to earn that prize.

He hated selling. He hated having to approach somebody and ask if they were interested in buying some of this super salve. But he swallowed his hate and made the effort. He was going to sell twelve cans, he kept telling himself. He finally did.

❖　❖　❖

Driving to the fourth bridge on our list led us to Young County and past hillsides with huge flat rocks lying on them. They looked like a dental chair positioned beside a giant who had most of his teeth extracted.

We stayed on Highway 114 and drove into Olney, home of the one-armed dove hunt. A huge sign in town shows two one-armed men smiling as they hold shotguns. I wondered how anyone could ever master holding a shotgun with one arm, aiming it at a flying dove, firing, and killing the bird. I never learned how to get my limit of doves using two hands.

We took Highway 79 toward Elbert, a small community in Throckmorton County, which the *Texas Almanac* said was the site of Camp Cooper, a Comanche Indian reservation. It was north of here that

General Ranald Mackenzie finally brought the Comanche Indians to their knees. He and his troops surprised the Comanche as they camped in the rugged territory of Palo Duro Canyon. It wasn't the success of the battle so much that led to final defeat of the Comanche. Instead, Mackenzie and his men captured nearly 1,000 horses from the Indians. They picked the best animals for themselves and slaughtered the rest, killing what had been the Indians' transportation system. For years the place where the horses were slaughtered was marked by acres of bones.

That page of history seemed far away as we looked at hay fields and green fields of cotton. The lushness of the countryside reminded me of a line I read in Julien Hyer's book about why ranchers wanted to settle along the Brazos River. One reason was the low cost of raising cattle here. One rancher said in 1854, "It costs $25 to raise a cow in Connecticut; $15 in Indiana; $2.50 in Illinois, while down on the Brazos you can raise one as cheap as you can raise a chicken."

We passed three buzzards, those kings of ugliness, feasting on a possum that had been killed as it raced across the highway. Several feet away a ditch ripped across pastureland. Pink evening primroses grew in thick clumps on one of its smooth banks. The flowers' small, cup-shaped blossoms looked like someone had spattered pink watercolors into them.

We went down a hill and there southwest of the community of Padgett was some bottomland and the fourth bridge on our list, another one of the modern concrete masses. We stopped, got out of the car, and stretched. I sipped from a cold cup of coffee as we walked across the bridge and looked in the bottoms. A tall pecan tree had its limbs stretched crazily to the sky, looking like somebody had given it one of those new modern hairdos.

The flood had reached here. The river carried logs, plastic jugs, and—ye gosh!—there was a western straw hat in the middle of all that effluent. I walked under the bridge and gazed at the abundance of graffiti. One read, "Two hearts make one that shall ride the waves of fantasy."

Aw, true love. I remembered when gathering under a bridge in the springtime was really a wild thing to do for a young couple who had stuffed their mouths full of Doublemint to try and hide the harshness of a country supper in hopes of a kiss.

I continued walking and looking at but staying away from the strong clumps of Johnson grass, those king chalets for chiggers. I kicked at the

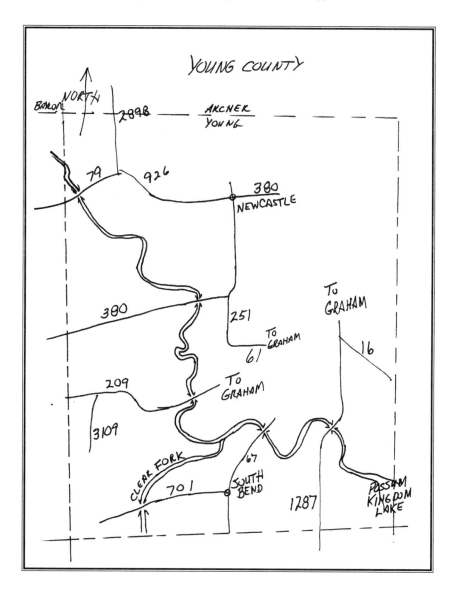

remains of a campfire and the bones from a wild turkey. Okay, somebody had dined well.

I thought of the other wild animals that once inhabited the Brazos River bottoms in abundance. Skunks, wolves, rattlesnakes, possums, squirrels, and prairie dogs all found their homes in these regions. The prairie dogs were so abundant, said one old-time rancher, that they ate enough grass in one year to feed out three million head of cattle.

A truck loaded with cattle thundered over the bridge. I heard the bawls of the cattle being taken to the market. Those sounds filled my ears, giving the bridge a heavy splash of character.

CHAPTER FIVE

Newcastle Bridge

❖   ❖   ❖

"But, where will you practice with a harmonica? You'll probably sound like someone dragging a nail across a piece of tin," his uncle said.

"I'll go to the bridge and play under it," he said.

"Oh," said his uncle. "Well, the bridge is a good place for everything from stray cats and dogs to people huntin' a place to dump thangs. I guess it can stand a few sour notes from a feller learning how to play a harmonica."

❖   ❖   ❖

The old bridge near the tiny town of Newcastle in Young County is the kind of bridge that I remember. It has steel girders that bend in the wind like an aluminum clothespin. The space beneath them became territory where a kid could play all sorts of fantasy games like Treasure Island and swear that Long John Silver really was looking out from those shadows, singing, "Sixteen men on a dead man's chest. Yo ho ho, and a bottle of rum."

The bridge west of this town on Highway 380 has been closed to vehicular traffic. It stands serenely by its replacement, one of those arching concrete marvels. The bridges offer a good comparison between the old and new since their locations are so close. The older model, built in 1932-1933, has five steel sections.

A plaque on the west end of the bridge reads, "The Brazos River Bridge." Huge piles of dirt block off any kind of entrance to the bridge except by walking. This hasn't prevented young lovers from coming. We read a hand painted sign that said, "3:45 P.M. Who says it can't be done in the middle of the day!"

Elms, junipers, and post oak trees have punched their limbs through the steel sides, giving it even more of a romantic look. Across the river we heard a rooster crowing. We looked down and saw the Brazos' flood had reached here, bringing dozens of huge logs and dumping them against its banks.

The locusts wailed at the nearby homemade grave marker for Matt Ford who apparently was killed or died June 25, 1999. Several bouquets of plastic flowers had been placed around the marker.

We drove to Graham and stopped at the *Graham Leader*, the local newspaper, asking for information about the bridge. They gave us several names of people, including the name of the regional engineer for the Texas Department of Transportation. "He can be a lot of help for this information since one of his many jobs is maintaining the bridge," said a reporter.

We followed his advice. But the people at the Texas Department of Transportation said they were just too busy with end of the month business to talk this day. Couldn't we, perhaps, come back some other time, the receptionist asked on behalf of the regional engineer? We said good-bye, returned to Newcastle, and stopped at Jerry's Meat Market & Grocery. Rich, pleasant smells that remind of old-time grocery stores with their open bins of potatoes and onions filled the building. We also found several people who had knowledge of local history as well as some of the bridges.

"My goodness, so you want some information about the old bridge," said Betty Harris, a cashier. "Well, I was born nearly at the foot of that old bridge. You can still see our house at one end. I walked across that old bridge and played under it. Good memories, oh, yeah, I have tons of good memories about the old bridge."

Micki Bullock, a customer, said she nearly cried when they built the new bridge. "I've driven over that old one so much. You get quite a feeling when

Even though this old bridge near Newcastle in Young County has been closed to automobile traffic, people may still walk across the bridge and get a feel for the sounds that once echoed from its steel-and-concrete roadway.

you go over one of those old ones. I don't know. It's kind of a feeling like you and it belong here," she said. "The new ones . . . you just speed over them and hardly know they are there."

Jerry Short, owner of the store, listened. "If you are doing a story on the bridges over the Brazos, you need to be sure and visit the Dark Valley Bridge. My daddy helped build that one," he said.

I confirmed that the Dark Valley Bridge was on our list.

"You also need to talk to Cariel Hardin. He has lived here forever and right out there at the bridge," said Short.

Hardin just happened to be in the store with his son, Danny Hardin. He had several stories about the bridge. "From the time he (his son) was big enough to crawl, I used to take him to that old bridge and let him crawl under it," said the father. "The new one . . . well, it's about ten years old, I think. But I think the old one looks a lot safer. I don't like that little short railing they got to keep people and cars from going off."

He said there once was a swinging bridge at the location. People said driving across that bridge in high winds could be a hair-raising experience. However, it fell into the river during a flood and was replaced by the steel-girder bridge.

Hardin, who was also born near the bridge, had some funny stories about things that happened near or on the bridge. He told one about trying to pull a combine across the bridge with a tractor. "I normally would have had a spotter with me. But I didn't have one that day. So I looked real good and just took off across it. Got about a third of the way across and here comes this car. I thought they would turn back. But they didn't and I didn't either. We got about halfway and stopped. Hell, this combine was twenty-four-foot wide and was taking up all of the bridge. Anyway, a little old gray-haired woman was driving that car. She said she wasn't about to back up. I wasn't either because I couldn't. We argued for a while and then she said, 'Young man, I will tell you the truth. I can't back up this car. If you will get off that tractor and get in this car and back it off the bridge, then you can have the bridge to move your tractor and combine on across.'"

He laughed loudly.

"That's what I did, and we both went on our ways," he said.

We drove back to the bridge for a final look. The sun caught its five sections in a brilliant display of light. It looked like a cache of silver. It made quite a sight. But I certainly would not have liked to back a car all of the way across it.

CHAPTER SIX

More Young County Bridges

❖   ❖   ❖

The harmonica came in the mail one day before he got home from school. He didn't open the package. He stuck it inside his coat and headed for the bridge.

When he got there, he carefully removed the wrapping paper until he saw the harmonica box. It had some kind of red, leatherlike covering on it. He brushed his fingers across this. Finally he opened the box. The harmonica was beautiful. As he looked at it, a bird that had a nest in the bridge rafters began singing.

He sat down and began playing. A large truck roared over the bridge, its booming muffler drowning out his music. He kept playing.

❖   ❖   ❖

Young County has been blessed with several bridges over the Brazos. The river makes its usual twists and turns in this county as its channel continues its nine-hundred-mile slice across the country to the Gulf of Mexico. We had seen the first of many bridges just as the day ended. So we returned to Graham, the county seat, to spend the night. The city has several nice places to stay and several good restaurants. And it has a wonderful museum in the refurbished train depot. For people who have memories of the old-time movies, the remodeled Main Theater is a must.

After dinner, I returned to my motel room and thought about one of my favorite books. I still treasure the memories from *The Adventures of Huckleberry Finn*, with Huck's adventures as he floated in a raft down the

Mississippi, his passage unencumbered by bridges. A person would have to go back to 1870 to find the period when the Brazos River had no bridges. I finally went to sleep and did not dream of bridges.

After eating breakfast and checking out of our motel, we took Highway 67 to FM 209 toward Woodson. The sun hammered us as we passed mesquite and live oak thickets and fields of bluestem grass that looked like a wave of water as the light wind hit its blades. We had reached scenic country. We played a game that we had just invented. Will this be a good, old-fashioned bridge or will it be one of those concrete-and-steel mammoth creations denuded of character?

I thought of those pioneers who faced this river without any bridges and the hardships they endured. As Verne Huser said in his book, *Rivers of Texas*, they had to build bridges. "Rivers blocked overland routes, sometimes by brief but serious flooding, which necessitated the location of fords, the development of ferries and even, eventually, the building of bridges," Huser wrote.

John Tushim suddenly said, "There it is. It is another modern marvel."

This modern model did have some pretty grapevines with purple flowers growing at the end of the bridge. We walked across and then I walked beneath the bridge. I have learned that "beneath the bridge" could be an insult to a person if you were describing his yard or landscape. You could say, "Boy, this looks as bad as a scene from beneath some bridge."

This one looked almost that bad. There were empty shotgun shell casings and some household garbage. There also was an old car generator and a freezing coil from a refrigerator. And, of course, the poets had left their messages on the walls in bright splashes of paint. Unfortunately, these were rated X.

We went back to the top and looked again at the flooding Brazos. I remembered a story I had written about a place not too far from here. The Brazos crossed through this man's place. But back in the 1920s, there was no bridge to get across. So people looked for what are called shallow crossings.

A man had bought a new car. He was going to town to show it off. The river was coming up but he thought he could make it across the shallow crossing. He didn't. The river caught his car and washed it away. He never found it. But years later, the man's relative was riding his horse down the river, and he looked into a sandbank. There was one of the wheels of the car sticking out, still attached to the axle.

"I suppose the whole damn thing is still in there," he told me. "I thought about digging it up but decided that it would be too much work. Besides, I think it's kinda neat having a piece of an antique car sticking out of the riverbank."

A bridge would have saved that car. Any kind of bridge would have fit the bill, even some of these modern marvels.

A monstrous red ant bed rose beneath this bridge. The ants were busy, one dragging what looked like a piece of a chicken bone toward the anthill. I was reminded of the time when we lived in Midland where numerous red ant beds marked the land. Even though they were certainly noticeable, many times a person intent on other matters might accidentally stop either in the trail of ants or in the middle of an ant bed. The person would be reminded of his ignorance by the sudden fiery explosions of pain on his ankles and legs.

So it was for me one day when I was about eight and was looking for coins in a sandy parking lot near the cattle auction my parents owned. I felt that scorching pain and looked down to see what had caused it. I was standing in the middle of a red ant bed. I screamed and began tearing my clothes off and throwing them to the ground. I don't know why I started with my shirt, but I did. Then I got to my pants and ripped them off. Then my underwear. By then some adult had come to help.

I thought of this because of the pair of some woman's undergarments lying close to this red ant bed. I wondered if she had ripped them off after discovering she was standing in a red ant bed. If she had, I'll bet she made some screams that couldn't be misconstrued as being from delight. Those shouts of agony probably rang through the bridge's steel girders.

We walked back to our car and drank deeply from our water containers. I watched the sun splash across the steel of the bridge. I had to admit it was kind of pretty even though it came from one of the modern bridges.

CHAPTER SEVEN

South Bend Bridge

His old man laughed and made coarse jokes when he heard him practicing the harmonica. One time he began pounding the kitchen table with a huge spoon and shouted, "Hey, baby, I think I sound better than you. You sound like a hawg that somebody had just denutted."

He laughed loudly and pounded the table some more. He began singing some old ribald song about sailors and prostitutes. That led the boy to make a decision. He no longer practiced at home.

Instead, he went to his own music chamber beneath the bridge. It smelled of wild onions, flowers, and clover. And nobody laughed at him.

We returned to Graham and followed Highway 67 south. We passed Treasure Valley and Toy Road and stopped at a historical marker that read, "The Tonk Valley Community." It said that the earliest known attempt at settling this valley permanently came in 1851 when Elijah Skidmore moved here. The valley got its name from the Tonkawa Nation, known in its own language as "the most human of people." This valley was a reservation for the Tonkawa. But in 1859 they were moved to Indian Territory in Oklahoma.

We continued driving and soon came to the next bridge, a concrete structure, which lacked any markings about when it was built or by whom.

I walked across and looked at the bottom of the river where limestone rocks formed massive pillars. I assumed they had once formed the foundations of the old bridge.

I walked down for a closer look at one of the foundations. Someone with obvious expert welding abilities had built a round steel gate that spins to allow persons to walk through a fence guarding the bridge. I reached the foundation and ran my hands over the rocks, admiring the work that had put them together. I walked back topside and looked again at the flooding Brazos. Evidence of the river's power came floating by. It was a large storage building that apparently had been ripped away by the water and brought downstream until it lodged against some trees sticking out into the river. The sweet smell of the thick growth of blood weeds and careless weeds filled our noses. So did the smell of a dead possum, lying on its back.

We drove to the home of Larry Barton, a talkative man with a graying beard tinged with nicotine. He has lived in the area for only four years but has been hunting in this part of the country for thirty. He said old-timers have told him there was a flood in 1978, and the water didn't get over the bridge.

"And that was some flood," he said. "See that little old rounded bush out there (about two hundred yards away). It got up to that."

He said he had a deer lease on down the river at Bunger and the water marks got up to eighteen feet on the trees there. "I think it must have washed a lumberyard away because there were brand new two-by-fours and two-by-sixes up in them trees. But the damndest thing was this oak school desk. It had been carried down that river and set down just as easy as you please, right in the middle of a clearing. It looked like somebody had carried it out there and set it down. It didn't have a mark on it."

We talked about that and how if the desk had been sitting in some public place for use, it probably would have gotten names carved into it as well as words and phrases written on it with pencils and ink. I thought about that and how a philosophical point could be made that Mother Nature can be gentle even when she is on a flooding tirade.

Barton interrupted my thoughts as he told about his company moving him to St. Louis for about two and a half years. He hated it there and said the people didn't know what brisket or Mexican food was. "But I tell you, by the time I left those folks knew what brisket and Mexican food was," he said. "Yes, sir. I cooked 'em batches of that food and they learned what cooking delights they had been missing."

He laughed a raspy laugh and then told us how much he loved the old bridges. "There's nothing like driving across one of the old iron bridges with wooden slats on it," he said. His eyes got a faraway look in them. "Listening to that when you are resting or just standing around, well, it's fine music. And nobody charges you admission to hear it."

We said our good-byes, and he said, "And, y'all come back."

We knew he wasn't kidding.

CHAPTER EIGHT

Bunger Bridge

❖ ❖ ❖

He practiced and practiced, but the notes never seemed to come
right. He was beginning to think that maybe his father was right. His
music did sound like the screams of a calf that had just been brand-
ed. Then one day he remembered a song he had heard when he was
four years old. He began humming the song.

"Many years ago, on a cold dark night. A stranger was killed,
'neath the town hall lights."

Then he put the harmonica to his lips and tried playing the song.
He couldn't believe this. He was playing the song.

"There were few at the scene. But they all agreed. That the man
who fled looked a lot like me." The locusts came in strongly on the
chorus.

❖ ❖ ❖

To find our next bridge, we headed south on Highway 16 out of
Graham. We turned onto FM 1287 and drove about two miles down this
road to the bridge, a concrete-and-steel creation of strength.

Locusts sang their warm-ups for an afternoon symphony. As I walked
through the grass, huge grasshoppers leaped upward and hit my pants, making loud "plop-plop-plop" sounds. I wished I had a throw line. I could catch
a couple of these huge insects that spit brown juice, bait my hook, and soon
see the line go stiff from hooking a big channel or yellow catfish. Such are

the dreams of a man who has spent too many hours on the river, as his father used to say.

"Bunk, your problem is you like that Brazos River more than you do your momma and me and respect it even more," was the chastisement he made to me many times.

Well, today effluent that looked like it could have come from a cesspool filled the river. Beneath this bridge civilization had left even more nasty reminders of what they do to nature. An armadillo tail lay near the remains of campfire. Empty beer cans and plastic sacks full of trash had been flung haphazardly around the ground, looking like baseball bases that had been left untied for months and had been scattered by the wind and animals. Also lying on the ground were an empty plastic ice tray and a stained western shirt. The shirt looked in good enough shape that I'd bet my longtime friend Doc Keen, who has traveled with me on many of my trips, would have retrieved it, washed it, and worn it.

We leaned over the bridge and looked at white cattle grazing in the bottoms. Many of them stood in the shade of the towering pecan trees, with branches already filling with pecans for a good fall harvest. Far down the river, backed up in a tiny slough, we saw a tall, skinny, white crane. The bird's flash of color and the brilliant greens of the river willows made one forget the nearby ugliness left by humanity.

We could also see some of the pillars from one of the old bridges. These lonely statues of the past are made from thick chunks of limestone probably mined from some nearby hills. I recalled that Darwin Spearing said in *Roadside Geology of Texas* the stone was hard, fairly resistant to erosion, and was abundant in this area. "Pioneers liked to build something sturdy, but they were smart and didn't drag their heavy building stones from long distances if good stone was locally available," he said.

The sickly sweet-sour smell of the new growth of blood weeds was almost overpowering. I walked back up the bank and looked in the distance toward where Eliasville and South Bend lay. I thought of the history these places have and how thousands of people once came to South Bend to bathe in the Stovall Hot Wells. Those wells were in the middle of a field and water that measured 101°Fahrenheit poured from the springs. At one time, cabins and a lodge there encouraged people to spend time in the wells. People did and claimed they were cured of a variety of illnesses including rheumatism, athlete's foot, eczema, kidney trouble, ringworm, soft gums, and poor circulation.

"You don't have to be in poor health to benefit from a bath and massage. It is a unique experience not to be experienced anywhere else. We have bathers in age from infancy to nearly the century mark," promised an advertising pamphlet somebody had given me.

I had taken a bath in the wells. I don't think it cured any chronic ailment from which I was suffering. But, as my friend Doc told me that night over the campfire, "It shore did improve your disposition for a while."

The wells closed when a fire destroyed the facilities. But right up the road is still another Texas treasure at Eliasville. There, near a remarkable old steel girder-and-cable bridge over the Clear Fork of the Brazos, are the remains of an ancient flourmill that once ground corn, wheat, and other grain. I have always wondered why the great state of Texas did not buy that place, restore it, and make it into a park.

During a visit to Eliasville several years ago, I stood near the dam that sent water into the gears of the mill, amazed by the number of alligator gars swimming in lazy-looking maneuvers near the surface of the water. The sight of numerous large cottonmouth water snakes also impressed me. But the preservation of such places is not the purpose of this adventure. We are looking for the bridges over the Brazos. So we headed for the next bridge on our list. We had thought that would be what is called the Dark Valley Bridge. But we made a rest stop at a roadside park just after we left the dam over Possum Kingdom Lake. A young man had parked his pickup truck there, with an empty cattle trailer behind it.

I walked over and introduced myself and told him what I was doing and asked if he knew anything about the bridges over the Brazos in this area.

"Well, you should be sure and visit the one just below the dam. It's one helluva bridge and make sure you park and look in under it. That is where the beauty is. My grandpa helped build it back during the Depression," he said.

"You mean, the one they call the low water bridge?" I asked.

"Yeah, some people call it that," he said.

"Well a woman at the BRA office at the dam said it wasn't much to look at," I said.

He shook his head.

"She must not have never gotten out of her car and looked in under it. That is where the beauty is," he said. "Take my word for it. It's worth your trip to go and see that bridge."

We thanked him. We wanted to see the bridge but the sun was becoming a muddy orange color in the west that meant we did not have much viewing time left. So we headed for home. But, the next day, we did take the young man's advice and headed for the Possum Kingdom Stone Arch Bridge that his grandfather had helped build. He was right. It is a helluva bridge.

CHAPTER NINE

Possum Kingdom Stone Arch Bridge

❖   ❖   ❖

The bridge had become his sanctuary. Sometimes he had full
orchestra support. That's when the locusts, grasshoppers, bees, and
old Rip Cheney's hound dog contributed a deep bass chord or two.

One day as he played, he stopped briefly. His heart thundered. He
swore he heard an echo. Or was it an answer to his music.

He looked under the bridge. He saw and heard nothing but the
warm, soft voice of the Brazos. He began to play again. Nothing
but his music touched the huge beams that looked like a steel
spider's web.

❖   ❖   ❖

When we first arrived at the Possum Kingdom Stone Arch Bridge, we
had proof of something several bridge experts have said about looking at
bridges . . . be sure and look under them.

This is certainly true with this bridge, which turned out to be one of the
most interesting of all of the Brazos bridges. It is a favorite bridge of many
people including T. Lindsay Baker, now curator of a wonderful museum
about the history of coal mining at Strawn west of Fort Worth, operated by
Tarleton State University. Baker is a well-known Texas historian and author
of many books including, *Building the Lone Star: An Illustrated Guide to*
Historic Sites, which features more than one hundred of the state's most
interesting and historic engineering feats. This old bridge made the book.

"It's an extraordinary bridge. I would call it spectacular," said Baker. "It
looks like a Roman bridge with its multiple arches."

The Works Progress Administration built this bridge in the early 1940s at a site that passes over Texas Highway 16 one mile below the Morris Sheppard Dam in Palo Pinto County. Baker's love of the bridge can be seen in the pages of history he provided about its construction.

Unemployed workers from surrounding counties did the work on the bridge. The men were brought to the site by the hundreds on cattle trucks that had been converted into public transportation vehicles. After a day of work, they were again loaded onto the cattle trucks and taken home. Many of these laborers had worked in the once-thriving coal mines in nearby Strawn, Thurber, and Mingus. They had learned how to cut stone in the underground mines so they were well experienced for cutting the slabs of rock from nearby limestone cliffs used in the bridge. Since engineers knew that the area would be subject to tremendous volumes of water released from the dam, they used a masonry arch low-water type bridge that would withstand flooding waters that would completely cover the structure.

An engineer who worked at the project said little machinery and few purchased materials were used at the site. Sand and gravel came from the site near the bridge, and lumber was salvaged from the dam that was finished about the same time. As a result of those efforts, the bridge was built for $760,000, an almost unbelievable figure for today's construction projects. The bridge has proved its worth. Its eighteen arches, measuring a total of 433 feet four inches long, have required little improvement or maintenance since its completion. The arches may appear to be the same size to the naked eye, but they actually vary from twenty-three to thirty feet across.

On the morning we arrived to look at the bridge, Cody Lain, twenty, unloaded fishing gear from his pickup truck to begin an hour or two of fishing.

"I'm no writer. But, if I were, and I were writing about bridges, I would choose this one to write about," he said. He pointed at the arches.

The Possum Kingdom Stone Arch Bridge in Palo Pinto County was built by the Works Progress Administration during the late 1930s. Workers mined the rock for its eighteen arches that stretch for 433 feet and four inches from local hillsides. Author T. Lindsay Baker named this as one of 100 of Texas' most interesting and historic engineering examples.

"Can you imagine the work those men put in cutting those and getting them laid so perfectly and so prettily?" he asked. "And what is kinda sad, unless you stop and get out of your car to look under the bridge, you would never know this beautiful work had been done."

We walked up and down some of the rock ledges held together with layers of mortar that look like graying rolls of bread dough. Some of the workers' footsteps had been left in the concrete. We could see massive rocks

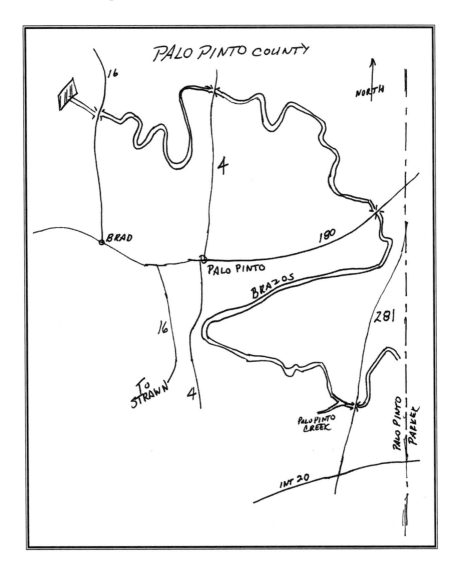

covered by the river, which on this day was clear. The rocks were covered with moss that looked like giant discarded sheets of film. We read a sign that warned about the river rising rapidly in minutes. "It (the river) may become very swift at any time. The river will rise without warning and you could be stranded or swept away by high water. Enter the riverbed at your own risk. Wear your life preserver," the sign warned.

The sound of oil field pumps making their "thunk, thunk, thunka, thunk, thunk" noises came from a nearby field. The grass and trees smelled earthy and strong on this day.

We saw Lain walking up the river, and he too warned us about the power of the river. "The dam's about two miles up this way," he said. "Be sure and be careful of that river because when they let water out up there at the dam, it can get to you pretty damn quick. They sound a horn most of the time when they let the water out, but it's nearly two miles to the dam so you might not hear it."

He looked up the river where geologists have long studied the rocks that have yielded oil and gas, water, coal, and clay. Darwin Spearing, who wrote extensively about this area, said that U.S. Highway 180 west of Weatherford travels across rolling countryside underlaid by limestone, shale, and sandstone of the Cretaceous Age. "This area is part of a cretaceous rim that stands high and surrounds the lower landscape to the west where the Brazos River has etched its way downward through the cretaceous to expose older Pennsylvania and Permian rocks," he said.

Those facts held no interest for Lain on this day; he was more interested in fishing. "Well, I'm going on up a little way and see if I can find me a striper hole. It was good talking to you guys," he said. "Hope I can catch me some catfish for supper tonight."

We looked some more and then drove about a mile to where Gene Yeager worked at cutting grass from around some gas well pumps. He was not aware of the beauty or the history of the Possum Kingdom Stone Arch Bridge. But he did say we should see the bridge near Bradford, Pennsylvania, where he was reared.

"It's called the Kinzua River Railroad Bridge. It's really something to see. But, you know it's like this bridge. I was raised up there and didn't think anything about that bridge until I left. I'll bet people are the same way down here about this bridge," he said.

"Yeah, I agree with that," said John Tushim. "I was raised in Punxsutawney [Pennsylvania], but I bet you don't know what Bradford, your hometown, is famous for."

He didn't.

"The Zippo cigarette lighter was made there," he said. "Yes, sir. That is what your hometown is famous for."

We all laughed. Then Tushim and I said good-bye and headed for the Dark Valley Bridge.

CHAPTER TEN

Dark Valley Bridge

❖ ❖ ❖

After he heard the echo, he could hardly wait to go to the bridge.
He had spent hours trying to determine what he might have heard
and misinterpreted for an answer to his music.

He didn't find an answer. But he had not heard the echo again.
So maybe he had not heard anything. Maybe it had been the sound
of the soft spin of tires about to lose their tread. Or maybe he had
become true to that label of what the kids at school had started call-
ing him; that crazy kid who plays his harmonica under the bridge.

❖ ❖ ❖

Palo Pinto County is a wonderful county in which to look for things like
bridges. Gray and black sandy lands lie in the rugged, ranching country.

Comanche, Sioux, and Apache who once lived in this area loved the
abundance of game and fish offered along the Brazos River. According to the
Texas Almanac, when the Anglo settlers began arriving in the 1850s, the
Indian tribes sought refuge in the river's bottomlands. The Texas Rangers
eventually removed the Indians.

We drove along Highway 16 on a sunny September day and took a fork
that led us to a magnificent view of ranchland. We could see small herds of
cattle and horses grazing in the pastures that had side oats grama and little
bluestem growing in abundance. Little bluestem turns a deep blue-green in
the fall and then becomes a soft, dark-brown color with white shining seed
tufts in the winter.

We drove past oil-field pumps going slowly up and down, making a "slish-sheezh-slish-sheezh" sound that means there will be money in somebody's pocket. We went over a creek with a flat bedrock bottom like a long bathtub. In the distance, the waters of Possum King Lake flashed at us.

We passed the Rusty Nail Saloon and Pauline's Hair and Tan and Nails and a colossal but gaudy rock entrance to some ranch. We finally saw the famed observation point at Possum Kingdom Lake. I am reminded of a saying from George English, a high-school friend, when he was beholding something impressive. He would say, "That's quite impressive, even though I must say so myself."

That is how I felt when looking off this ten-story-high point above Morris Sheppard Dam. We read facts about the half-mile-long, nineteen-story-high dam. How it required more than 1,000 boxcar loads of cement and almost 2,000 miles of reinforced steel. The observation point is called Jack Smith Observation Point, named after a registered public surveyor who worked thirty-five years for the Brazos River Authority.

We did our "oohs", and "ahs," left, and drove past a hill that looked like a woman's breast covered with green felt, a result of all of the rain that had recharged the grasses. We drove through miles and miles of mesquite flats until we finally reached FM 4 and headed south. And there, in front of us, sat the Dark Valley Bridge, another new modern concrete concoction. Rochelle's Canoe Rentals sits almost under the bridge.

We talked to Buddy Rochelle, one of the owners, who was wearing shorts and sandals. Two black cats slept in chairs on the porch. "I've been coming here ever since I was a kid," he said. "My grandpa bought this place in 1928. He started shuttling people and canoes up to the dam in the 1950s. We have gone from six canoes to two hundred, which we rent and shuttle today."

He had heard many stories about the old cable bridge that once stretched across the Brazos where the new bridge is now. "I saw some pictures of it that once ran in the *Texas Highways* magazine. I think it was in 1955. But that bridge was something else. It sure was," he said. "My grandpa said he used to watch that old bridge when people would come across it. It would creak and rattle and sound like it was coming to pieces. People with cattle in trailers would start across it and that old bridge would nearly touch the river, it would dip down so much. By the time they'd get to the other side, they would be almost looking straight up in their trucks and trailers."

But, a flood in 1981 brought a good-bye to the old bridge. The storm hit Graham on Halloween night dumping up to seventeen inches of rain. The water swelled the river beyond its banks, engorging the stream into a dirty chocolate wave of destruction. The river, which had been calm like it was on this day, swept downstream and into farmlands, tearing houses from foundations, trapping and drowning cattle in massive limbs of pecan trees. The water overturned tractors that had been left in places that had never flooded before. Then it reached the old swinging bridge. *Adios*, old bridge.

"I'm sure this new one is much safer. But, does it have the character of the old one . . . . Lord no," said Rochelle.

I looked down at the bridge and remembered Jane and me canoeing from Possum Kingdom Dam to this location a few years ago. We had made the trip fine and thought we were expert canoeists by maneuvering successfully through several whitewater places. Then just as we skirted under the bridge, some swift water grabbed our canoe and dumped us in front of about one hundred spectators standing on the shore. I told Rochelle the story, and he laughed and said he had seen similar accidents numerous times. Then we said our good-byes.

"You boys ever need a canoe, be sure and come to our place," he said. "We give good service."

And you can rest in the shade of the Dark Valley Bridge when you finish your paddling even if you turn over before reaching the bridge.

CHAPTER ELEVEN

Palo Pinto County Bridge

❖   ❖   ❖

He heard it again. Only, this time it wasn't an echo. It was an
answer. He had been playing, "I'll Fly Away" and had reached the
part that goes deep like a bucket falling to the bottom of a well. The
answer, "I'll fly away, fly away in the morning," resounded beneath
the bridge.

He looked to a spot about twenty feet from him. Some thin trees
made a chapel-like formation, and there she stood. She looked like a
piece of beautiful sunshine splitting the clouds after a rain.

❖   ❖   ❖

As we headed for the next bridge in Palo Pinto County, I thought of
some of the old-time cattlemen who once ranched and lived in this area. I'd
bet they would have loved to have had some bridges to head their cattle
across when they were taking them to market.

I heard a story about how they got cattle to cross the Brazos or any river.
They would drive them for hours, making certain they did not get a drink
of water. By the time they got to the river, the cattle would be almost dying
from thirst. The cowboys would keep the herd milling for an hour or so
before letting them go. The cattle by now had a strong smell of the river in
their nostrils. They would charge forward to the stream. After they had
satisfied their thirst, they were relatively easy to move on across the water.

Near Palo Pinto, we spied a historical marker and stopped. It told about
George Webb Slaughter who came to Texas in 1830. He fought in the Texas
War for Independence as a courier for Sam Houston. His marriage to Sarah

Mason in October 1836 was the first marriage sanctioned under the laws of the Republic of Texas. They had eleven children and moved to this country in 1857. He organized a Baptist church and preached and practiced saddle-bag medicine.

My Grandfather McConal worked for Slaughter. He used to tell stories about helping him take cattle up the trail to Kansas in the late 1860s. I looked across the road at a set of old corrals and an old barn, wondering if my grandfather had once worked cattle there. I also remembered a story he told about cowboy justice on the trail. A young cowboy had been caught stealing some money from one of the other trail riders. Though it amounted to only a few cents, the trail boss ordered the thief tied to one of the wheels on the chuck wagon. Then the boss thrashed the offender with a bullwhip.

"It was severe. You betcha," said Grandpa McConal. "But the young colt never stole nothing else on that drive and I'll bet he never stole nothing that didn't belong to him for the rest of his life."

Of course, justice seemed severe in those days. Some of the old bridges became not only scenes where justice was dealt but provided places for executions. One such event occurred on a sultry April night in 1869 at the jail in Richmond in Fort Bend County. A mob with vengeance fanned by its consumption of homemade rotgut whiskey stormed into the local jail and removed a man charged with stealing horses.

"Whar in the hell we gonna string this sorry outlaw up?" yelled one of the mob. He answered his own question. "Ain't no trees with good long limbs close that I know of."

"How about the braces on that new bridge that they are building across the Brazos?" shouted another person. "If they are built to support a wagon, they sure as hail will support the weight of a horse thief."

The iron supports proved the man right. They barely echoed as the thief was hanged with a thick rope around his neck. Other bridges, including the suspension bridge in Waco, have been used accordingly.

Those thoughts faded as we headed south and west on Highway 4. We passed just-plowed fields waiting for fall grain planting. They reminded me of a young kid who had just had his haircut for fall classes. We drove past sheep grazing beside a mare in foal. The horse's belly was larger than the sheep standing beside her but they didn't seem to mind. We passed fields where helicopter pilots stationed at Fort Wolters trained for service in Vietnam. And then we reached the county seat, tiny Palo Pinto with its picturesque old courthouse and the old jail museum made of native sandstone. Finished in 1880, its top floor held killers, cattle rustlers, rowdy cowboys, and other prisoners. A sign said that a trapdoor installed for hangings in 1907 had never been used.

The jail closed in 1941 and in 1968 the Palo Pinto County Historical Association became its owner and restored it as its headquarters and a museum. Thank goodness for the local historical groups that save so many of our Texas treasures. May those preachers who load up on fire and brimstone in summer revivals in the old tin-roofed tabernacle across the street go kinda easy on them.

We drove east on Highway 180 toward Mineral Wells. We passed hay fields with huge round bales of hay waiting for winter and hungry cattle. Our next bridge appeared near a chunk of the historic old Bankhead highway on Highway 180.

Walking down the banks to get a better look, I snapped one of the blood weeds and showed John the liquid that looks like blood pouring from its stem.

"I can see why they are named that," he said.

A miasma of stuff including empty plastic oil jugs, potato chip and Scoop packages has been left beneath the bridge. Portions of a campfire with pieces of bologna skin that looked like sunburned lips protruded from some gouged-up dirt. I could see the remains of two other bridges, one upriver and one downriver with thick pieces of steel beams that had been cut off and several huge round concrete pillars.

I walked up the bank to the home of Vonita Liles. She and a friend were working on her mobile home, but she took a break to smoke a cigarette and talk about her family, who lived on the Brazos for years.

"I've seen that river get up right to that bank," she said, pointing to a line of grass only a few feet from us. "That's when I would talk to God. I would say, 'God, it's getting a little deep here. Can you do something about it?'" She sucked on her cigarette and smiled. "He always stopped it."

She said her uncle, J.C. Liles, who is eighty-nine and has lived on the river all of his life, said the river got to within six inches of the bridge one time before it stopped. She didn't know if it was the prayers or if it had just quit raining upriver.

"You need to go and see Wilese Warren," she said. "She lives right across over there and has been on the river all of her life. She is ninety-one."

So we drove across the river and met Wilese Warren, a delightful person with a face tanned mahogany by her years spent outdoors.

"I've only known one other person with that first name," she said. She smiled. She has white hair and cobalt blue eyes. "I've lived on this river since they built that bridge. But don't ask me when that was because I don't remember. I came here when I was a little girl. Moved here from Naples, which is in East Texas, and I still don't know why we came to this country. Maybe it was the river. I've played in it and fished in it and played under that old bridge. So yes, I love it. And, let me tell you something else. Right below that bridge, that river has saved many people. Our church, Indian Creek Baptist Church, used to bring people here and baptize them. Wash away their sins right there in the Brazos, right below that old bridge."

And as the water that sometimes looks like rust has been mixed with it rolled down the saved foreheads, people joined hands and sang:

Are you washed in the blood of the lamb, in the soul cleansing blood of the lamb.

Are your garments spotless, are they white as snow, are you washed in the blood of the lamb?

"Then they'd gather under the shade of the bridge and the pecan trees and eat fried catfish, pickled okra, sliced tomatoes, and watermelon. Hopefully, maybe the Widow June would bring some of her special pecan pie that had a lace of chocolate right under the pecans. Those delights made going down before the congregation and professing your sins much easier."

CHAPTER TWELVE

Bridge near Mineral Wells

❖　　❖　　❖

They met but said little to each other. They simply played music on their harmonicas. He had been instantly impressed with her ability to pick up on any song he played and bring a harmonious response to the tune.

At first he just accepted that she would know any song he played. Then he had tried to stump her, reaching way back in his memories for old, old songs. She had always responded perfectly. At the end of each song, she always smiled. Those smiles were like sneaking a shot of his uncle's homemade wine. They left him full of fire and warmth.

❖　　❖　　❖

Before heading south on Highway 281 for our next bridge, we drove around Mineral Wells. The city is full of interesting things, like the old Baker Hotel, which has seen many unsuccessful attempts at restoration to its once-elegant state. Here at the Baker, people came in droves to have their aches and pains banished by bathing and drinking mineral water that came from nearby wells.

There is also Charlsie's Beauty Shop, owned by Charlsie Sparks, a true Texas character. She is friendly, and if you don't need a hairstyle, buy a dozen fresh eggs or look at the antiques sprinkled liberally around her beauty shop. And if none of that interests you, well, help yourself to a piece of homemade pound cake. For nothing.

"Honey, I just love talking to people," she told me one day. I had become "honey" after our second meeting. "Too many people worry about making sure somebody who comes into their store spends some money. You start worrying about that all of the time and you miss out on some of the most beautiful things in life."

Also in Mineral Wells is a man I call the boatman. He has been working for years on a monstrous boat made of steel. When completed, he plans to haul it to the northwest, and he and his wife will spend the rest of their lives cruising around the world.

We drove south on Highway 287, past Gonzo's Paint and Body Shop and fields of sunflowers, wilted by the ninety-eight-degree heat. The day would have been a good one to sell deodorant or go swimming.

We drove past Hog Mountain Road and stopped at what I think is one of the prettiest roadside parks anywhere. The park is about five miles south of Mineral Wells. It's nicely kept, and the tables overlook the Brazos River bottom. On this day, clouds looking like chunks of cotton were in the sky. A bit of a breeze stirred and dried the sweat on my shirt. Some people call that homemade air-conditioning.

Not too far from here, a person can barely see a crossing of the Brazos. A roadside has been cut through the thin, light gray, crinkled beds of limestone. According to author Darwin Spearing, many marine fossils from earlier geological times, including brachiopods, can be found in this limestone, which probably represents one of the longest strings of shelf limestone that extended westward when the water level was high and sediment supply was low on the Pennsylvania shelf cut.

We looked and then continued south, passing a barn with four gables and a tin roof. And, just for the hell of it, we drove down a road called Old River Road. Not much is along the road but two houses.

Just beyond this road, the next bridge, an old-time steel marvel, greeted us from coastal Bermuda grass fields. Lo and behold, it had a marker that said it is the Brazos River Bridge and was built in 1939 by the Texas Highway Department and the Bureau of Public Roads. Brown & Root, Inc. were the contractors. A car came across the bridge, causing the old structure to rumble and tremble, sounds that I love.

We looked upriver at a brown house built on stilts. Flood insurance, some call it. We looked at pecan trees so large they probably were here one hundred years before the bridge was built. Their limbs were already full of fall pecans. As a huge truck thundered by, I put my hand on the steel and felt it hum. I looked at the river, an emerald green color and kind of clear today, looking like a woman's lime-green hose, revealing so much but not everything except those faint traces of lace.

We drove to Deborah Dunaway's house on the river. She wore shorts and hiking boots and was tanned and nice looking. She invited us in for a drink of ice water and talked about her love for the bridge. "I don't know much about the bridge other than I love it. There's talk about it being torn down or adding on to it. I certainly hope that isn't going to happen," she said.

She said her husband was reared on this land. And so were their great-grandparents. So they feel at home out here some thirteen miles south of Mineral Wells. She refilled our water glasses. "A new bridge. Oh, my goodness. It just kills me to think they might tear this old one down. There's not another bridge like it in Texas. So from a historical viewpoint, as well as a personal viewpoint, I think they should leave it," she said.

We stepped outside. We could see the bridge gleaming through the pecan trees like a piece of silver. "I'll tell you, when that river gets up, it does roar. It sounds like a freight train. It's scary. It's awesome," she said. Those sounds bring the same feelings to her as when she sometimes looks at the old bridge just as early morning light is chasing the darkness away from its steel girders. That sight, well, it's like looking at a magnificent painting.

CHAPTER THIRTEEN

Parker County Bridge

❖   ❖   ❖

One day their music session was stopped by one of those rain-
storms that explode with thunder. The bridge was a good place to be.
As the rain came down in dripping sheets, she motioned for him to
join her in her timber chapel.

"I'm Ely Benningfield," he said. He stuck out his hand.

"I'm Essie Mae Johnson," she replied, grasping his hand. She
smiled. "You make good music."

He felt like he had taken a giant gulp from his uncle's wine bottle.

❖   ❖   ❖

Blessings came to James and Sandra Griffin even before they bought
and restored the Brazos River Camping & RV Resort and Catfish Café.
Those good tidings came when a local group interested in preserving this
area's history closed down the old Brazos River Bridge on I-20 west of
Weatherford. But instead of dismantling the 1934 structure, the group paid
to have it restored.

"I love that old bridge," said Griffin. "It's a part of the scenery. It's a part
of the history. It's, well, a part of life around here."

The bridge has a marker that says it was completed in 1934. The
Buckner brothers were the contractors and John Wood was chairman of the
State Highway Commission. It has been beautifully restored and furnishes a
pathway across the Brazos to part of old US 80. The bridge also offers a good
comparison between the old and new bridges. The new four-lane bridge
over I-20 is only a short distance away.

We had driven past the Rattlesnake Ranch, Gilbert Pitt Road, and the Highway Church of Christ at Millsap to get on the access road leading us to the bridge, which is on I-20 and about fifteen miles west of Weatherford. Between here and Cisco, which is west, Darwin Spearing said colorful red bands of Permian rocks could be seen. Although rocks may not be exposed at the surface in much of this area, the vegetation is frequently a clue to the underlying strata. Mesquite commonly grows over clay stones, while post oaks favor sandstone terrain. Junipers and live oaks prefer limestone country. So, says Spearing, if you see green trees and shrubs in the winter, you will know you are on calcareous coils and rocks. We could see plenty of green trees and vegetation at the bridge site.

As we looked at the steel girders painted white, Griffin stopped in his pickup truck. "If y'all trim trees, then I sure would like to hire you," he said. When I told him what we were doing, he laughed and invited us to the Catfish Café for a cold drink. "I've got a great selection of photos from the old days when they had a filling station and catfish café here," he said.

We listened to a few more cars make thundering echoes across the bridge and then went to the café. The Griffins' son, Austin, welcomed us with our choice of soft drinks. We looked at the wall filled with photos taken when the place was known as the Catfish Café and Filling Station. Other photos showed gasoline selling for 22.9 cents per gallon and advertisements for Frostie root beer, tire repair, and a wide variety of brands of oil.

I could vaguely remember the old Catfish Café from when I was a child. We had stopped on some of our treks from West Texas. I remembered the sign saying, "Fresh catfish caught from the Brazos. Pick your own fish to be cooked." Griffin laughed at that.

"They did have a water tank with catfish in it. A person would come and pick one of the fish and they would remove it in a net, walk through the café to the kitchen," he said. He smiled. "They would keep on going out the back door and then go back to the tank and put the catfish back in the tank. No telling how many people chose that one fish for their meal."

The business thrived until the coming of the interstate. When it was constructed, the Catfish Café and Filling Station, like so many other businesses, came on hard times and eventually closed. Griffin said he was managing a marina on Eagle Mountain Lake near Fort Worth when he saw the boarded-up facility. It was a kind of love at first sight. So he and his wife, Sandra, bought the facility and reopened it. He talked about that day when they first saw it.

"I knew I was gonna buy it. It was on a fall morning, and it was misting rain and water was leaking through the roof and onto the wooden floor,

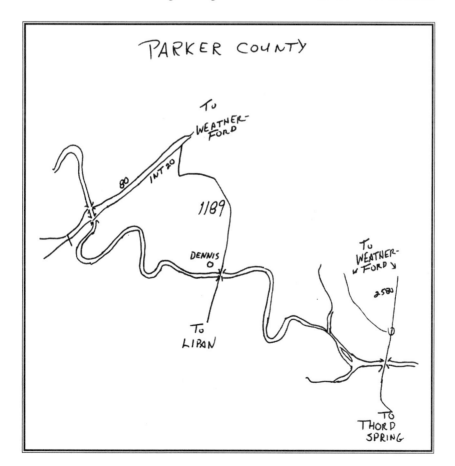

which had already rotted out," said Griffin. "But there wasn't any doubt in our minds about what we were going to do. We bought it. That was in 1997."

He thought he had never seen the place before. His mother corrected him. She said the family used to travel from Fort Worth to Abilene. The old Catfish Café and Filling Station was the first stop the family made. They probably were some of the customers who saw the well-traveled catfish being taken from the tank, through the café, and out the back door.

Regardless, Griffin and his family were motivated. They did most of the work themselves, and today have the Catfish Café back in business. They also offer plenty of camping and RV sites. One of their employees is Frances Johnson, who lives in the nearby community of Soda Springs.

"Yeah, I am happy they got this going again. Preserving that old bridge, well, that was like saving a member of my family," she said. She shook her head. "You know, you see something like that all of your life and you just come to accept that it is there and will always be there and you don't think anything about it until somebody starts talking about tearing it down."

Her husband Wyndell feels the same way. "I've been coming here and fishing all of my life," he said. "I'd just tell Frances that I was going to the old Brazos River Bridge to go fishing, and she knew where I'd be."

We went outside and walked about halfway over the bridge. We looked down at the Brazos, which looked like somebody had dusted it with green paint on this day. Certainly not a bad place for a husband or anyone to be hanging out.

CHAPTER FOURTEEN

Bridge at Dennis

They both had loved music for years. But whereas he had strug-
gled to become better, her ability came naturally. She just one day sat
down at a piano and began to play. She could do the same thing
with any instrument she chose.

"Including the harmonica?" he asked.

"Yes," she said. The smile came. "I did practice some before I
came down here."

"Why did you come here?" he asked.

"That's another story," she said. "Let's play 'Foggy Mountain.'"
They did. The bridge seemed to hum that day.

❖   ❖   ❖

We learned many times during our adventures looking at bridges that
often it is not the bridges that are so interesting but the people who live
around them. Such was the case in our coming to the bridge at Dennis, a
tiny community in southwest Parker County. As with many bridges, nobody
seemed sure how old this bridge is.

We looked unsuccessfully for a marker or some kind of identification
on the bridge's massive concrete pillars and beams. The scene beneath the
bridge was typical. An old sofa had been dumped here, along with many
empty beer bottles and soft drink cans, bottle rockets, and Roman candles.
I found a bit of irony in a sign that read, "Don't Mess With Texas. $10 to
$1,000 fine for littering." I estimated that somebody had run up about a
$5,000 bill.

There was a healthy growth of gourds with bright yellow flowers. Eddie Lane walked over to where I stood and said, "I've driven my boat all the way from Granbury to this bridge. That's about thirty-two miles. And, right across from us is the Sugar Tree Golf Course. They say it's a pretty tough course. Regardless, it is pretty."

Walking along the bank lined with wilting blood weeds, we waved at two fishermen across the river. They waved back.

"How did you become interested in bridges?" I asked Lane.

"I'm really more interested in the Brazos River. I got interested in it after I read John Graves' books. Then I read *The Bridges of Madison County*, and that whetted my appetite for bridges," he said.

You could tell birds were interested in this bridge, as a line of swallow nests that looked like tiny mud castles clung to the edge of the bridge. Nearby was a tin building that reminded me of an old cotton gin building. Age had brought a lean to it. A fence near the building was covered with Mustang grapes, noted for their powerful taste in jams and jellies. They also produce a purple-colored wine that won't win any fancy wine sipping contests but it will knock your head off with a hangover if you drink too much of it.

We walked to Balentine's Bakery, only a short distance from the bridge. The smell of ham-and-cheese rolls, breakfast burritos, and sausage rolls was pleasant. Kristy Perry, who managed the bakery that day, said she knew little about the bridge. "But I'm from Peaster, and I just drove across it the other day just to see what it is like to drive across it," she said.

We left and walked to the post office to talk to Robyn Reed who was also from Peaster. She didn't know much about the bridge either but she did know that Buster Brown, the character who once traveled around the country promoting shoes, was from Peaster. Brown was a midget who came to towns with his dog, Tige, and urged people to buy Buster Brown shoes.

"Hey, if you are writing bridge stories, I've got a bridge story for you," said Mary Bynum, who had come in to check her mail. "This is probably one of the most hair-raising experiences of my life. As I look back, it probably was the closest I've come to having the Lord's angels looking out for me." It happened north of here as she and her husband Bobby were trying to get home after getting off their night shift at work. The night had been marked with torrential rains that caused flooding. As a result, the bridge they normally crossed over had been shut down.

"But we didn't want to spend the night away from home, so we decided to go over this little one lane bridge that we knew about," she said. Driving her small sports coupe, they started across the bridge.

"We'd been across this bridge many times. And normally, when I looked down, the creek was just a tiny trickle," she said. "But, this night, we got about halfway across and I looked down and the water was coming up over the bridge. Bobby kept driving and then we saw this huge wall of water coming toward us. He (Bobby) had fought in Vietnam so he doesn't get scared. But, I asked him if he were scared when we saw that water, and he said, 'We are in a very grave situation.' So I told him, 'You'd better get us the hell out of here.'"

She stopped and smiled. She's a pretty woman with long, rust-colored hair and blue eyes. They twinkled as she continued. "He began backing up and just as we made it across, the water hit that bridge and it began making screaming sounds. The impact of that water just twisted and tore that steel into pieces. As far as I know, we were the last people to ever go across that bridge," she said. "Bobby said he had some close calls in Vietnam but nothing as scary as that. You should go up there and look at the place today. I think some of the old bridge is still there."

She gave us directions and we headed several miles north toward the creek that today has a new bridge. On this day, the creek was a meek spiral of green liquid. It was hard to imagine that during flood stage, it can get so wild and rambunctious. But, pieces of its power lay below us, huge chunks of concrete that looked like a boxer's teeth knocked out with a strong right cross. In a nearby field, several donkeys stood. They began braying that loud "eeh-onka, eeh-onka" noise that could have been translated to cries of danger on the night the Bynums made it across the old bridge.

CHAPTER FIFTEEN

Shackelford County Bridge

❖   ❖   ❖

She eventually told him why she came to the bridge to play.

"You have become famous. All the kids talk about the crazy guy who goes to the Brazos bridge to play his harmonica. So I started looking for you. I looked under every bridge in this county. I was beginning to feel like an idiot and that maybe they had been kidding me."

She stopped.

"Then I came here and heard you play. Your music is beautiful, simply beautiful. I knew then they had been telling me the truth, at least about your playing."

❖   ❖   ❖

Eddie Lane suggested we add some bridges that technically could not be called bridges over the Brazos.

"Jon, there are bridges that are not over the Brazos but over the Clear Fork of the Brazos or the Salt Fork of the Brazos that are well worth people driving to see. So I think we should put in a section about some of those," he said.

I agreed and found facts about two of these bridges in T. Lindsay Baker's book, *Building the Lone Star*. Two of those bridges are in extreme northeastern Shackelford County. One of these, when Baker did his research, was still being used and he called it "one of the oldest operational suspension bridges in Texas and a structure very worthy of inspection by visitors to this area."

My wife, Jane, and I found the area indeed a pleasure to visit. We came here by following Highway 351 north of Abilene. We drove past ranchland with long horizons and pastures with small creeks that had clots of frogfruit growing on their banks. These plants have flowers as tiny as june bugs. We reached Albany, the county seat and a large sign proclaiming it "the home of the Hereford."

We read a historical marker that said the county was created in 1858 and early residents included Dr. John Shackelford for whom the county is named and W.H. Ledbetter who came here in 1859 and started the Ledbetter Salt Works. Several of the old buildings on the courthouse square have been restored. As we looked at them the clock in the courthouse steeple boomed out the time. Huge mesquites sent curtains of shade onto the courthouse lawn and the buildings.

We asked a local resident about a place to eat. "Go down past the light and turn right and go to this convenience store. Inside is the Prairie Star and their cooking is good," he said.

We took his advice and found the Prairie Star to be a delight, with an interior furnished with many old signs. Heavy oak furniture and a tip-top bar made a pleasant atmosphere. The menu features homemade sandwiches and plate lunch specials like home-cooked meatloaf and vegetables. We finished our lunch, which was delicious, and then followed Baker's directions to the suspension bridge.

"Take Highway 283 some nine miles north. Take a right on a country gravel road and go 7.9 miles to the bridge," he said.

We drove past the Nail Ranch and clumps of cactus with huge caches of red pears. "Those are called tunas," said Jane. "They taste like dehydrated pineapple in a trail mix."

We reached the gravel road, turned right, and drove past oil field pumps and an old telephone line with two wires that sagged like elastic that has lost its strength. We topped a hill and suddenly the bridge loomed in a distant valley looking like the remains of an old castle, a mass of wood, iron, and steel. A cradle of mesquites and other native trees surround the bridge that, according to Baker, was built in 1896 by the Fluice-Moyers Company of Weatherford. The contract called for a suspension bridge with a total length of three hundred feet, including a one-hundred-forty-foot-long suspension span forty feet above the river.

When T. Lindsay Baker first saw the bridge in about 1980, it was still being used. "The most significant alterations to the bridge were undertaken in the 1930s when the steel towers were filled and covered with concrete and when the truss stiffening on the sides of the roadway between the towers was replaced," according to Baker.

The bridge is not used today. A sign in flaking red paint warns that the bridge has been condemned to all trucks by the county commissioners' court. Bullet holes riddle the letters.

I walked across the thick wooden planks that still have places where pitch oozes from them. Nails that look like spikes hold the boards in place. Cables made by twisting steel wire about twice the size of coat hangers droop on each side. Baker said that a wooden catwalk was built across the river so workers could carry these individual wires back and forth as they plaited the huge cables.

On this day the river flowed milky green, lacing a thin covering over massive limestones near a small waterfall that made a low echo. I looked at it and then to the west and amazingly, the moon appeared, looking like a faded silver dollar; it was only two in the afternoon.

We took photographs and then headed back. Because of time restraints, we did not visit the Fort Griffin iron-truss bridge in the same area near Fort Griffin on Highway 283. But, Eddie and I did return in the fall for a look at the bridge. We were not disappointed though the temperatures were in the forties and rain and mist hit our faces and ears as we crawled from our car for a look at the old bridge in some beautiful Brazos River bottomland north of Albany. A flock of wild turkeys twisted their heads toward us as they picked for seeds and insects in some freshly planted farmland.

We stopped as we reached the end of the bridge and looked at its thick, massive timbers used as a roadway. "Those are two-by-twelves," I said as I looked at the boards held in place with nails as large as railroad spikes.

"They are more like two-by-thirteens," said Eddie.

We looked in under the bridge and saw marks made by axes on boards that apparently had been hand hewn. The size and weight of the timbers could be better measured from this position.

"I'll tell you one thing," said Eddie. "The mules they used to haul those in here got up one helluva sweat."

A large oak tree with twisted limbs that made it look like the set for a horror movie stood near the bridge. The tree had leaves as pale as yellow popcorn balls.

Baker, who also visited this bridge, said that the King Iron Bridge Company of Cleveland, Ohio, one of the largest of the nineteenth century firms specializing in building prefabricated bridges, built that bridge in 1885.

"The bridge was built as a result of demands from people using an all-weather crossing over the Clear Fork of the Brazos between the towns of Albany and Throckmorton," he said. "Two large piers were made from limestone blocks cut from the area. The bridge has a total length of 226 feet," he said.

When Baker did his research, an ordinance passed by the county in 1886 that regulated traffic across the bridge still remained in effect. The ordinance authorized the placing of a sign at each end of the bridge, warning travelers that they were liable for a $5,000 fine if they drove or rode across the bridge "faster than a walk" or drove more than twenty head of cattle or horses across the span at one time.

That fine may sound severe. But this county once handed out even more harsh justice. Consider the vigilante group that rode across the countryside handing out large portions of their own justice. A man caught stealing a horse in 1876 met that justice when he was hanged from a pecan tree. The men in the group showed their disdain for anyone who might have disagreed with them by leaving below the body a pick and shovel that could have been used to bury the body should anyone desire. That horse thief became a warning for others who might choose to follow his deeds. The group shot two more horse thieves, hanged six, and then shot a former lawman caught rustling cattle.

I thought of those stories and about something Jane had said in the event that we ever returned to see the bridge. "We definitely will bring only fifteen head of cattle," she said.

CHAPTER SIXTEEN

Tin Top Bridge

❖ ❖ ❖

They soon could play anything together. Sometimes she would
start and sometimes he would start.

Sometimes one would stop and begin singing the words as the
other kept playing. Then one day they both stopped at the same time.

She looked at him. She offered her hand. He took it and they
looked at each other. Both smiled. He could hear explosions going off
inside his head. They sounded like the booms made by the big trucks
as they roared across the bridge.

❖ ❖ ❖

The deep feelings for old bridges can be found in the stories about the
collapse of the aged Tin Top Bridge in southern Parker County. That happened one night in 1980 after a flood ripped the bridge from its cables. Mary
Kate Durham of Granbury remembers the event and the next day well.

"When we heard about it, a group of us went up the next day. We stood
there like a bunch of mourners and looked at its wreckage lying there in the
Brazos. It was old and wooden. It was just like an old man who is standing
outside and a good stiff north wind hits him and just blows him over," she
said. Her voice became soft. "But I still grieve when I go over the new Tin
Top Bridge. I loved that old bridge."

Earlier, we had driven north of Granbury to FM 2580 and then headed
for the tiny community of Tin Top, which is better known today for the
fact that several winning lotto tickets have been sold at a convenience store

there. Eddie Lane told about coming to the site after a flood some five years ago.

"I saw a trailer ripped loose and dumped right on the edge of this road," he said. "Let's see, that would have meant the old Brazos carried it more than a quarter of a mile."

We reached the new bridge. A tiny kitten with a flag of white across its chest greeted us. I petted her, and she exploded into purring. She followed us as we walked in under the new bridge. Somebody had erected a barrier made of wrought iron. I thought about how time has brought those changes to territory around the bridges.

When I was a youngster living in Glen Rose, the property near and under the bridges remained open to anyone. We camped out in these places many times. But today they have been closed with all sorts of fences and structures. Near this fence the willow trees grew at angles in their search for moisture. The north winds apparently had helped put a slant in their trunks. Numerous huge grasshoppers ate the vegetation. We looked at the new bridge, built strong and sturdy but lacking atmosphere. I thought about what Donald Linney, Hood County road administrator, had said about old bridges and their character. "Yes, I love them and the personalities they have," he said. "The new ones are certainly stronger and last longer. But they don't have the feelings those old bridges did."

The old bridge here had character and history. But this whole area seems wrapped in history. Near Mary's Brazos Café, a favorite eating place in this area, is the New Prospect Baptist Church and the Church of Christ. A historical marker in the front yard of the Church of Christ says that the oldest log school in South Parker County was built near here in 1852 and among the pupils to attend that school were Drs. W. M. Campbell and Alf Irby, two early leaders in the Church of Christ denomination.

We drove across the bridge to the development of Rio Brazos. Al Magness was working on a swimming pool. He pointed to a nearby clump of vines and weeds, where in the shade of a monstrous native pecan tree a sign from the old bridge still stands and reads, "Slow. Weak Bridge. Gross weight, 26,000 pounds."

"I love the old bridges. They are just like this area, so full of history of the Indians and the old west. But you should go talk to Jan Esslinger. She can tell you about the old bridge," Magness said. "She just lives up the hill."

We drove up the hill and met Esslinger, who had a few stories about the old bridge. "I can remember driving across that bridge in a little '59 Volkswagen one time. It was just about dusk, and I was nearly all the way across when this pickup full of young people came onto the bridge," she said. She smiled. "You got to remember, the old bridge was only one way. Anyway, this young driver puts his bumper in front of my VW and then starts pushing me backwards. He pushed me all the way back across the bridge. Scared me? It absolutely petrified me."

She recalled the night the old bridge collapsed. "When I saw it, I was thanking God I was not on it," she said. She shook her head. "You need to go talk to my daddy. He and my mother were watching TV the night it happened and they heard it."

We drove a few blocks to the house of her parents, Mary and Johnny Anderson. They bought property here several years ago. He recalled driving across the old bridge. "It was one way and there was a lot of meeting in the middle. And, yeah, it was kinda rickety. That came from the old two-by-twelves and two-by-sixes they used to build it. I was always apprehensive when I drove across it. But, that certainly didn't stop me because it was the only way we had to get across the river to our property," he said. "But, you really didn't have much maneuvering room on it."

Then he recalled the night that the bridge collapsed. He and his wife were at home watching television. "We heard this kinda roaring noise. I can't really describe it. But then we found out it was the old bridge that had been torn from its cables and had collapsed into the river," he said. He said the new bridge had just been opened a short time before that so there was no real problem caused from the collapse. "But, a funny thing about all of that. There had been talk they were going to come in and make the old bridge into one of these scenic things . . . you know, a park. They were going to have a bike and hiking trail across it," he said. He shook his head. "I guess it was in worse shape than they thought."

That may have been true. But there was a man from Parker County who built bridges that lasted for generations. His name was William Flinn. Kate Nowak of Gordon, who once published the magazine, *Painted Post Crossroads,* told me about Flinn, a Kansas native, who came to this area in 1880. He apparently learned how to build bridges while working for the rail-road, and, from 1885 until he died in 1904, Flinn—known as Billy—built bridges in Parker, Palo Pinto, Erath, Mills, and San Saba counties. One of his partners was E. E. Runyon, who patented the design that involved coupling pipe with heavy strands of twisted wire to hold the weight of the bridge. Runyon's design also involved forging special fittings to hold the thick strands of cable. Old photographs show the size of these huge strands of cables.

Flinn took his bridge building seriously. In fact, he was so serious about being on the site that he purchased a large tent that he put up where a bridge was being built. The tent housed a kitchen, a commissary, his office, and three bunk beds fashioned so that they could be disassembled in a matter of minutes for shipping to the next job. The tent's sides could be ele-vated during hot weather and had a special attachment to stretch the canvas taut in bad weather. The structure provided good housing at any location and was as important to Flinn as the huge cranes used to hoist the steel beams into place.

Flinn's obsession about supervising construction may have con-tributed to his early death at the age of forty-four. His demise came while he was working on a bridge between Mineral Wells and Weatherford. Flinn developed an abscessed tooth but, rather than go to a doctor, he went to a blacksmith.

"I've shod mules and horses, but I ain't ever pulled a tooth," said the smithy.

"If you have done those, then you can certainly pull a tooth," said Flinn. "Have at it."

The blacksmith removed the tooth. But following the extraction, Flinn developed blood poisoning and died at his home in Weatherford. A resolution was passed, recognizing his work as a bridge builder and a leader in the community. Within a year of his death, favor turned from suspension bridges to trussed structures. By the end of World War II, the era of the short-span suspension bridge had ended.

In a bit of irony, pylons from some of Flinn's bridges can still be seen today in the thick brush that grows along the banks of the Brazos River. They are testimony to the fine craftsmanship he engineered.

CHAPTER SEVENTEEN

Hood County Bridges

❖   ❖   ❖

His old man boomed out the question even though he knew the answer. His sour breath came in fogs as he demanded, "Where in the hail you been going, boy?" He didn't wait for the answer. "I know. You been goin' to that bridge to play that mouth organ you got. Well, we got other thangs to do. Got land to plow. Got cattle to work. No time for thangs like going to that bridge and sucking on that musical instrument. Besides, I got that mouth harp and hid it. You want to practice somethin', then practice plowin' or workin' cattle."

It was a long time before he made it back to the bridge.

❖   ❖   ❖

Hood County has been blessed with history.

This colorful miasma of the past has stories about John Wilkes Booth, assassin of Abraham Lincoln, having lived in Granbury, the picturesque county seat located some fifty miles southwest of Fort Worth. Another page in local history says that Jesse James, famed train robber, is buried in a Granbury cemetery.

The stately old courthouse still has in its towers one of the old clocks that has to be wound by hand. Just walking around it gives visitors a taste of that past. There are plenty of interesting shops, antique stores, a bookstore, ice cream parlor, and the Granbury Opera House, a beautifully restored theater where musicals and plays are produced.

Included in the city's colorful past is an item of which few people are aware. Granbury had the only suspension bridge across the Brazos other than the first one built in Waco in 1870. That was a toll bridge, which at one time had the grandson of Davy Crockett, famed Kentucky pioneer and hero at the battle of the Alamo in 1836, acting as toll taker.

Unfortunately, that Hood County bridge, like two other of the old suspension bridges, has been demolished and replaced. Those replacements came after bridge inspections done by Texas Department of Transportation revealed deterioration that had caused unsafe conditions. The bridges are rated on scores from zero to nine on such things as decks, superstructures, substructures, and approaches. Nine means the item is in excellent condition, and zero means the item is in a dangerous condition and beyond repair. Many of the older bridges have only one or two lanes, and expensive restoration cannot be justified.

Therefore, on our quest to look at bridges over the Brazos we looked at the new bridges and the sites of the older ones. The bridge on Highway 51 has been called the Weatherford Bridge for years. As I stood beneath its massive concrete beams reinforced with no telling how much steel rebar, I was impressed with its apparent strength but its lack of character.

I thought of a story I heard about a cowboy watching an exceptionally strong Russian in a weightlifting contest. The Russian had just hefted what appeared to the cowboy to be weights the size of his horse. He asked the Russian how much he had lifted.

"Five hunnert pounds," said the Russian.

The cowboy was impressed. So he asked him what he ate to achieve such strength.

"Five hunnert pounds," said the Russian.

The cowboy was puzzled. So he asked him where he was from.

"Five hunnert pounds," said the Russian.

That's the way it is with these new bridges. After you say they are massive and strong looking, there is not much else you can say. As I pondered the situation, Eddie Lane had a suggestion.

"Call Mary Kate Durham. She can give you all kinds of information about the bridges in Hood County," he said.

I did. Mary Kate, as she is known locally and with whom I had talked about the Tin Top bridge, is a walking book of historical facts about her

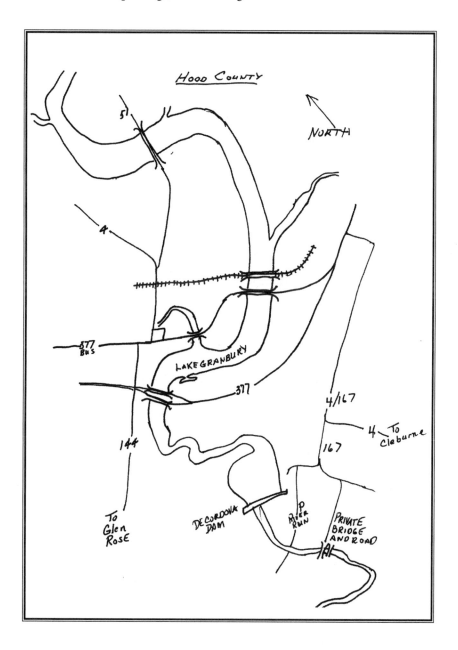

home county, including loads of facts about the old bridges. She learned many of her stories from something her late father taught her.

"He always encouraged us never to take the same route when we left home to go somewhere. He said by taking a different route, you just might discover something new and different," she said.

That came in handy for at least one man when the Weatherford Bridge washed out in the 1950s. Mary Kate, who has photographs of the bridge's wreckage, recalled that story. "I asked a man, named White, who lived on the other side of the bridge how he got to work that morning because he didn't have a bridge," she said. "My husband thought that was a dumb question because Mr. White knew all of the back roads, which he followed to get to work that day. He'd learned those by doing exactly what my daddy had taught us to do and as a result, the washing out of a bridge did not deter him in the least."

She told another story about the rickety Weatherford Bridge and a friend of hers. That friend's father was a doctor and calls late at night would require him to go over the old bridge. "That worried her to death. She just knew that the bridge was going to collapse and send her father to his death in the Brazos River when it was flooding," said Mary Kate.

The flooding of the Brazos, which happened many more times in those days before dams had been built across it, did cause problems with the bridges. Powerful floodwaters totally washed out some bridges. On other occasions the bridges' approaches were washed out, which prevented crossings. That could cause a dilemma like the one that confronted the family of Jim Randle, Mary Kate's grandfather. The family had come to Granbury to buy groceries and supplies. They headed home in a horse-drawn wagon after heavy rains began saturating the area.

"They made it to the north side of the bridge when the approach fell," said Mary Kate. "Grandfather took the family back to town, put them on a train, which took them across the river because the train bridge was okay.

He had called a friend to pick up the family. He could have stabled the team in town but he thought too highly of those horses to do that. So he got into his wagon and headed for the next and only other bridge over the Brazos in the country then. That was at Waco. He drove all the way to that bridge (about eighty miles), paid the toll, and then headed home for Granbury."

Bridges caused another problem back in the days of horseback travel.

"Many horses did not like to go over a bridge because of the overhead steel or wooden girders," said Mary Kate. "It would scare them so bad that they often would hurt themselves." Her father, the late Keith Randle, would never ride a horse in a parade after what had happened to him one day when he was leading a horse by himself. Randle was driving a pickup and had a bridle on the horse, which he held from the vehicle's cab.

"When they started across a bridge, that horse balked but Daddy kept going, literally dragging the animal which had set back on its haunches and refused to budge," said Mary Kate. "When he got home that horse looked like it had its neck broken. After that, he said he would never ride a horse in a parade because the parade route often went over bridges."

Mary Kate said that before and after the construction of bridges, ferries carrying people and their supplies across the Brazos flourished in Hood County. "We had two ferries here," she said. "Burton Burks [a local resident] has a big rock in his front yard. That rock still has a steel ring embedded in it. I understand Burton had the rock dug from the riverbank before the lake covered it. That ring is where they tied the ferry."

Does she like the new bridges?

"Well, they are more serviceable," she said. "But, they aren't nearly as picturesque."

A person can still get a glimpse of the remains of one of the more picturesque bridges in Hood County if they catch the Brazos when it is at low stage. Many people are not aware of this bridge, located less than a mile from a bridge built in 2001 by the development known as Pecan Plantation. We met Courts Cleveland, a Hood County native, at his home at Pecan, and he drove us to that early bridge built by residents of the Kristenstad community.

Kristenstad, a sort of commune, developed in Hood County in the late 1920s. Cleveland remembers the bridge because his family then ran cattle on land leased in this area. "I've tied a cow to every tree in deCordova Bend," said Cleveland as we drove to the site of the old bridge. "There used to be a family from the commune who still lived here. They were bossed by an old woman that I called Granny. I would ride up and ask if they had seen any of my cattle. She'd scream curses at her boys, demanding that they tell me if they had seen any cattle."

We'd reached the site. Cleveland parked his car. Gerald White, his son, Danny, Eddie Lane, and I walked down to the river. Because it was low, parts of the old bridge were visible, including logs that had been placed on top of

Jon McConal walking on the remains of a bridge built in Hood County in the late 1920s by residents of the Kristenstad community, an early-day commune. Pieces of old farm equipment and automobiles were used to reinforce the concrete.

Both of these bridges in the Pecan Plantation development in Hood County were built with private funds. When the bridge in the foreground was declared unsafe, members of the development association appropriated $1.3 million to build the new, 540-foot bridge.

rocks cemented together. Beneath there are pieces of steel that came from such things as old motors and transmissions.

"They must have used everything they had to make the foundation," said the elder White. "Look at this. It's an old axle either from a Model T or an old row binder [a piece of farm equipment]."

"I think they must have put everything that was heavier than water down for their foundation," said his son. "And, to think, I've lived here for nearly ten years and had no idea this bridge was ever here."

We returned to the car where Cleveland told about seeing his father drive the family Model T across the bridge. "It was a good low-water bridge," he said.

We could see the new bridge down the river, built by Pecan Plantation after another bridge built by the Leonard family, which owned and developed the land where Pecan now is, had been declared unsafe.

"Actually, one whole end fell down," said Jim Miller, project manager for the new bridge. "The new bridge has a H40 rating, which means it will take anything you want to put on it."

That new bridge is 540 feet long and cost $1.3 million. That includes money to remove the old one, which has not been done. As we drove across the new bridge, Cleveland looked downriver at the Kristenstad bridge site.

"I've ridden a horse across that old bridge many times. I've got many memories of that bridge and this area," he said. Most of them are good memories like coming to the bridge for picnics and eating fried chicken, freshly sliced tomatoes, cucumbers, watermelon, chocolate cake, chocolate pie, coconut pie, strawberry pie, biscuits layered with homemade butter, and fresh peaches, blackberries, and grapes. Then there came the days when Cleveland would ride his horse to the bridge in the summertime when both he and the horse had sweat dripping from them and he would order the animal into the Brazos for a delightful cooling off. Yes, those are good memories.

CHAPTER EIGHTEEN

Breckenridge Homemade Bridge

❖   ❖   ❖

The first day when he had not appeared had been the worst for her. She had played and there had been no answer. She had played again. Still no response. Fear and anxiety began to shadow her emotions.

She wondered why he had not come. She had a good idea. But, still, she ached to see him. Her music sounded hollow and shallow as it hit the bridge. Nothing answered it but a barn owl that said, "Who? Who? Who?" A motorcycle blasted across the bridge, killing the owl's answer. Where was he? Only the muffled echoes from the motorcycle came.

❖   ❖   ❖

The strong spirit of Texas individualism can be found in abundance in the people who live along the Brazos River. There is no better example than Lester Clark, a Stephens County rancher. When he grew tired of driving eight miles to get to the other side of the Clear Fork of the Brazos and the rest of his large ranch, he solved the problem in a rather unusual way. He built himself a bridge over the river.

That bridge is still being used today though in order to see it, you have to have a private invitation from the Clark family. Eddie Lane had obtained one for us after talking to Troy Taylor of Granbury about our Brazos bridges project.

"You should go to Breckenridge and look at the bridge on the Clark Clear Fork Ranch. It is really impressive," he said. "If you are interested, call Eddie Clark in Dallas and tell him I told you about the bridge."

Lane got an invitation, and here we were headed west on Highway 180 to Breckenridge, returning to country we had already visited. The morning was smoky with fog caused by an overnight rain. Lane talked about his interest in bridges and rivers.

"Actually, I was more interested in rivers," he said. "I was reared in Ohio. Where I went to high school, the school was built in the bed of the old Maumee River. I can remember saying as a kid that someday I was going to come back and float that river. I never did, but I became really interested in rivers, particularly the Brazos. That naturally led to my interest in bridges."

Ironically, shortly after he had told that story we looked at some barricades erected across a county road in the southern part of Stephens County. The sign read, "Road closed. Bridge out."

We continued driving west, reaching a wide expanse of ranching country where a deer ran across the highway and leaped a barbed wire fence in a beautiful ballet. We passed an old two-story wood-frame house, graying with age. An elderly man stood in the front yard with no shirt. Muscles flashed on his arms as if maybe he had built a bridge or two across the passages in his life.

We came to Breckenridge, a town made into a hot spot by the discovery of oil. Evidence of the oil industry remains in the presence of huge trucks, painted red and yellow, with oil rigs welded and bolted onto their trailer beds. There is also an oil derrick downtown, and oil pump jacks for sale line many streets.

We headed north to the Clark Clear Fork Ranch. Ron Jones, ranch foreman, greeted us. He's a big man with a deep voice that sounds like the foghorn on a river barge. He said the ranch, which encompasses several thousand acres, is tonic for Eddie Clark, the owner. "It's so peaceful and quiet out here at night. You don't hear anything but birds calling and deer and coyotes talking. It is relaxing," he said.

He told about Eddie's father, the late Lester Clark, teaching school in this area in the 1930s. He saved his money and bought land. When oil was found on a parcel of that land, he used part of his profits to buy more land. An oil painting in a game room suggests he became friends with some powerful people. He is standing with the president of Mobil, and Sam Walton, who started Wal-Mart.

"The reason he built the bridge? Well, he couldn't get to the other side of his property without having to drive eight miles. Another reason, when you got a real strong rain here, that river comes up and starts flooding quickly and you can't get out of some of that property," said Jones.

He said Jack Ray built the bridge by welding oil-field pipe together. Only one other man helped him. They started in 1970 and finished in 1972. And, the bridge is still used regularly. "Oh, yeah. I use it all the time. In 1980, they added some suspension to it for strength. I'd estimate that it will hold about ten thousand pounds today," he said. "Come on. Let's go look at it."

So we drove north from the ranch house, which today is used as a weekend guesthouse. We passed a rock house built in 1852 that is still being used. "The door has the initials of the people who built it and the year carved into it," said Jones. "There's a strange thing about that. There is that date of 1852 and on the side is a satellite TV dish." We drove through pastureland that has a long line of electric light poles. Jones pointed at one of them. "Every night that pole will have about 100 buzzards on it. And, they always come to just that one. We don't have any idea of why they chose that pole," he said. He laughed. "The only reason we can figure is it's cheap rent for the buzzards."

We drove across a hay field that Jones said is often covered with as much as three feet of water when the river floods. "It also gets that high in that house," he said.

When Lester Clark, a Stephens County rancher, tired of having to make an eight-mile trip to haul his cattle to market, he solved the problem by building this bridge out of oil-field pipe. The bridge, possibly the only private bridge over the Brazos, is still used regularly.

That's another reason for the bridge, which is a short distance from the house. The bridge allows its residents to drive to safety during a flood.

"Well, here it is," he announced.

He pointed at the bridge, painted a rusty red color. Mesquite trees leaned across portions of it. We pushed them back as we began walking across the one-lane bridge made from six-inch and two-inch pipe. The welds are perfect. Looking below at the yards and yards of pipe that had been used reminded one of a steel jigsaw puzzle.

Jones stopped in the middle and we looked down at the river, which today was a thin, green line. Huge limestone rocks form the riverbed and are only partially covered by the stream.

"This is the normal size of the river. It stays like this unless it floods," he said.

Downriver, a deer had stopped for a drink. She stood near the shade of some huge mesquites with gray on their trunks like the growth of a beard on an old man's face. The smells of a recent rain and the new growth it had triggered were sweet like a woman's fine perfume. The river made a tiny echo with its stream.

"You know, when the oil boom was really going, the pipe used in this bridge would have been worth a fortune because there is so much of it," Jones said.

We walked back to the pickup, and he drove us across the bridge. There was no sound or wobble from the pipe frame as we crossed. "I'm repeating myself, but I've pulled a trailer across this without any trouble," said Jones.

We stopped on the other side and looked at some huge dogweeds with thick, white blossoms that looked like explosions of sacks of cottons. A road-runner with its typical crazy scarecrow haircut darted across the road. A jackrabbit was lying near a mesquite tree with its long ears stretched along its back.

I thought of what a photograph that rabbit would make if it could be caught dashing across the bridge. No doubt, it would hold him.

CHAPTER NINETEEN

A Brazos River Ford

❖ ❖ ❖

A month passed. Still nothing responded to her music but the echoes from the cars and the cries from the bats and owls. Then one day she played a special rendition of the old gospel tune, "I'll Fly Away." When she reached the chorus, a deep answer resounded. Only he could make music like that. She cried. The Brazos cried with her.

"I'll fly away, oh glory. I'll fly away, fly away in the morning," the words went.

Great sounds and great times dwelled beneath the bridge again.

❖ ❖ ❖

Eddie Lane has made many interesting discoveries during his years of exploring the Brazos River. One is the ford across the river at Oaks Crossing in Palo Pinto County.

"I don't remember exactly when I discovered this," he said as we drove to the ford, which is about five miles south of Mineral Wells. "I have since heard that it was one of few natural fords on the river."

Back before the bridges finally came across the rivers, fords were extremely important to cattlemen and residents. To find what was considered a natural ford brought them a blessing, because ranchers could drive herds of cattle across the river without the fear of the animals being caught in the current and swept to their deaths. The same places brought feelings of comfort to the early settlers. A natural ford with shallow water meant the settler with his wagon and team of horses or mules could make it across the stream without having to unhitch the wagon and possibly take it apart before getting to the other side.

We had come north on Highway 281 to find this crossing, stopping to ask directions from a lanky woman who looked like she could have been a model for an "after" in a weight-loss program.

"Yeah, go up here to the gas plant and take a right and go on down to Willow Pond Cemetery and take another right. That road will lead you right to it," she said.

We followed her directions. We drove past some goats in a pasture. One stood on the back of another in an attempt to reach some leaves from a leaning tree limb. We passed one of those old rock fences that had been hand laid and are still in good condition.

"There it is," said Lane.

The Brazos ran wide but clear over the gravel bottom and did not look very deep. The river water looked much cleaner than the trash left in what has to be a local treasury. Empty beer bottles, cans, old socks, and insect repellent cans lined the shore where people had stopped for no telling what reason.

"It looks shallow enough. I'd bet we could drive across it," said Lane.

It did look inviting but we didn't drive across. Instead we drove to the home of James K. Glover, who was born and raised in this area. He's built lean and has a short beard and moustache. This day he sat outside in a gazebo he had built, with his dog J.J., a miniature Dachshund, nearby.

"So you want to know about Oaks Crossing," he said. "Well, it was named after Old Man Oaks. He had some relatives here that I knew when I was a kid. I used to go across it on a motorcycle. Let me tell you, that was fun."

He excused himself for a moment. "I've got to clean my mouth out. I'm dipping," he said.

Soft-looking white clouds floated overhead. Then the scratchy cries from a mockingbird interrupted him momentarily. He grinned and continued.

"My wife and I lived here many years. She's gone," he said, and his voice softened. "She died from that breathing stuff. I sure do miss her."

He told about going to school in nearby Prospect, of working a variety of jobs, including laying brick, being a machinist, and working at filling stations.

"I worked in them old stations, the kind that had the glass container that looked like a giant fruit jar and had brass rings around it marking the gallons of gas. You'd push down the handle until it reached the amount the customer wanted and then you'd take his money. And, maybe he'd step inside and buy one of those coconut rainbow candy bars," he said. His eyes flashed as he recalled those days.

"I'm seventy-one, so I've been around here awhile," he said. "As for that old river, I've seen it get up over that second bank. Yes, sir. You didn't go across that crossing then, unless you had a boat. I never did cross it in a car. But, I certainly did many times on my motorcycle."

He said he had heard his great-grandfather talk about bringing cattle across the river at that location. "He married a Choctaw Indian. She was a strong woman," said Glover. "He raised cattle and I heard him say that Oaks Crossing was one of the main ones for driving cattle across around here."

He petted J.J. and then announced that he is a licensed ordained preacher. "I have been for thirty years," he said. Again his voice softened. "But, nobody wants me to preach anymore. And I can play the piano, too. I'm a Baptist, but that don't make any difference. I can preach and play the piano at any church. Like I have played at the Assembly of God church and the preacher there let me preach some, too."

A huge truck roared by and interrupted his story. As the smells of its diesel hit our noses, he continued. "I sure do miss preaching and playing the piano in church. I used to try to get them livened up with my playing. You know, get them to singing and clapping their hands and feet. Get some life in the service," he said. "And, I only charged $15 to play the piano."

He stopped and picked up J.J. Then he continued. "I love that river. You know at night, me and J.J. go to bed and he doesn't say anything unless somebody drives up. And, sometimes I dream about that old crossing and going across it on my motorcycle," he said. "J.J. just lies there and he doesn't say anything."

He stopped talking and stared into the distance. I closed my notebook, and we said good-bye. As we headed for home, I could imagine Glover in his younger days, climbing onto that motorcycle, driving like hellfire to the crossing, and then roaring across it with the wind blowing through his hair.

CHAPTER TWENTY

Somervell County Bridge

❖   ❖   ❖

The years passed quickly like the notes from their harmonicas. High school graduation neared. They received their high school yearbooks and wrote messages of promise and hope in the pages that contained photographs of Derrick Hatcher and Lyda Merrick, named most popular of the entire high school that year.

They were going their separate ways. They talked about where their lives were leading them and about how important it was for them to stay in touch. They promised that they would always be together, as mates as smooth as the notes they made beneath the bridge. Yet, as they looked into each other's eyes, they both knew that their promises were shallow like the old Brazos during a drought.

❖   ❖   ❖

As drivers head south on Highway 144 for Glen Rose, glimpses of the white limestones of the lower cretaceous Glen Rose formation can been seen. Author Darwin Spearing said the few road cuts and natural exposures along the highway are all Glen Rose limestone. "The typical Glen Rose alternations of hard limestone beds and intervening soft marl or mud stone weathers to distinctive stair-step topography that characterizes Glen Rose outcrops across central and north central Texas," he wrote.

Those ingredients and the abundance of cedar junipers, mesquite, and live oaks make for a scenic drive to the steel bridge on Highway 67 six miles east of Glen Rose. That bridge answered the needs of motorists and young

This bridge in Somervell County stands on FM 200 where another bridge collapsed when an army convoy drove over the 400-foot structure during troop movements in World War II. One soldier died and two others were seriously injured in the accident.

people when it was built in 1945 after the collapse of Somervell County's only other bridge.

The new bridge was needed, said an official with the Dallas Chamber of Commerce, to "promote the extension of Highway 67 across the Rio Grande to Chihuahua and eventually to the West Coast."

Those needs ranked high, particularly after an army convoy caused the old bridge to collapse. But youngsters of that era soon found the steel structure's shade a great place for Sunday gatherings. I spent many hours there showing off cars and listening to the latest sounds caused by "Smitties," which when added to the exhaust systems were supposed to cause the engines to make an impressive deep rumble.

And sometimes, spontaneous activities took place at the Brazos Bridge as it was called in those days. As youngsters we always looked for ways to entertain ourselves. We often found that entertainment on Sunday afternoon when we gathered at the bridge. We marveled at the strength of the bridge as "semis" pulling trailers loaded with a variety of goods roared across the structure. One day as we stood there philosophizing about such matters, I remembered that I had some boxing gloves in my car.

"Anybody interested in boxing?" I asked.

Only one other person stepped forward and slipped on a pair of the gloves. I can't remember where I had gotten them, but I do remember that

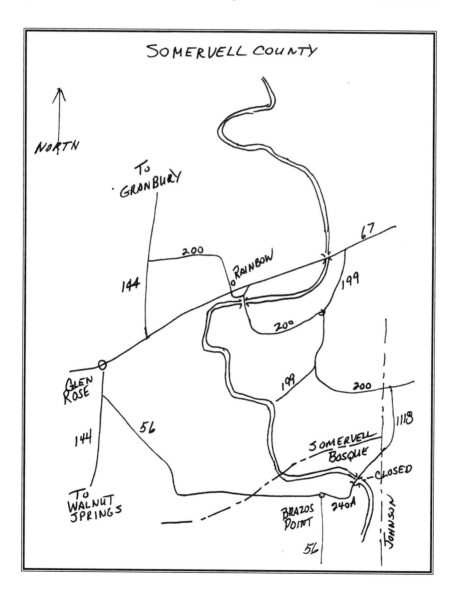

they were so worn that the padding in both left gloves had slipped and hardened. Which meant a left jab became a powerful weapon. I grinned to myself as I put on my pair of gloves. We stepped to the center of the ring, which was nothing more than the other guys standing around us. They began hollering.

"Sic 'em, Bunky," yelled one of my buddies.

Though I weighed only 118 pounds, I had no fat on me and was a pretty fair boxer. Pure muscle stretched over my five-foot five-inch frame. Or at least that is what I told myself when I looked in a mirror. I quickly rocked my opponent with a left made even harder by the massed up padding. He dropped his right hand in pain. I landed a right jab and then a left cross that knocked him off his feet. He looked up at me and said, "I've had enough."

I helped him to his feet. I probably strutted some when a guy named Cheek, who was two years older than I, announced that he would like to put on the gloves. Cheek always had a kind of crazy look in his eye and was known to be without fear. But I had no fear that afternoon either. Heck, I had just knocked one man down and had gotten my soul refreshed that morning in our little fundamental church. The preacher had ranted and bellowed that I should believe and if I did believe "in the Lard Jasus Christ with all yur hart, then you can accomplish miracles and whup yore enemies."

Well, I did believe in Jesus and I had just decked someone, so why not take on old Cheek? I did. I began to wonder about my decision as his buddy tied on the gloves and I could see that crazy gleam in his eye. Then somebody yelled, "Go to it." Cheek immediately began moving toward me. He abandoned the fancy stuff of circling each other and feeling each other out. He was by gawd ready.

As he moved toward me, he had his gloves almost hanging at his side. I thought this rather unusual so I hit him with a right. I hit him so hard that my shoulder shuddered in pain. I looked at Cheek and realized two things. He had been drinking homemade whiskey and that stuff was a liquid enforcer that made people lose their inhibitions. It also made them mad as hell when you hit them as hard as I had hit Cheek.

Raw anger flashed in Cheek's eyes as he came at me. Suddenly, I knew this was not some Sunday afternoon boxing for him. Instead, this represented a downright fight in which he grabbed me and slammed me to the ground. Then he got on top of me and began pounding my face with the boxing gloves. About then, I realized two other things about Cheek. One was, he was as tough as rawhide, and the other was that you had better forget about having Jesus on your side and run like hell when he got after you. He had bloodied my nose and caused a large purple whelp on my right cheek before the others could pull him off.

As they held him, he stood for a moment looking at me with that crazy look. Finally, Cheek calmed down, shook my hand, and apologized.

Anyway, such adventures happened regularly at the Brazos Bridge during my childhood. Obviously, it still is the site for adventures today. But, looking at the evidence of those escapades brought a feeling of sadness to me. I guess I had thought that since I had always taken my trash with me when I had departed this spot where I spent so much of my youth that it would still be the same way. It isn't. It is typical of so many of the bridges we had seen, the ground stained with empty beer and soft drink containers, discarded undergarments, and old shoes.

I walked to the banks and looked at the water that ran so clear on this day that I could see a channel catfish darting near a ledge. I thought of a time when the late Dale McPherson and I camped out here and caught some catfish. We cleaned them, rolled them in cornmeal, and cooked them by dropping them in a skillet of smoking grease.

As I looked across the river, four people from Dallas arrived with some huge tire tubes.

"I've been coming down here for about eight years," said Roy Marzynski. "This is a great place to have some fun."

I agreed and told him about coming down here as a youngster and boxing.

"So what are you doing today?" he asked.

"Oh, I'm writing a book about the bridges over the Brazos," I said.

"Hey, really," he replied. "Well, you look like Ernest Hemingway."

I thanked him as they shoved off into the river.

I walked under the bridge and looked at a growth of wild mustang grapes snaking up one of the concrete pillars. Wild rye with heads of grain about an inch long punched through some grass near cottonwood trees, their whitened trunks looking like sheets of silver in the sunshine.

I stopped at the ashes of a campfire. I saw old nails, a piece of a lock, and part of a valve from an engine. Right on the edge of the ashes, two dimes sparkled. I picked them up and put them into my pocket. If I had found them the day Cheek whipped my ass, I would have had enough money to buy four soft drinks to sip and heal my wounds . . . and pride.

I walked to the highway and looked at the bridge. It is one of the older ones, with its long lines of steel arches secured by rivets as big as mashed plums. I looked through the steel beams at the huge pecan trees that would have limbs loaded with pecans in the fall. I thought of the times I had come to this place, picked some of the pecans, peeled them with my pocketknife, and then marveled at their rich taste. I just might do that again when the next fall rolls around.

CHAPTER TWENTY-ONE

Glen Rose Bridge

❖   ❖   ❖

They met for one final playing. They talked of the future. She was going to medical school. He was going to study plant pathology.

They looked at each other. She said no more. They played. Then he sang the song that was now so popular. "Oh, my love, my darling. I hunger for your touch. The long rolling tide."

They played the next verse.

"That's beautiful," he said.

"It will not be the last," she said.

But it was for a long, long time. And, as the song goes, "Time goes by so slowly."

❖   ❖   ❖

A person would never guess when standing on this bridge on this day that this had been the scene of a World War II tragedy.

But at this site on FM 200 three miles east of Glen Rose off Highway 67, part of an army convoy crashed into the Brazos River when the bridge collapsed. The accident, caused by the weight of the convoy passing over the bridge after floods had weakened it, happened in January 1945. One soldier was killed and two others were badly injured.

"The crash of the falling bridge made a great noise and shook the windows in all of the nearby houses," said a report from the *Glen Rose Reporter*, the local newspaper.

The collapse of the 150-foot section of the bridge is still remembered by residents who went to the scene. "I couldn't believe it," said E.E. (Eddie)

Flanary, who lived with his parents on a farm less than a mile from where the accident occurred. He and many others, including his wife, Billie, flocked to the scene for a look. "That was the biggest thing that I had ever seen. And, being just a kid, it did impress me." He and his wife had come to the new bridge that was built in 2002. There's a story in that. "Yeah, they built the old low-water bridge after the accident. It was supposed to be temporary. Funny, but it temporarily lasted more than fifty years," said Flanary. He showed photographs of the old bridge before it collapsed. The one-lane four-hundred-plus-foot structure had been built in 1908 with money from a $15,000 bond fund. The bonds had been paid off less than a year before the accident occurred.

One newspaper article said the bridge was not built for car traffic and signs had been posted for a long time warning that loads of more than 5,000 pounds should stay off the bridge. However, one of Flanary's photos shows several cars coming across the bridge.

"They also had quite a park there," he said. "Look at this photo." The photograph shows a concession stand and a large swimming pool near the river's banks. A postcard referred to the pool as the place of "laughing water." That label probably came from the fact that the swimming pool was fed with water that poured in such great quantities from a natural spring that it made a sound that resembled laughter. The cold water often caused swimmers to exclaim in loud reactions that ranged from shivering to laughter.

Flanary and I walked across the new bridge built exactly where the old one had been. He pointed to some thick undergrowth on the river's banks. "There's the spring. It's still flowing," he said. "I never swam in the pool here, but we used to come and look at the crowds that came here to swim."

The county had several other attractions that drew crowds by the hundreds. The Flanary postcard collection shows many of those—things like sanitariums that promised to heal a myriad of ailments with baths and the drinking of sulfur water that naturally flowed from wells. One of those cards

This bridge on Highway 67 six miles east of Glen Rose in Somervell County was built in 1945 after the army convoy caused the collapse of the bridge on FM 200, about two miles east of Glen Rose.

showed a churn being turned by a flowing well as it made butter. Another card showed an ostrich standing in the front of one of the sanitariums.

"I know a woman who cooked for that place, and she said they used that ostrich's eggs for cooking," said Billie. She smiled. "She said she could make an unbelievable number of pies by using just one ostrich egg."

Such attractions furnished fodder for plenty of stories for the local residents. They got something else to talk about on that January day in 1945. Let the old newspaper article from the *Glen Rose Reporter* tell the story. It reads:

> One soldier is dead and two others were badly injured last Monday when an entire span of the Brazos River bridge on Highway 67 about three miles from Glen Rose collapsed.
>
> A convoy of soldier trucks was passing over the bridge and other trucks had a narrow escape. About nine of the heavy trucks

had passed over the bridge and the tenth almost made it across when the 150-foot span of the bridge gave way and dropped some 50 feet into the water about four or five feet deep. The fall of the bridge section was rather a gradual one and the floor went down together, but the steel frame was badly twisted and broken. Some of the steel girders fell on the back part of the carrier pinning it down to the floor, which was under water.

The soldier receiving the most serious injuries was said to be riding in the gun turret (of an armored vehicle) [and] was reported to have a multiple fracture of the hip and thigh bones and other injuries.

Efforts were started at once to make some arrangements to take care of traffic. For the present it is being routed by Eulogy or by Granbury and Godley, which makes a long out of the way trip for people in this section.

Machinery is already being moved to the old Rock Ford crossing where construction will start at once on a concrete slab crossing which will be used except during high water.

I looked at photographs of the steel of the old bridge that looked like twisted pieces of bailing wire. Then I looked upriver where the old low-water bridge had been, the one that was supposed to be used for only a few months but lasted nearly sixty years.

We talked about how as youngsters we would come down and watch the Brazos flood and send huge logs crashing into the temporary structure. We also talked about friends who would put inner tubes into the river above the low-water bridge and float down to it during these floods.

"It's a wonder several didn't get drowned," said Billie.

But the low-water bridge was a place for other activities. We would go there on weekends to camp out and cook over campfires that heated skillets filled with grease for frying catfish and potatoes and bologna. Those activities changed in recent years and the low-water bridge became a hangout for drinking and drugs. Those became such a headache that the decision was finally made to build the new bridge and demolish the old low-water bridge.

"Feel bad? Are you kidding? I was elated," said Billie. "It had become nothing but a place for drinking."

Lloyd Wirt, a Somervell County commissioner, also was glad to see the old low bridge demolished. But he has ambivalent feelings about its demise. He also remembers the stories that his parents told him about the springs and how people came to bathe in them and have picnics.

"It was really a family place back in those years," said Wirt, a native of the county. He shook his head. "But a few years ago, it became more like a cesspool than a place for people to swim and have fun. I became a member of our rescue squad on our volunteer fire department and the number of calls we responded to out here was unbelievable. It's unfortunate but sometimes you have to make changes to protect people. If you could have seen how this place looked after a weekend of partying by that bunch, you would know what I mean."

Those scenes are hard to fathom on a day like the one I had chosen to look at the new bridge. It's also hard to imagine the river, which today had water so low that a person could safely wade across, becoming so powerful and strong that it ripped a bridge from its foundations, causing it to collapse as it did on that day the army convoy began its crossing. But, as Wirt's late father, Loyd Wirt Sr., had told me many times, "Don't ever underestimate the power of this old river. You do, and it'll kill you."

CHAPTER TWENTY-TWO

Brazos Point Bridge

❖   ❖   ❖

*Her family moved. So did she. She became engrossed in her
school, as deeply attached to her studies as the mustang grapevines
that twisted themselves onto the bridge braces.*

*She kept telling herself she would go back to the bridge some day.
The day did not come. But she did keep her harmonica tucked
beneath her undergarments in the antique oaken chest in her bedroom. Every so often she would lift the clothing, look at it, and
think of him.*

❖   ❖   ❖

We drove south from Glen Rose and took FM 56 to Eulogy and the next
bridge on our list at Brazos Point, a tiny community on the edges of Bosque
and Johnson counties.

The farm road cuts into Highway 6 near the southern edge of Glen
Rose. It leads through some beautiful ranching country and is full of curves
and hills. Those curves have long figured in stories about the Eulogy community back when it was considered a rather wild place where a person
could get about anything he asked for, including whiskey and a black eye. I
thought of some of the wild stories about Eulogy that I heard as a youngster
in Glen Rose as we drove through pastures parched by drought. Recent rains
had turned them instantly green like a pair of white shorts that had been
dipped into a bucket of green dye.

One story concerned two local men who were older than I. They had a
reputation for having an insatiable thirst for strong spirits. That led them

to buy an old Plymouth two-door sedan for $6. They cut the top off the vehicle, painted it a bright blue, and announced that they had a convertible. They called it the Blue Bird.

As was the custom, one night many of us gathered on the courthouse square to exchange deep bits of wisdom: did Juicy Fruit, Dentine, or Spearmint chewing gum make your breath smell better? As we talked, we stepped over to the flowing well that gushed sulfur water and took a drink. After many of those, you needed something much more powerful than Juicy Fruit to stem the smell that water left in your mouth. Just about midnight, we heard this long honking of a horn. Then we heard the rumble of an engine with twin pipes.

"That's the Blue Bird," said someone.

He was right. In a couple of minutes the Blue Bird and its owners roared onto the square. They made a couple of circles around the courthouse before a loud explosion sounded from the Blue Bird. The driver, holding a glass of liquor in his right hand, eased the vehicle over to the side of a street. Then he and his partner, also holding a glass of liquor, climbed from the Blue Bird.

"We've been over to Eulogy," pronounced one of them. "Been having a good time. But, we think the old Blue Bird might have got its feathers burned."

They yanked open the hood. By then we all stood around the car. We gasped when we looked at the head of the Blue Bird's engine. It had turned a melting red color, looking like a piece of the sun as it rises in the morning.

"I knew it was low on water and tried to get him to stop and let me pour some of our beer in the radiator," said one of the partners. "But, he said, 'Hail, we only paid $6 for old Blue Bird and we paid $9 for that beer.' That made sense so we didn't stop."

Needless to say, the old Blue Bird went to its final resting place in a wrecking yard.

Such were the stories that came out of Eulogy. Today it has a couple of houses, a mobile home or two, and that's about it. I circled once and then headed on to Brazos Point, another sleepy community. We drove to Bosque County Road 1175 and headed for the bridge that forms the line between Bosque and Johnson counties. A new bridge has been constructed but the old steel bridge has been left. It is well worth a drive.

We walked across it. Briars with dashes of red berries that looked like someone had spit a mouthful of shotgun pellets painted red grew out of

Visitors can see some of the aging, rusting rivets that anchor the steel beams in this old bridge at Brazos Point, a tiny community that straddles the line of Bosque and Johnson counties. The three-span structure has been closed for several years, but sightseers can still walk across the bridge.

rusting railings. A sign read, "Weight limits: gross 6,000 pounds; axle or tandem, 3,000 pounds." People had been detoured to this bridge when the army convoy caused the Glen Rose bridge to collapse. Thick rusting rivets anchor the steel beams together. As we looked, crows made their "ca-ca" cries from a nearby pecan tree.

The Brazos ran shallow today. My friend, John Tushim, looked down and spotted what looked like an old boat barely covered by the water. "Wonder how long that has been there?" he asked.

We watched a snapping turtle as large as a bucket lid glide over the boat. We continued walking, and I spotted a high-top shoe that looked like it had been dipped in concrete and then tied to one of the steel beams. As we walked, a hollow sound came from the bridge. I thought Tushim had been hitting the sides. He hadn't.

"We'd better get off this," he said.

I laughed, walked to a side, and saw what had caused the noise. The wind apparently had caused one of the steel cables to scrape a steel beam.

Fluffs of clouds drifted overhead as we looked at a large spider spinning its web. Its belly was as big as a marshmallow. I wondered if that was because of eggs it carried. Life continues.

I followed a trail that led beneath the bridge. Concrete girders with tops like giant bottle caps hold the structure firmly. Tall cocklebur weeds with limbs full of tiny demon claws threatened me. Near the top of the bridge, caught in a beam, was a huge tree trunk, testimony of how high the river gets in flood stage.

We left and headed for Brazos Point, passing large sand and gravel operations that had eaten up much of the rich bottom farmland. We reached the community and drove to the Brazos Point Cemetery. Land for the cemetery was given by Joseph and Susan P. Day in October 1869. The cemetery has several handmade concrete markers. Before the concrete dried, the creator had sketched outlines of flowers and crosses. These had then been filled with broken blue, green, and yellow glass and big marbles. One of the markers was for Tamsie May, born February 9, 1904, died January 10, 1926. An inscription read, "Dear Tamsie, twas hard to give thee up. But, thy will, O God, be done."

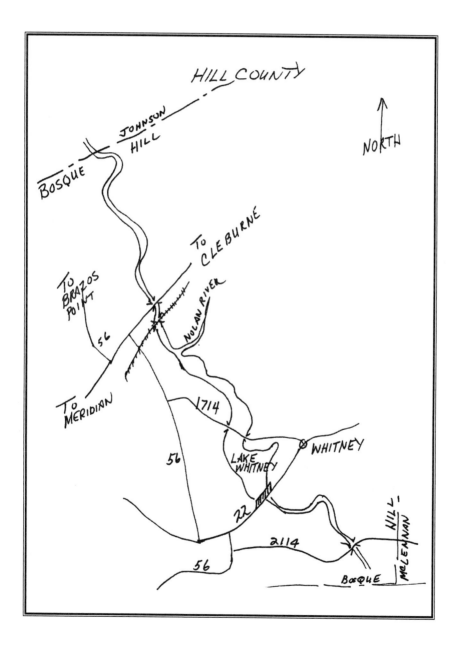

Suddenly, from a nearby house a rooster started its screeching "kerr-kee-err-uh" cry. The temperature had shot into the mid-90s, causing sweat to plaster my shirt to my back. I wondered if that rooster was as hot as I was or as hot as the old Blue Bird had been that night.

CHAPTER TWENTY-THREE

Bosque County Bridge

❖   ❖   ❖

He eventually chose ranching to make a living. But, he never married. He lived by himself. And, regularly he went to the bridge to play his harmonica.

He thought of her when he played. How her breath smelled like the soft-spun honey he had once found in a hollow tree near one of the bridge pillars. He played deeply during these sessions. The only echoes came from his own breath as he drew on the harmonica.

The huge pecan trees continued to grow. One had thick grapevines twisting around its limbs with graying streaks of moss hanging from them. Sometimes when the sun caught the tree near sundown, it looked like a lonely guard walking his shift. Those times seemed fitting for the feelings he had in his heart.

❖   ❖   ❖

One of the Brazos River bridges in Bosque County has seen herds of Longhorn cattle swimming the river at flood stage. We drove to this bridge from Glen Rose, taking FM 56 through Eulogy and Brazos Point. Dew came up from grain fields like smoke from campfires on this cool, hazy morning as we headed for the bridge on Highway 174, at the site of an old town known as Kimball Bend, some twenty-one miles southwest of Cleburne.

The Chisholm Trail once crossed the Brazos River at this bridge, as ranchers pushed thousands of Longhorns north to market. On this day the Texas Chisholm Trail Cowboys Heritage Celebration, sponsored by the Alliance for Justice Foundation, Inc., was being held. Chuck wagons, tepees, and other frontier regalia as well as pieces of old rock buildings dotted the old town site of Kimball Bend, which was established in the early 1850s. At one time when the Chisholm Trail was heavily used, more than 250 people lived here, operating hotels, general stores, cotton gins, and gristmills.

As we walked around looking for Ivanne Farr, one of the event organizers, we passed Longhorn steers with western saddles. I wondered what the old cowboys who drove the Longhorns from Texas to Missouri would think of seeing somebody riding a Longhorn instead of driving the animal.

I talked to Barbara Hamel who said her mother Ouida Mearl Bateman attended school at the Kimball Academy here in the early 1900s. "From what she told me, it was a nice place. I don't like the fact they have built a bridge here and changed it so much. I wished it was still like the old days," she said.

We hitched a ride on a hay wagon being pulled by a tractor driven by Raymond Cheek (no relation to the Cheek I had fought). He said he was glad to see the bridge built but he has seen some bad floods come over it. "I saw the highway department use a cherry picker on that bridge during one of them bad floods. They were picking up debris that had lodged against the bridge and was moving it. They were afraid that there was so much stuff stacking up against it that the bridge would be gone by the next day," he said. "But, I guess they got enough off of it because it held." But, he said he has seen several floods cover the bridge as well as the bottomland where we stood. "There's still debris from the last one along the shore over there. And there are old tires still up in the tops of some of the trees," he said.

I remembered a comment Steve Frye—who was reared in Johnson County—made about the flooding Brazos. "We used to take our rifles and stand along the river's banks and shoot holes in barrels that were coming down the river. We were trying to sink the barrels before they came to the bridge and lodged there," he said. "They gave us a quarter for every barrel we sunk."

Many residents in the area have strong memories of a recent flood. John Shaw, who lives on the road leading to Indian Lodge Resort, said he felt like he was looking at an ocean when he watched the flooding Brazos go over the bridge. But his friend Tom Wright said it was not that flood that impressed him so much but another freak of nature that occurred in 1960 in this area.

"On that night, the temperature went up to 140 degrees. That's what I said . . . 140 degrees. I know it's hard to believe. But, it happened. Cotton wilted and turned black, and people thought the world was coming to an end. Parents wrapped their children in quilts, just knowing that the end was coming," he said. "That's a true fact. Harold Taft [the late weatherman for KXAS-TV Channel 5 in Fort Worth] even sent a television crew down here to photograph it and then he reported it on the news."

Taft and Ron Godbey, who at that time was also a meteorologist for KXAS-TV, wrote about the incident in their book, *Texas Weather*, published in 1975. They entitled the chapter about the occasion, "The Strangest Storm in Texas or The Night the World Almost Came to an End in Kopperl." They attributed the phenomenon to a downward thrust of heated air from an old dried-up thunderstorm. "Mothers wrapped their crying babies in wet sheets to protect them from the intense heat. Fire sprinkler systems were set off, car radiators boiled over, and panic-stricken women were crying, thinking the end of the world had come," Taft and Godbey wrote.

Shaw agreed with that description. "You just knew that this was it as far as life going on," he said. He paused and stared off at the cedar trees. "Well, enough of that. If you want some more information about the flood go on down to Indian Lodge. They got a bunch."

So we drove to Indian Lodge Resort, owned by Tim and Barb Jones. They are friendly and full of stories about the 1992 flood. He said it is still hard for him to fathom that much water being in the area.

"They were actually driving boats over the bridge," he said.

"Yeah, and I saw a boy fishing from his bedroom window. And, he caught a couple," said a neighbor, Paul Griffith.

Well, they weren't catching any fish on the day of the Chisholm Trail Celebration. But they certainly were trying to capture scenes from the frontier days. We watched a man dressed like an old pioneer throw a hatchet with a steel blade at a target made from a tree trunk. The weapon spun end over end and stuck into the trunk.

We walked under the bridge, built in 1951, backed off, and looked.

"It's hard to imagine the river getting over that when you look at it today," said Eddie Lane.

I agreed that imagining that would be like some kind of a dream. Ivanne Farr described the event today, which originally was going to include driving some Longhorns across the bridge, exactly that way. She had picked us up in her van to show us scenes of various events.

"Oh, my goodness, this is a dream come true," she said. "This is the cowboy's way."

She explained that driving the Longhorns over the crossing once made on the Chisholm Trail had been changed because of the problems the Texas Highway Department feared it would cause with traffic on Highway 174.

"But, we are bringing them across the highway and are going to water them in the river where the crossing was," she said. She's tall and wore a long suede dress, in keeping with the frontier atmosphere. We waited for the herd beside the road. Suddenly she said, "Oh, my goodness, here they come."

We watched as some twenty-five or thirty longhorns came across the highway. The people riding snorting and sweating horses in the noon heat outnumbered the cattle.

"It's symbolism . . . a chapter from our tradition and heritage. We've got to do things like this to give people an idea of where we are going," she said. She had rolled down her van window. "Here they come. Isn't this awesome?"

The riders yelled at the longhorns. "Hyeah. Hyeah. Hyeah, cattle!"

The cattle moved past people dressed for the event and standing in the shade of the huge pecan trees. One woman had on black pants and red suspenders with her pants legs stuffed into a pair of yellow boots. "Hyeah, hyeah, hyeah, cattle," yelled the riders.

I looked at the bridge. A pickup pulling a long trailer thundered across. Bawling cattle packed the trailer. Regardless of history, I'd bet that rancher preferred taking his cattle across the Brazos that way.

CHAPTER TWENTY-FOUR

Ferries for the Brazos

❖   ❖   ❖

He became known as the old man who plays under the bridge.
His music became famous. Sometimes people would come and hide
in the undergrowth so they could hear him play.

"His music is so powerful," said one man.

"Yeah, and it is so lonely," said another. "It's like finding a good
steak, finely cooked in the middle of a forest. Only you know there's
nobody within fifty miles to share it with. So you just light a candle
and watch it melt away as you eat it yourself."

❖   ❖   ❖

In the days before bridges were built across the Brazos, people depended
on ferries or just wild courage to get them across the river. According to the
Handbook of Texas Online, before modern bridges were built to cross Texas
rivers, ferries were maintained at most points where roads crossed streams
or rivers that were not fordable.

"From the beginning, ferries were subject to regulation by the community they served," says the handbook. "Ferries had various styles of construction, but perhaps the most common type was a flat raft-like barge
onto which a wagon or cart could be driven from the inclined stream
banks. Many ferrymen stretched a bank-to-bank cable for a guide and ferrymen were allowed to raise their fares for crossings at night or in bad
weather."

Ferries were the preferred way to cross a river if a person had the money
to pay for the crossing. That money did make a good living for those people

who built and operated ferries, such as the one that crossed the Brazos River at Kimball Bend. Old photographs of that ferry show it transporting an army wagon across the river in 1865. Two other photos show the ferry loaded with people.

"The information I've gotten said the owners charged fifty cents a head for livestock and ten cents for a person," said Lem Young of Whitney who has built a model of the old ferry. He smiled. "You either paid the price or swam the river."

Young does not exaggerate with facts. "I'll tell you I don't know rather than tell something that I'm not certain about and have history scrambled," he said. So when he was asked to build a model of the ferry that operated here, he found few facts. "We think it started about 1860. But, I am not certain who owned it or when it closed," he said. "But in looking at photos, I would estimate it was about fourteen feet wide and thirty-five feet long."

Young said he agreed to build the model ferry because he has always been interested in history. "I've spent a lot of time studying the old masters and how and why they built things," he said. He explained the working of his model ferry. It has a wooden wheel in the center of the boat. "This has a lot to do with ancient Egypt design," he said. "There is a single wheel in the middle which was turned by hand. And, that is how you changed the attitude [direction] of the ferry."

Actually, the Brazos River's current pulled the ferry across the river. "Of course, back then, they had a whole lot more water in the river," he said. "But, anyway, here is how it worked. They had a cable that stretched across the river. It was anchored to towers on each side. The towers, of course, were higher than the river. The ferry was attached to the cable with this."

He pointed to an item that had steel pulleys on each end. This was attached to the center wheel of the ferry. By turning that wheel, the ferry's course could be altered, which pulled it across the river. Turning that wheel, which was huge, demanded strength from the ferry operator. Many times customers would help crank the wheel, particularly if the current of the river was strong.

"When they neared the landing on the other side, they let down one of these platforms," said Young. The platform stretched wide and looked like a portable walkway. He pushed down the model's platform that fit inside the landing on the shore as the ferry neared the shoreline.

"It made a pretty neat operation," he said.

Eddie Lane agreed. "I've ridden on one just like that up in Maine," he said.

As we looked at the model's various parts, Young told why he thought the project was so important. "The main thing is educating the kids," he said. "I used to work on the dam here at Lake Whitney. Kids used to come through on tours, and they would look at the turbines that were buried underground and they didn't seem to understand them. Then I would say, 'Well, they work like a waterwheel.' A light would come on in their eyes because then they understood the principle of the thing. That impressed me so much, I decided to build a waterwheel that would work so the kids could get a really good look at it. "

As we talked, a man stopped to look at the model that was on display during a frontier celebration. When Young mentioned that he worked in the dam, the man said, "What did you think about the cracks in that dam . . . did it scare you?"

Young looked disgusted. "There were no cracks in that dam. That is just an old wives' tale," he told the man, who left immediately. Young shook his head. "I've heard of bodies being buried in the cement in the dam and all sorts of wild things. I get sick and tired of history being disturbed by stories like that." Then he turned back to the history of this ferry.

"We think they abandoned the ferry about when they built this bridge. They think it was about 1910," he said. "The old cable was still across the river until about twenty years ago. And, the old towers are still there. You can walk down and look at them."

We thanked him and followed his directions to one side of the bridge. There, peeking from a heavy growth of vines, stood one of the old rock towers, leaning with age from its position on the edge of the Brazos. A beautiful wild leafy rose bush with a large white blossom punctuated by a dot of red in the center grew nearby.

You could just imagine a young lover crawling from the ferry, picking one of these, and taking it to his sweetheart.

CHAPTER TWENTY-FIVE

Smith Bend Bridge

❖   ❖   ❖

Her name ranked high among heart surgeons. She could stitch
new valves into place as quickly as the notes that poured from a
maestro's violin. Or as smoothly as the notes from a harmonica being
played beneath the old Brazos Bridge.

Gosh, how long had that been? How long since she had heard the
rackety symphony from the crickets and other insects as she and he
played. How long ago had that been? Too long, maybe.

❖   ❖   ❖

The area around Lake Whitney about fifty miles south of Fort Worth
has an abundance of lodges, fishing camps, a beautiful state park, and four
bridges over the Brazos River.

We had numbered the bridges from the beginning and as we
approached the next bridge in sequence, we would announce that we were
coming to that particular bridge. Bridge 20 on our list, which is called the
Katy Bridge, amidst limestone cliffs that nature has gouged out of the surrounding hills, offers a spectacular view of the lake. To get there from Lake
Whitney, find FM 56 and head south past old barns with tin roofs and
fading red paint. We saw a beautiful red-tailed hawk sitting on a skinny
tree trunk stretching its wings and puffing its white-feathered chest like a
weightlifter flexing his muscles.

As we drove, I remembered what Tim Jones had said about the Katy
Bridge, named after the Katy railroad that once passed over it. "It started out
as a railroad bridge and then was closed. Then they opened it again to rail

traffic and then closed it again. Then they opened it again, this time for vehicles," he said.

We drove through tiny Kopperl and over Mesquite and Steele creeks and turned east on FM 1713. The lake sparkled in the distance, and then we were on the bridge.

"This is a long one," said John Tushim. "I think it's the longest one we've gone over so far."

I didn't know about that, but the bridge measured some .6 miles on our odometer.

We headed on to Whitney to try to find some facts about the bridge. Horace Findley, chamber of commerce manager, who has lived here all of his life, knows lots of area history. "One of the more fascinating bridges that I know about was what we called the old Wagon Bridge," he said. "It was named because that was what it was built for . . . wagons and teams. I saw it as a kid. They covered it up when they built the lake. Durn shame because if they could have preserved it in some way, it would have been quite a sight today."

He said his grandparents homesteaded here and his uncle Charlie Overton once operated a ferry across the Brazos. After talking to Findley, we looked around Whitney, a picturesque town with several buildings that have historical markers. One of those is the Cumberland Presbyterian Church, a handsome white frame structure with a steeple and bell.

We took Highway 22 west looking for the next bridge. Actually, it is a road built on top of the dam. But it is worth making the drive for another beautiful view of the lake, which was blue and smooth that day.

We drove through Laguna Park, which is on the edge of the dam, and turned south on Highway 56, reached FM 2114, and turned east to Smith Bend and Coon Creek Cemetery. Here, we stopped to read a historical marker that said the site contained more than five hundred graves. "The Smith Bend Community was founded in 1856 by John Jackson Smith and his wife Margaret when they moved here from Mississippi," it read. The Smith's daughter and her husband, Ann and Silas McCabe, started the nearby settlement named Coon Creek. We looked at the markers of families of Prathers, Raines, Hix, Welch, St. Clair, Kellum, and Burrus before continuing on our way.

Fat Hereford cattle stood in the corral of an old red barn with their heads thrust into a large round hay bale. Shortly after that we topped a hill and there below us was the Smith Bend Bridge which looked fairly new. We got out and walked across it. A huge red ant bed was at one end, the ants getting ready for winter by one lugging a piece of a corn kernel to the center of the bed. Skid marks caught our eye. A car apparently had smashed into the steel posts, bending two of them and a section of railing and leaving those marks.

On the north side of the bridge a road led to a huge sign that proclaimed a canoe rental place. Some large trees shaded the road, and a sign nailed into one of the trees read, "This River is enchanted."

That's how Dick Weinkauf, who lives on the banks of the river, feels about the place. "When I came down here thirty years ago, I was supposed to be totally disabled," he said. He is a tall, slender man with gray hair and beard. He laughed. "So I invented my own business—a canoe and kayak rental place." He moved here when he tore loose most of the muscles and nerves in his shoulders and arms by keeping a steel bookcase from falling on a fellow worker at a plant near Dallas.

"They declared me disabled and let me go. They gave me a small check. If you didn't eat much, use any electricity, or drive a car, you might have been able to make it," he said. Again came the raspy laugh. "But, as I said, I started my own business. I love it here. I got the riverfront. I got trees. They call me old Crazy Dick from the city."

His wife, Jeanne Sydell, also loves it here. She has short red hair that matches some of the colors of the pottery pieces she has been making for twenty years. "Being this close to the Brazos is so conducive to creativity," she said. "And being close to the bridge, well, that is like being on the bridge to success." Her work has certainly become that. From her business, called Sydell Riverplace Pottery, she ships creations all over the world. "And, everything is handmade. There are no presses or machines that do it. We do it ourselves," she said.

Many of her productions have a religious theme. But there is little doubt about the work that goes into the stoneware and porcelain angels or the Majolica items that are fashioned with a technique using red terra cotta clay. She showed a foot washing bowl and pitcher used for pouring water into the bowl during that symbolic religious activity.

"I spend nearly a day doing those," she said. "And, those, like most of our items, are sold wholesale to merchants."

We bade our farewell, walked to the nearby riverbank, and took one last look at the bridge that is so near her place of business. I thought of how easy it is for today's customers to come from Waco, drive across the bridge, and arrive here where they can either rent a canoe or buy some pottery. I remembered reading several tracts about how the construction of bridges meant booms to local economies.

Of course, that meant bringing in the unbridled herds of humanity with their cartons of plastic containers, old refrigerators, and other trash to be hurled beneath the bridges and left as ghastly and smelly stains on nature. That's a price we pay for advancement. I shoved those thoughts from my mind as we headed south for Waco and its cache of bridges and stories.

CHAPTER TWENTY-SIX

McClennan County Bridges

❖   ❖   ❖

He continued going to the bridge to play his harmonica.
Sometimes his fingers still had the smells of the strong potions used
in doctoring the various ills of his cattle.

People started telling a story about him. They said he came to play
beneath the bridge because his heart had been broken and playing
lonely melodies was the only way he could find any emotional relief.

Regardless, he still played. The only answers to his music came
from the memories of those warm, summer days so long ago when
she had been there.

❖   ❖   ❖

McClennan County has bridges galore. Not only is Waco, its county
seat, home of probably the oldest and most famous bridge in Texas, but
some ten other bridges cross the Brazos River as it twists its way through the
county where tribes of Tonkawas, Wichitas, and Waco Indians once lived.

We came to this bridge mecca by getting on Highway 6 in Meredian
and following it south. The drive leads through pretty farm and ranch lands
and Clifton, which used to always be a football power and is the home of
Bobby Joe Conrad, famed all-pro wide receiver for the St. Louis Cardinals
and former high school star. I told my companion Eddie Lane a bridge
story that happened when Conrad, who finished his career for the Dallas
Cowboys, was steamrolling toward the high school district championship
in the 1950s. My high school team, the Glen Rose Tigers, had a Friday night
date to meet the famed Clifton Cubs. Our coach had promised that we had

the power to beat this highly touted team. The *Fort Worth Star-Telegram* thought otherwise.

"The only way the Tigers can hope to beat Clifton is for someone to burn the bridges between Glen Rose and Clifton so the Tigers cannot make it to Clifton," the sportswriter opined.

We didn't burn the bridges. Clifton beat us 52-6.

Lane laughed and looked at our map at the number of bridges we had come to see in McClennan County. "Holy Moses, this is going to be a day of bridges," he said.

We turned east on FM 185 and went across the head of Lake Waco. Then we crossed the Bosque River that on this day flowed dark like spilled chocolate. At FM 1637 we turned right and the Waco skyline appeared out of a haze. We reached FM 3051 and headed east past Steinbeck Bend, across fertile bottomland to the first bridge we would look at in this county. The bridge stands at the edge of a hill.

We parked and looked at a beautiful old ornamental iron fence that had some white paint peaking out from layers of rust like the white in eyes of kids peeking from the darkness of a porch. Just beyond the fence stood tall pecan trees near piles of dirt practically covering some massive blocks. "There used to be one helluva house in there," said Eddie. "Can you imagine the stories it could tell about the days when they picked cotton and packed it into wagons and then took it to the old gins."

We walked under the bridge and were greeted with the usual splotches of graffiti. One read, "Viva Tomorrow." Roofers had left loads of old shingles, a sight that would become even more common as we worked our way down-river. As I looked at the piles of composition roofs and twisted pieces of roof edging, I wondered what people thought when they came to a beautiful river like this and dumped their trash. Did they perhaps think it was some giant commode that the next rain would cause to flush and spill the trash and junk into some giant cesspool? Aw, well, forget it, I told myself.

There was a Chinaberry tree with big clumps of berries that made the lower limbs lean nearly to the ground. The red berries and the tree's green leaves were a welcome respite of beauty placed by nature in a mat of ugliness left by humanity.

I found a piece of a guitar pick barely sticking out of some sand. I picked it up and tried to imagine somebody coming here and playing so hard they snapped the pick. Or maybe they snapped it in anger because whomever they were playing for turned their head away. Someone drove a huge John Deere tractor in the nearby bottomland, planting fall grain. Soon there would be new growth and new life.We headed south for the next bridge near Cameron Park East. Later, a worker told us that this park, which follows the river from here all the way through town, is the state's largest city park. It is a beautiful spot and has thirty-two horseshoe pits.

"This must be the Super Bowl for horseshoe pitching," said Eddie.

And, if you don't like horseshoes, they have holes dug for washer pitching. Three men standing nearby watching their fishing lines laughed about the crowds those games draw every weekend.

"Sounds like somebody is constantly dumping shovels of horseshoes into a steel barrel," said Jeff Burgess. He and his buddies, Leroy Barnes and Alvin Wydermyer prefer the fishing here. They looked like and had the smell of workingmen.

"The bridge there, hey, it's a bridge to catfish kingdom," said Barnes, a short, stocky man. "When we catch 'em, you talk about some good cooking and eating. Them catfish from the Brazos are like food from a king's table."

The river on this day was calm. It's smoothness caught the reflections of the trees, making them look like a fine oil painting. "This kind of calmness, this is what draws the speedboaters down here," said Wydermyer. "They come in here and race. They got boats that do 220 miles an hour. Forget fishing when they are here. But, they're fun to watch. And dangerous.

We saw one of them famous speedboats called the *Pink Panther* blow up in here one day. Absolutely blew itself all to hell."

But, it's the river and the shade of the bridge on hot days that these men love. "I've been coming here for thirty years. No better place in this country," said Barnes. He smiled. "Funny how I found Waco. I was raised in San Angelo. You know how dry that country is. One time I was just driving through in a 1958 Oldsmobile 98. Pretty car. Painted a light purple. Anyhow, I got to Waco and the transmission went out. I had a brother living close to here, so I just stayed. Never regretted it."

They looked at Eddie who on this day wore a black western hat and jeans with red suspenders. His gray hair crept from beneath the hat. "Hey, you look like old Walker, the Texas Ranger on TV. You could pass for him. Did you know that?" asked Burgess. "You're not going to arrest us, are you?"

"Not if you share those catfish with us," said Eddie. We all laughed. Shook hands again and headed on for the next bridge, another fairly new structure called the Herring Parkway Bridge. We followed more of Cameron Park and drove through groves of huge pecan trees to reach this bridge. Tall cattails grew along the banks with cottonwood trees so tall you had to lean backward to see their tops. We drove past Lawson's Point and Lover's Leap.

"When you were a kid full of piss and vinegar did you ever wish you could find a lover's leap after some girl you thought you were madly in love with and couldn't live without gave back your high school letter jacket?" asked Eddie.

I thought of those days as we parked. The car radio was playing "The Great Pretender." Gosh, the memories that song triggered. I hummed part of it as we walked to the bridge. Several ducks rested in a shade made by the structure. The site brought pleasant memories to Eddie.

"I came down here, near this very place, when Jerry Levias was inducted into the Texas Sports Hall of Fame," said Eddie. "He played for Southern

Methodist University when I was athletic trainer there, and he and I became very good friends."

Levias, a tremendous football player, eventually went to the NFL where he made quite an impression. "But, the thing I liked about Jerry was he always remembered where he came from and never got on a high horse," said Lane. He smiled. "We still call each other several times each year."

We looked up at the bridge's concrete supports, then backed away and gazed downstream. In the haze we could see the famous Waco suspension bridge. So we headed south for that bridge. But, we reached another bridge

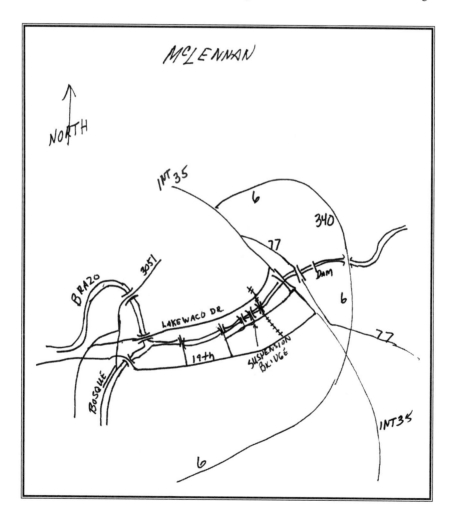

first, one near the St. Francis Catholic Church, a beautiful, graying structure well worth taking a look. We walked inside and gazed at what a brochure called "the celebrated Rose Window, probably the most celebrated window on the Western Continent that has been duplicated and is located on the side wall of the Baptistery Transept."

That work is impressive as is the half dome of the ceiling, covered with a symbolic oil painting by Reggi depicting the history of the Franciscan Order. Again I read from the brochure that said, "This painting is very well executed. It is 42 feet wide by 33 feet in height."

The building with Roman, Moorish, and Spanish Gothic motifs in the ornamental details was completed in 1931. That book says since its dedication, the walls have been decorated with almost life-sized paintings representing the Stations of the Cross, the glorification of St. Francis, and scenes of the arrival, predication, and martyrdom of the first Franciscan missionaries in Texas. "The paintings are the work of a painter from Mallorca, Spain, and good friend of the Franciscan Fathers, the master Pedro Juan Barcelo. The architect was Mr. Roy E. Lane."

We walked outside and looked at a house sitting on the same grounds. A historical marker there said that Capt. R.W. Lusk built the house in 1866. In 1885, his widow Margaret Henry Lusk married her brother-in-law, Dr. W.R. Clifton, a pioneer Waco businessman who lived here until 1925 when the Franciscan fathers purchased the property for a monastery. The house, painted white with massive white columns, looks like the setting for a movie about the Old South and its plantations. We walked to the street and took one final look and then headed for the famous suspension bridge.

Actually, for bridge enthusiasts, there's a twin delight at the suspension bridge near the downtown section of Waco. Of course there is this structure which, though closed to automobiles, still accommodates pedestrians. The second bridge within shadows of the suspension bridge is a steel structure built in 1902. Gazing at the two bridges and letting your imagination run, you can conjure up the people from Texas history who have passed over these bridges. A nearby historical marker tells one such person was Jacob De Cordova. He came here in 1847 to survey and sell property acquired by John S. Snydnor.

De Cordova hired George Bernard Erath, and they laid out the town of Waco. De Cordova later formulated a scheme to industrialize the Brazos River Valley, but he died while working on this project at Kimball Bend in Bosque County about forty-five miles northwest of here.

I moved onto one of the walkways of the steel bridge known as the Washington Avenue Bridge. It is a majestic structure built in 1901 by John H. Sparks of St. Joseph, Missouri. Resident engineer was John W. Maxcy of Houston. This is my kind of bridge with cutouts of stars, pears, clover leafs, and hearts in its massive supports. I felt one of the huge rivet heads and

The Washington Avenue Bridge in Waco is located close to the famous suspension bridge. This steel bridge, built in 1901 by John H. Sparks, has cutouts of stars, pears, cloverleafs, and hearts on its massive supports. One-way automobile traffic still passes over the structure.

steel bolts holding all of this together. The bridge still accommodates one-lane traffic.

Then I moved to the suspension bridge that is listed in the National Register of Historic Places by the U.S. Department of Interior. I walked across its wooden floor and stopped in the middle and looked down at the Brazos, so calm on this day. A long line of turtles rested on a log in the sunshine, perhaps taking their afternoon siesta.

I read another marker that said the Waco suspension bridge contained new innovations that made it an important forerunner of the longest-span suspension bridges of the world. Jim Chavez, an employee of the city park department, took a break to talk about the bridge and the area.

"Look down there. That is what used to be called Indian Springs Park. Those springs are still running, and they have furnished water for many for so long," he said. He loves his job and loves sharing his knowledge with people. "It is so important to preserve history like this. Preserve it for your kids and my kids so they can someday come here and bring their kids and walk across this bridge where so many of our early heroes once walked," he said in a burst of words.

He talked about the rumor that the Brooklyn Bridge was modeled after this bridge. "It's not true." He smiled. "But, one time I went to New York, and I had to drive across that bridge. It is much larger. Much larger."

Amy Iverson of Silver Lake, Minnesota, stood nearby. She once lived in this area but had never walked across the bridge. So when she came back to visit her parents, she made this one of her first stops. She is a pretty woman with two lovely children. One of them is Courtney.

"We saw this in a little booklet about Texas history. I told Mother that I wanted to come here and walk across it," Courtney said. Her mother nodded her head.

"I am and have always been interested in Texas history," said the mother. "Plus I have a special interest in this bridge. My grandfather said

The oldest bridge across the Brazos was built in 1870 and is still being used by walkers today. This majestic suspension bridge is 475 feet long and more than 2.7 million bricks were used in its construction. Fees that included charging a ride on horseback ten cents for crossing triggered instant criticism and eventually were dropped.

that he once got his hair cut in a barber shop that was located in one of those tower buildings."

There are four of those, two at each end of the bridge. The thick cables that support the bridge are anchored into these buildings. I watched as Iverson led her children onto the bridge and past the towers. Courtney and her sister suddenly started running on the wooden planks.

"That's a nice sight," said Chavez. "Children discovering history. Hey, you need to get some books and brochures and read all of the history on this bridge. There's been a bunch written about it."

I had already discovered that in reading several books and magazine and newspaper articles about the bridge. Here's just a portion of what I found about Texas's most famous bridge. Roger Conger, well-known Waco historian who has written a history of the bridge, called the conception of the bridge, which suggested a suspension bridge be built across the Brazos in 1866, "unquestionably one of the most remarkable epics of Texas frontier enterprise."

> At the close of the Civil War, Waco was a poor but pulsing little community of some 1,500 inhabitants lying directly on the west of the Brazos River at the site of the long celebrated Waco Indian Spring. Capt. S.P. Ross's ferry connected the village to the east bank, from which landing the state road lay eastward to Waxahachie and Dallas, and forked south to Springfield and Marlin. In the year 1866 there was not a single bridge across the sprawling stream, from one end to the other, something like a full 800 miles without a bridge.

Verne Huser Press cited other reasons for a bridge in *Rivers of Texas*, published by Texas A&M University. "Rivers blocked overland routes, sometimes by serious flooding, which necessitated the location of fords, the development of fords, the development of ferries, and even eventually the building of bridges," he wrote.

According to newspaper articles, after the end of the Civil War, Waco was dependent on the wagons that linked the rapidly growing town to Jefferson in East Texas and Houston in the south. Waco was situated on the west bank of the Brazos, which meant that every wagonload of goods had to cross that often-flooding stream to reach its destination.

Still other reasons for a bridge were cited in a magazine article in *The Developer*. That article listed the benefits of Texas.

> No other state has the temperature, humidity, and soil quality suited to the distinctively southern crops in conjunction with all the grains, fruits, truck, and forage plants of the more Southern

states, likewise to the prolific breeding of all kinds of farm animals
and at the same time can furnish practically all the products of
the mines and forests that mankind requires. In fact, many
authorities have stated that the state of Texas can come nearer to
producing everything required for man's needs and happiness
than any similar sized territory in the world.

But, of course, Waco needed bridges because ferries like those operated
by Captain Ross were doing their best to handle the growing traffic but were
frequently thwarted during times of flood and high water when no boat
could cross the river for days and sometimes even weeks.

According to an article from the *Waco News Tribune*, on May 8, 1868,
Joseph W. Speight, along with other well-to-do businessmen, organized the
Waco Bridge Company; they were granted a charter. They sold stock at $20
a share. The 2,500 shares issued had been bought by the end of a month.
Col. John T. Flint, a lawyer and banker who during his youth had worked on
the Erie Canal, was elected president.

According to Conger, there was some discussion over what kind of
bridge should be built. Some wanted an ordinary iron bridge but others
favored the new suspension bridge being developed by the Trenton, New
Jersey, firm of John A. Roebling & Son. Flint decided upon the suspension
bridge because it was the cheapest and the best.

He hired Thomas Griffith as the engineer and went to New Jersey to buy
materials. The Roebling firm had already spent two years working on plans
for the famed Brooklyn Bridge so the romantic tale about the Waco bridge
serving as a model for the suspension bridge linking Manhattan with
Brooklyn was not true. As Conger said, "It's like comparing a rabbit with a
horse or an elephant."

"The Brooklyn Bridge is such a monumental bridge that it just dwarfs
any other suspension bridge in America. The Brooklyn Bridge's main span

was 1,595 feet long. Waco's was 475 feet. The two stone towers holding up the Brooklyn Bridge are each 271 feet tall. The Waco's bridge's four brick towers were each 49 feet tall," read an article in the *Waco News Tribune*.

There was some discussion about using stone for the bridge's foundation, towers, and anchor houses. But because of the expense and availability, builders used bricks. Eventually, 2.7 million bricks were required to build the bridge.

Oxen brought the steel cables from the nearest railroad at Millican, some 140 miles south of Waco. That cost $8,276.70, said Thomas C. Turner in an article in *Texas Parade*.

In 1937, a *Dallas Morning News* reporter interviewed Emanuel Vreeland, a construction worker and blacksmith and supposedly at that time the only living man who had helped build the bridge. He said, "It was a mighty big job welding the huge cables to the anchor dogs. We first had to get them in place and they weighed many tons. Then we tied them so fast that they are still holding to this day. I guess we done a pretty good job, all right."

A *Waco News Tribune* article said the bridge officially opened January 6, 1870. Miss Kate Ross, the first white born in Waco, was the first citizen to cross the bridge. But, historian Conger says that many people actually had crossed the bridge earlier, including "oodles of boys and girls who climbed across the scaffolding of the bridge before they put the floor in."

Many stories came after the bridge's completion, including the tendency of the bridge to sway in high winds or when heavy loads of material or livestock moved across it. The late Miss Elizabeth Hughston told about the time during her childhood that a circus came to Waco, unloading at the depot on the east side of the river. The elephants refused to set foot on the bridge after being led to it. So they crossed the river at the ford just south of the bridge.

There were also some ugly stories about the bridge. Julien Hyder tells one of those in the book, *Texas: The Land of Beginning Again. The Romance of the Brazos*. He said at least one lynching was held at the bridge and another was planned in 1916. But the crowd, after capturing a black defendant accused of killing a white rancher, was heading for the bridge, stopped at a tree, and hanged the man there. "That was the last lynching of record in the Brazos Valley," he wrote. He also mentioned how wild Waco was in those early days. People like Jim Miller, Clay Allison, Bill Longley, Ben Thompson, Tom Star, and even Billy the Kid visited there.

"Warnings were given to men, don't bring a wife to Texas. Wait and find one here. Then she'll be used to the climate," he wrote. "As for Waco, it was so wild it was known as six shooter junction."

Fees charged for crossing the bridge brought immediate criticism. Those fees, according to the *Texas Parade*, charged horse-drawn vehicles with more than two horses twenty cents per wheel and five cents for each animal; vehicles with one or two horses paid ten cents a wheel and five cents per horse; a mounted rider paid ten cents; and large livestock were charged five cents each. Smaller animals were charged three cents.

But, the late Judge Walter Cocke said that the fees were avoided by crossing the river at the old fords. "We forded the river many times," said Cocke, whose father was a doctor and made his calls on horseback. "Lots of people did that to save the nickel or dime that it cost to cross the bridge. There was a rock crossing at the old ford in those days. The ford traveled almost directly under the bridge. But when the upper sections of the river were opened to farming, the river soon filled with sand and silt (covering the rocks) and forced everyone to use the bridge."

Even though McClennan County residents were charged half price, within two years of its completion, local grumbling grew about having to "pay to git into town." The grumbling continued until September of 1889 when the county conveyed the bridge to the city of Waco and fees no longer were charged.

As Waco has grown, more bridges have been built across the Brazos. And, when the old suspension bridge was closed to vehicular traffic, there was some consideration of tearing it down. Fortunately for history and bridge fans, that thought was abandoned. Waco's suspension bridge has survived and gained recognition and honors. It was featured as the only "non-building" in *Texas Public Buildings of the 19th Century*. That book's author, Williard B. Robinson, quoted Dennis Hart Mahan, an instructor at the U.S. Military Academy at West Point, who said:

> **A bridge should not only be secure, but appear so it should conform to the features of the surrounding locality. . . . This point of view was beautifully embodied into the bridge across the Brazos . . . a suspension bridge supported by wire cables, this work was already dramatic by virtue of its structural form. Nonetheless, to further enhance the work, the brick piers that thrust skyward supporting the thin cables were decorated with string courses, recesses, and other features resembling medieval crenellations. Later numerous other wire-cable suspension bridges were built in the state, but none was as spectacular or as ornate as the one at Waco.**

Some of that history flashed into my mind as I stood there with Lane admiring the suspension bridge. I made one last walk to the middle of the structure and again touched the huge steel cables. Then I moved to the center of the wooden planks and, just for the sheer fun of it, I broke into a trot toward the end. My footsteps made faint, hollow echoes. Someday my grandkids could say their crazy grandpa trotted across this bridge.

Lane and I loaded into the car and, as an afterthought, checked out the final bridges in McClennan County. Three of those lay within the shadows of the suspension bridge. We had been so overwhelmed by the suspension bridge that we gave little time to those.

Instead we drove to George's, a local restaurant on the city's south side famed for its steaks, chicken, Tex-Mex dishes, fresh vegetables and homemade breads. We talked about the bridges we had seen and those still on our list. "It's turned into a good adventure," I told Lane.

We headed for the bridge crossing Highway 491, which lies in the shadows of Baylor University, and parked near the university coliseum with its dome that looks like a bald-headed man with his head painted gold. We walked through some thick grass toward the bottom of the bridge.

Typical graffiti greeted us. I also found a woman's high-top lace-up boot lying on one of the concrete foundations. I walked around the foundation and found the other shoe. A tree limb had been cut off at a fork and stuck down into the shoe. I wondered if there was any significance in that.

We looked downriver and saw a huge factory surrounded by piles of river sand. The plant's engines made a loud hum. "Hey, look at this," said Eddie. He pointed at a fishing line somebody had tied onto part of the bridge under the covering. He pulled it. It remained slack. "Nothing on it," he said. We sat down and rested in the shade of the bridge. Cars and trucks roared overhead.

"You know the best thing about this bridge?" said Eddie.

"What?" I asked.

"The roofers can't get in here and dump all of their trash," he said.

I laughed. I thought of a story I wrote within shadows of this bridge several years ago. I had met a man named Cooper who could twist a steel horseshoe like it was a piece of string. After I wrote the story, he called me one day and invited me to go to Waco with him to meet Sugar.

"Sugar is an old horse now. But I used to own her and for years I would go out every day and pick her up," he said.

"Pick her up?" I asked. "With what?"

"With my hands and arms," he said.

"You mean lift her up?" I said.

"Yeah, that's what I mean," said Cooper. "I sold her to a man down in Waco, and he told me where he is keeping her so I thought we could go down there and I could pick her up again or just see if I could still do it."

We traveled to Waco and found the barn about a mile from this bridge. Inside a corral stood a brown-and-white horse. She neighed as we walked up.

"This is old Sugar," said Cooper. "Sugar, baby, I'm going to see if I can still pick you up." Sugar was a mid-size animal. I don't know what she weighed but I figured it was several hundred pounds. I thought all of this as Cooper walked inside the corral. He leaned over, reached around Sugar someway, grunted and by gosh, he lifted her until all four hooves cleared the ground.

"Well, thank you, Sugar. I thought I could still do it," said Cooper. "Okay, let's go home. I'm through." And, with that, we returned to Fort Worth.

Eddie smiled at the ending of the story. "He should have played tackle for the Dallas Cowboys," he said. We laughed, left the shade, and walked back to our car. We drove for the next bridge, a few miles away. It spans Highway 6. We parked at a fence that had a beautiful gate made from steel with a wagon wheel welded into its center.

There was another sand-and-gravel operation in the vicinity. As we walked toward a trail that led to the river, I looked at the giant waves of sand mined from the Brazos. That product is like gushers of oil. The huge pieces of equipment sucking the sand from the bottomland sounded like oil-field equipment. The trail led us through high undergrowth. We walked over scattered beer cans. Berries that had fallen from a Chinaberry tree crunched under our shoes. We finally parted the brush and looked at the bridge, another modern structure. Remains of catfish bait hit our noses with a strong, sour blast.

"So what do you think of this bridge, Mr. Eddie Lane?" I asked.

"I think someday we will read a story that says, 'The bridge across the Brazos River on Highway 6 collapsed today when a truck drove across it in a driving rainstorm.' I get that impression by looking at those footings.

I am no bridge expert, but they certainly don't look in very good shape," he said.

I am no expert, either. But, the footings did look like a big piece of bread that had been nibbled on the edges. As I looked, I reached into my pocket and pulled out a silver medallion that I had found near the Catholic church. I walked close to the river and tossed the medallion into the river. Maybe it would bring somebody good luck. As I watched the tiny ripples it made, I realized something. Before we had begun this great adventure, we had counted the bridges and given each one of them a number. By my count, this bridge meant that we were more than half completed in our quest to look at all of the bridges over the Brazos.

"Eddie, do you realize that we all we have left is about thirty more bridges before this old river empties into the coast?" I asked.

He stared at the bridge and the black line of Highway 6 as it headed south. A faint smile came onto his face. "Yeah, I realize that and something else," he said. "I have not made one attempt at fishing during all of this. I have never been down this much river before without buying me some earthworms, baiting a hook, and trying to catch me a fish."

I laughed. "Well, we still got a few more miles to travel before we end this. So maybe you can remedy that situation sometime soon," I said.

We crawled into our car and headed south.

CHAPTER TWENTY-SEVEN

Falls County Bridges

❖ ❖ ❖

A young band heard about his playing. So one day they went to hear him. After ten minutes, the bandleader said, "Hey, dude, you're good. Why don't you join us and make yourself some big bucks? Plus, maybe you'll meet some chicks, even at your age."

He shook his head. He said, "No, I only play for my sweetheart."

He put his harmonica into his pocket and went home.

"Crazy old coot, ain't he?" said the bandleader.

"No, maybe he ain't," replied his lead guitar player. "Maybe he has found something that we still are looking for."

❖ ❖ ❖

Fall's full grip had arrived the day we left for the bridges in Falls County. Temperatures had leaked into the lower thirties by the time I got up. I looked at Lake Granbury and thought of the old song, "There'll be smoke on the water." The morning cold caused clouds of mist, which looked like smoke, to float from the top of the water. The sun tried to punch through the early clouds making some eerie and weird shapes. Gawd, what a day to go look at bridges.

We drove south and went through Crawford on Highway 317. A sign near the middle of town read, "Home of George W. Bush." Within seconds we had reached another sign that read, "You are leaving the home of George W. Bush."

We drove through McGregor, home of the McGregor Bulldogs and Kidd's Bakery. We hit some ranchland with pastures that had been eaten off almost smooth to the ground by hungry cattle during the recent drought. I could picture them looking for bites of grass and jerking their heads up with dirt on their noses as they scratched wounds into the ground in their efforts. Recent rains had already started the healing process with ribbons of green winter grass covering the raw earth. An old barn with a tin roof leaned with age. As we continued, I thought about a story I had read about how bridges actually started. My good friend Doc Keen, who once prowled the state with me, sent me a copy of this story from one of the many publications he has collected. I think this must have come from some encyclopedia. It said the first bridge builder was probably a primitive superman, dating back to as early as 15,000 B.C. He may have strolled along one day and come to a stream that had risen so much from flooding that he could not cross. So as he stood there with his stone axe, he got a brilliant idea. He would cut down a tree and drop it across the channel. He did and walked across without getting his feet wet. Hence, the first bridge builder.

That process grew when somebody else thought of dropping stones across a stream, making a ford. Eventually somebody thought of placing the log beams across the stones and so we got a multiple span beam bridge. In the northern territories where timber was in short supply, early man used slabs of flat, thin stones to make the piers. This kind of bridge became known as the clapper bridge. Some of these still exist in more primitive areas.

As humanity grew so did its ability to figure out how better to cope with the surroundings. So in southern climates where there was an abundance of grass and ferns, man figured out how to make a suspension-type bridge by plaiting and weaving the grass and ferns into ropes. He secured one end to a rock or tree and swung himself across to the other bank. The next logical step involved making two ropes and covering the space between them with some kind of mat, thus creating the true suspension bridge.

One of the earliest of these in America was the Newburyport Bridge over the Merrimac River in Massachusetts, built in 1810 by John Templeman with a span of 244 feet.

Another early American bridge builder was Theodore Burr, a descendant of Aaron Burr, the vice president under Thomas Jefferson. Theodore

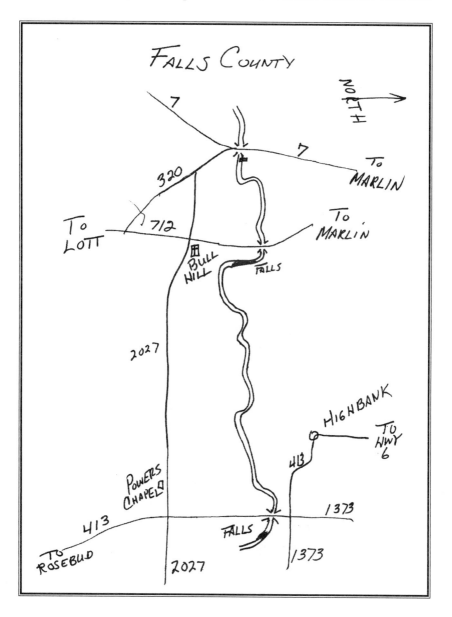

Burr developed a truss called the Burr truss and one of his bridges was a 360-foot structure built in 1815 at McCall's Ferry, Pennsylvania. Still another new type of bridge came into being in 1779 when Abraham Darby and John Wilkinson built an iron bridge in West Central England. It was fashioned from five semicircular ribs of cast iron and was still standing after 167 years.

I thought of these firsts in bridge building when we passed a first for Texas near Moody. Mother Neff State Park, the first state park in Texas and a delightful place to camp, is located near this town. We drove through Eddy. "Gosh, a town named after me," said Eddie. "I want to stop here."

We stopped at Worm Lady's Tackle to satiate Eddie's appetite for fishing gear. But, Worm Lady's, with an old Coca-Cola sign in front, was closed. It looked like a neat store. We headed into Falls County to look at its three bridges over the Brazos. The first bridge is on Highway 7, about seven miles west of Marlin.

On this day the Brazos's waters stretched calmly in a thin covering over the riverbed and looked like green Jell-O. Some old bridge piers still remain there. One of those looms from the middle of the river and looks like massive twin cannon barrels. I walked toward another pier on the river's west bank. Thick vines and branches from elm trees covered it.

I looked again at the pier in the center of the river. Sheets of steel were wrapped around the concrete legs and spanned across the middle of each, holding them together. A huge hole had been gouged out near the top of the steel plate.

Massive logs had wrapped themselves around the piers of both the old bridge and new bridge supports. I thought of the power of the river when floods fueled it and brought those monstrous logs down the river like wooden torpedoes. That's what happened here in May 1922 when six people drowned while watching the flooding Brazos as they stood on the bridge.

That story is a wild one, as information given to me by Carolyn Contella, former director of the Marlin Public Library, reveals. The tragedy occurred during one of the many floods that turn the Brazos River from an almost-gentle stream into a dangerous torrent. Records of those floods go back many years and include the high waters that came in 1899 and 1913. In those years, the Brazos spilled from its banks and reached a width of three or more miles. In 1913, people got into boats at Bean's Hill, a half mile from the Falls County Courthouse, and got out eight miles downstream.

According to a report written by Roy Eddins for the Old Settlers and Veterans Association of Falls County in 1947, several bridges over the Brazos did not survive the strength of the river during flooding before 1922. He told about an old wooden bridge built in the 1870s. Its piles had been driven into the riverbed and were only a few feet across. "People always crossed with some foreboding of danger, especially after the bridge had been in use for awhile," he said. "The bridge was short-lived, naturally, because its foundation was unstable and the pilings were subject to damage by driftwood and debris . . . the bridge required constant watching and frequent repairs and, even then, was not always considered safe."

Then came the spring of 1922. Abundant rains had soaked the countryside and the Brazos had been at flood level for several days. The flooding caused damage to the approach on the western side of the bridge at the Chilton-Marlin road. But a discovery of oil had probably caused people to downplay the danger erosion had caused.

In Eddins' history, the news of an oil well coming in near Chilton caused Falls County citizens to avoid any traffic interruption to the area. A headline in the *Marlin Democrat* on May 10, 1922, read, "Brazos Bridge Safe—Travel Not Interrupted." Two days later another headline read, "Oil Runs Over at Top—Gray Wildcat Holds High Attraction of Oil Scouts and Public."

Shortly after that, a six-inch rain drenched the area. The river continued its rise and people of Marlin were urged to go to the bridge to help protect its western footing. People gathered on the bridge to help pour cement, sand, and other material around the weakening standards. About 1:00 P.M., a loud sharp noise like a huge wooden beam shattering exploded from beneath the bridge. T.H. Smith, an eyewitness, said the bridge appeared to twist as a pier collapsed, the southwest edge bending downward. Then the northeast corner of the span bent downward.

The strength of the flooding waters was so great that the entire three hundred feet of steel and iron, which weighed many tons, tumbled into the river and was washed fifty yards downstream. Only a few pieces of steel jutted out of the water where the bridge fell.

"It only took ten seconds for the whole bridge to fall into the water," reads a report from the Marlin newspaper. "With the collapse, it hurled all of those on the west span into the swollen stream. Many were able to grab huge planks in the water and survived, although some men were in the water for several hours before they could be rescued.

Several were not so lucky and drowned. They included Marlin Mayor F.M. Stallworth, Dr. Walter H. Allen, seven-year-old B.J. Briggs, William Harris, Mrs. C. Mosely of Beaumont, and a man named Willokowski. Eighteen days after the collapse, the last body was recovered fifteen miles below Navasota."

Survivors included Dr. H.W. Knickerbocker, pastor of the First Methodist Church of Marlin. He managed to crawl from the water about a mile downstream. Other survivors were either rescued or crawled from the river several miles downstream at the famed waterfalls across the Brazos, for which Falls County is named. Eyewitness accounts of those who died numbed family members.

"The body of Mrs. Mosely was taken from the water a few hundred yards below the bridge. A deep wound on the lower part of her face and large bruise on her neck indicated that she was killed instantly," reads an account from the *Marlin Democrat*. "Mayor Stallworth, when last seen out in the stream, bore a deep gash in the face. He seemed unable to swim, apparently on account of the wound. He is believed to have been caught in a whirlpool."

As a result of the bridge collapse, Marlin was cut off from the west, except for a road through Waco, for several weeks. Finally, an appeal was made to Fort Sam Houston in San Antonio. The army sent fifty-five men who installed a pontoon bridge used for several months until a new bridge could be built.

Writers spared no adjectives in describing the Brazos after the tragedy. One, in the *Marlin Democrat,* said: "The Brazos once again has proved its claim as a treacherous stream. The channels and its current are constantly shifting. Its caprices are weird, peculiar, and tragic. In this horrifying instance it has more than maintained its gruesome history."

It seems unusual but few local residents remember or even know anything about that event. Jana Waters, twenty-three, who works in a store near the scene, said her father who has lived here for years had never mentioned the story to her. "I'm certain he never heard it," she said. "But, let me tell you, I've seen that river on a rampage and I have no doubt about its power."

Still, two other people who once lived in this area said they had never heard the story. They are Kenneth and Mary Hall, who today live in Jacksonville. "My granddaddy was raised in this country and though he never told me that story, I know the line he would have used to describe the river on that day. He would have said, 'That river is going to Kosse,'" she said. She laughed and then explained the term, "Kosse is really the name of a town about twenty miles from here. When I was a little girl, he would tell us when we were doing something wrong that we were going to 'Kosse.' I thought it was a curse word. It was years before I finally went through Kosse and realized it was just a town." We all laughed. We asked directions to the falls, a renowned landmark of this area.

"Yeah, you got to be sure and go see the falls. They are worth the trip. My granddaddy used to grabble for catfish just under the falls. Caught a bunch, too. And, they were good eating," she said.

We thanked her and headed for the falls.

CHAPTER TWENTY-EIGHT

The Brazos River Falls at Marlin

❖ ❖ ❖

One day her daughter found the harmonica. It was wrapped in a piece of velvet and stuck beneath her mother's undergarments.

"Mother, what is this?" she asked.

Her mother took the instrument. Her fingers touched it softly like she was holding an infant. A faraway look came into her eyes. She began to play. The notes were so sweet yet so lonely. She only played about two minutes and then she said, "Here, put it back."

Her daughter started for the bedroom. She turned and looked back. Her mother was crying.

❖ ❖ ❖

To reach the falls, we drove to Marlin and then headed south on FM 712. We drove through bottomlands with huge pecan trees. I remembered driving in this country in the spring when black-eyed Susans with bright yellow heads and a dash of black in the center filled the fields. We passed the William Hobby Correctional Institute that anchors a large swath of the rich bottomland.

"Wouldn't you feel honored to have a penitentiary named after you?" asked Eddie.

"Well, it would be better than having a warthog named after you," I said.

"A warthog?" he asked.

I explained. Once, my good friend Doug Clarke had been dispatched to the Fort Worth Zoo to write a story about a warthog they had just added to

the zoo. The director at the time was a wild and crazy guy named Lawrence
Curtis. He loved to jest with the local journalists.

"Mr. Clarke, why don't you name our new warthog," he said.

And, Mr. Clarke, who has a serious line of jest in his character, said,
"Certainly, let's call him, 'Bunky.'" They did. And, since that is my nickname,
that is how I came to have a warthog named after me.

I finished the story just as we reached Bridge 35, a huge concrete
structure lying almost within the shadows of the Hobby prison. We parked
and walked under it. A spider web stretched to the bridge's steel supports.
As the spider crawled upward, it stopped and then gathered itself into a
ball. The wind gently swung the spider in its knot of freedom. I thought
there must be some kind of philosophical meaning in this since we were
so close to the prison housing hundreds of inmates. I wondered what they
would think of the spider and its freedom.

In the river, green moss clung to rocks and fallen logs. We could hear a
soft roar downstream. "I think that is coming from the falls," said Eddie. So
we drove to the Falls Park. Several nice camping sites are available. One had
signs that included warnings about performing bodily functions there.
Another said, "You stay, you pay."

We worked our way down the bank of the river to the falls that by then
were making a loud roar. We walked past mushrooms as big as coffee saucers
and looked at the middle of the falls where a seagull and another bird that
Eddie called a water turkey stood.

"That thing will eat its weight in fish in one day," he said.

He began studying the course of the river for a possible canoeing trip.
"You could approach the falls from the center and then go around down
here and I think you could make it without taking out," he said. "Do you
know any history of these? They are quite impressive."

I didn't, but a historical marker did. It said the falls were located two
and a half miles southwest of where we stood when the original settlers

came to this area. "At that time water fell about ten feet over a rock ledge," the marker read. "The falls served the Indians and early settlers as a landmark and campsite. In 1834 colonizer Sterling C. Robertson established the town of Sarahville De Vesca here. It was abandoned in 1836 because of Indian hostilities."

Several other towns sprouted in the area, including one known as Bucksnort, which lasted only a few years. But the falls became a natural gathering place. "The falls also formed a natural landing place for frontier travel. The rocky stream bed was the only hard-bottom crossing on the Brazos within 200 miles of the coast," read the marker.

The rapids gained another note in history. When steamboat travel started at the mouth of the Brazos on the coast, it worked its way north until it reached the falls and could go no further. "The rapids marked the limit of the river's 19th-century steamboat traffic," said the marker. "The Brazos River changed course in 1866, moving the fall line to its present site and lowering the rapids to about two feet."

We returned to the river's banks and looked at the falls. Spray from the water danced upward in a fine mist. Carolyn Contella, a resident of Marlin, had told us about coming to the falls when she was a child.

"My father would drive our car across the falls. We would get about to the middle, and he would deliberately stall the car and my mother would start screaming," she said.

She said that fish known as alligator gar reached lengths of seven feet in water just below the falls. "And, you want to be careful in that water. Actually, it's no place to play. The bottom has volcanic rocks that form whirlpools. Once you get sucked into one of those, it may be three days before it spits you out," she said. "That river is a dangerous place. But, some days, it doesn't look that way. That is what fools a lot of people."

On this day, it didn't look too dangerous. But, as Eddie noted, the water roaring around the edge of the falls had much more force than one would imagine. We stared at the falls for several minutes, savoring their beauty and power. Just outside the park we found another historical marker with information about Bucksnort. It reads:

> This area was first settled in 1837 by the Marlin and Menefee families. The settlement grew and was known as Jarrett Menefee's Supply Station. It had a school, several blacksmith shops, a stable, saloons, post office, stagecoach stop, and a racetrack. According to local historians, Bucksnort was coined by an inebriated patron at one of the saloons. By the 1850s, settlers moved into other areas and Bucksnort no longer was a viable community.

We drove on to Marlin, looking for a place to eat lunch and for seeking information about an unusual tombstone I had seen several years before in a Marlin cemetery.

We found both.

CHAPTER TWENTY-NINE

Marlin and the Highbank Bridge

❖ ❖ ❖

Some youngsters had hidden in the growth beneath the bridge.
They listened to him play.

"I know his secret," whispered one. "He's playing for a fairy. He
claims that sometimes another fairy plays back to him."

"I know that," said his buddy. "You hear all sorts of noises under
the bridge. Even screeches made by ghosts."

"Oh," said the first youngster. "I hope I never hear that. I like his
music better."

❖ ❖ ❖

I knew I had found my kind of cooking when we walked into Latricia's
Café in downtown Marlin. The smells pouring out of the kitchen from pots
of homemade vegetables made that evident immediately. Eddie chose a
plate lunch of liver and onions, mashed potatoes, cabbage, and pinto beans.

"Delicious," he said.

I chose a bowl of navy beans, a salad, and cornbread. I agreed with his
assessment and complimented the owner, Latricia Broadus.

"I cook from the heart," she said. "I had always wanted my own business
so after I retired from the air force, I thought, why not come home and do
the one thing that I knew I could do. So I came here and opened Latricia's
two and a half years ago. It's the realization of my dream."

I told her about the tombstone that I had discovered at a local cemetery
several years ago while passing through here. The marker is shaped like a
double bed.

"That must be Calvary Cemetery," she said. She gave us directions.

We found the cemetery and quickly found the tombstone made out of cement and shaped like a bed. Many stories have been told about the unusual marker. One said that the people buried there loved to sleep so the family shaped the tombstone like a bed so the couple would always be in bed, even after death.

We also heard about other unusual markers in the cemetery. One is shaped like an electric light pole and marks the grave of a man who died while working on electric high lines. Another is an angel who is pointing her finger to heaven. Supposedly the angel changes her position, which is the basis for ghost stories about the cemetery. A historical figure buried in the cemetery is Capt. Edgar Collins Singer, who is credited with inventing the torpedo and whose uncle invented the Singer sewing machine.

"We've got one more bridge to look at in this county. Let's go to the Marlin chamber of commerce and get directions to it," said Eddie.

We drove through downtown where once thousands of people came to bathe in the mineral waters that offered cures for practically everything. A history from a chamber of commerce pamphlet tells about those healing powers. It reads:

A great majority of common ailments are caused when toxic poisons accumulate in the body and resist the attempts of the excretory system to throw them off. Such collected body residues breed all sorts of functional disorders, often proving the direct cause for painful diseases that might otherwise have been avoided.

Many patent laxatives are undesirable because of their harshness and habit-forming tendencies. What a welcome blessing it is to discover a mineral water that when taken internally functions to promote the natural elimination of body waste, and, when administered in the form of hot mineral water baths, draws through the pores of the skin the sluggish impurities that clog the bloodstream. These are but two of the reasons why thousands upon thousands of sick, run-down people who come to Marlin suffering and discouraged are able to leave feeling better, stronger, and happier. Even the most stubborn cases find relief through Marlin's famed resort features. Nowhere in America will you find more beneficial mineral waters than those which flow hot from these deep artesian wells.

Those wells still flow. Several spigots gushed the hot mineral water near the chamber of commerce's office front door. And, nearby is a foot tub where people can sit and bathe the many disorders that might have settled in their feet.

A woman inside the chamber said that yes, people still come to the wells and fill jugs with its water. "I've had people tell me that their ancestors had been coming here to drink and bathe in the water to cure any number of ailments," she said. "And this is the site where the original wells were discovered. Across the street is the eighth hotel that Hilton built. There used to be an underground tunnel from the wells to the hotel, which stayed full most of the time."

"Can you give us a cup for a drink of the water?" Eddie asked.

"Oh, yes," she said. "But, I warn you. If you aren't used to it, it can have a laxative effect on you."

We took the cups and stopped at the well. The water was hot and tasted, well, like the old-time medications my mother used to pour down me for any number of ailments. As for the laxative effect, we didn't drink enough to find out.

We headed west to Reagan and then took FM 413 through Highbank. West of there is the third bridge in Falls County, a fairly modern structure and number thirty-six on our list. A massive pecan tree bore evidence of the power of recent flooding. The waters had twisted the tree almost into two pieces.

Under the bridge we found another example of humanity's ways to denigrate the country. A three-inch thick layer of broken beer bottles stretched in a line against one of the concrete pillars. We looked at the river, which gave a testament of its capricious nature. Whereas only a few miles upstream, the river had been low and lime green in color, the stream here was muddy and lapped at the banks.

We left and drove to the nearby community of Wilderville, stopping at the general store there, owned by Carlo Salvato. He had told Linda Brothers, a friend of mine, several bridge stories. One happened during World War II when two crop dusters decided to fly under the bridge, wing to wing.

They accomplished the almost impossible feat, said Salvato. But they had not planned on seeing workers hanging from scaffolding and painting the bridge. As a result, paint cans and workers were scattered.

Salvato related another incident that happened during construction of the bridge. A man who had worked on Salvato's father's farm quit his job there where he was earning $1.25 a day to take a job earning $1.50 a day to work on the bridge. "He was killed while working on the bridge," said Salvato.

We heard more stories from Renee Tacker, a friendly person who works in the store. She gave us coffee as we talked. "I don't know any stories about the bridges but my grandfather studied rivers all of his life and he told me to stay out of the Brazos because it was dirty and powerful. I've seen it all the way up to the top of the bridge," she said. "There's a lot of history here. Right over there is a house that was built in the 1830s." She pointed across a nearby cotton field.

"And, you need to stop at Powers Chapel. It's just right down the road. Real interesting place," she said. We drove north to Powers Chapel, a white frame church that originally was built in 1850. A sign said that the Rev.

Joseph P. Sneed, a Methodist circuit rider, started the settlement. We looked inside the church with its tall ceilings and straight-backed pews. You can imagine all of the old blistering sermons that had been given there, urging people to "repent of your evil ways and accept Jesus as your one and only savior."

A huge mailbox near the church held a guest register. Guests from several different states had signed their names. One had left a note that said, "I need help. I cannot find my father's grave or marker. It was right across the street (in a cemetery). If you have any information, please contact me."

The cemetery is neatly kept. On this day, bright yellow broomweed blossoms made a striking picture. From a nearby house a rooster crowed its ragged sound. It was 3:15 P.M., time to head for home and have a drink of Scotch and hope the brethren at Powers Chapel would not hold that against me.

CHAPTER THIRTY

Robertson County Bridge

❖ ❖ ❖

*A niece asked him to play at her wedding. He did. His music
filled the country church. Some people said they felt like crying.*

*"Sounds like him when he plays under that bridge," said a
cousin. "That music does something to your soul. It reaches down
deep inside you and you don't know whether to cry or laugh. It sure
does move you."*

Yeah, it did.

❖ ❖ ❖

Bridges are a gathering place not only for fishermen but also for area
characters. If you want information about the people and towns in a certain
area, go to a bridge and you are bound to find people who not only will tell
you if the fish are biting but also give you a clue to local history.

We learned that after driving south of FM 2027, turning east on FM
979, and finding the next bridge on our list in Robertson County. After
parking, we saw evidence of the good fishing at this bridge. Several huge
catfish heads had been stuck over the fence posts nearby.

There were several pickups, a van, and a car parked near the bridge.
Stories about fish were as abundant as the bites. One concerned a man who
fishes here quite often. "That old boy will come down here and camp out
under the bridge for a month," said Charles Poole. "He uses grasshoppers for
bait. Some of them are so big you'd think they could eat the catfish. But, one
day I came down here and he had caught a catfish that stretched all the
way across his pickup."

He shook his head and then told about a retired game warden who is famous for making stink bait.

"You can't beat that stuff for catching these catfish," he said. I asked him what he thought about the bridges over the Brazos.

"I love them," he said. "They are great gathering places and easy places to come to for fishing. And there are some interesting things around these bridges. Let me show you one at this bridge."

He led me under the bridge and pointed at a line of several dozen bird nests made from mud. "Okay, here's my question. You come down here when them birds are nesting, and they will fly out and get some bugs or something and then they come zooming back and they go right to their nest. Now here's the question . . . how do them birds know which nest to go to? Can you tell me that?" he asked.

I couldn't, so I moved on down the bank to look at some old pillars of a bridge that had been replaced. They were made of rock and had huge concrete blocks on their tops. Nobody had any idea when that bridge had been replaced.

Below these old columns another group of four people sat fishing, including Willie Johnson of nearby Cameron. "Yes sir, I am from big-time Cameron. Population 4,600 if you count all of the cows," he said.

Suddenly his fishing line went taut. He jerked the line strongly and began reeling. He had caught a small channel catfish. "Aw, well. What I really want is a good gasper goo," he said. "Some people call them trash fish. But, they're big like a carp, and you clean them right and they make good eating."

Delores Campbell, who sat next to him, smiled at me. "Why don't you interview me and maybe I'll catch a fish," she said.

They all said that they liked bridges because of the access to fishing they offer. "If it weren't for these bridges, we'd have to drive many more miles," said Johnson.

We said our good-byes. As we were leaving, one of them said, "If you want to see a place full of history, go on up to Calvert. Yes, sir. It's a nice little town and lots of things happened there."

I had read about the wildness that the Brazos begot along its banks during the early settlement of this area. Several of these stories came from Julien Hyer's book, *The Land of Beginning Again: The Romance of the*

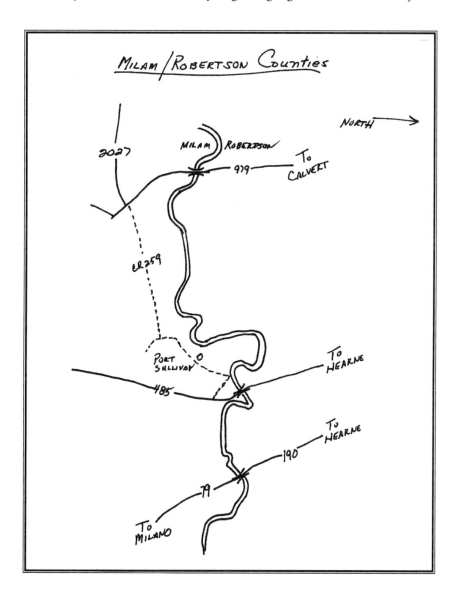

Brazos. He tells about the early settlers from Baden, Bavaria, Bohemia, and Czechoslovakia.

"Bremond in Robertson (County) was a wild place in the old days and one hears interesting tales . . . few strangers arrived from the outside except those who were running from something and going nowhere . . . fugitives from justice, fleeing the old states, formed a regular colony around Duck Creek in the 1860s. They would come into Bremond armed and in parties, defying the law," he wrote.

Paul Bremond, for whom the town was named, once said, "The fellow who traded a hack and two ponies for this town was one mule-skinner that got skinned himself."

Hyer said that the towns in the area were once known as "Houston, Hempstead, Hearne, and hell. Gambling, desperados, lawlessness thrived along this part of the river. But they sent a young Methodist preacher in, Horace Bishop, who started holding services over one of the saloons. He kept on until he had rallied the law-abiding in a campaign to clean up the town and build a schoolhouse and a church."

Calvert, which is a few miles east of the Brazos bridge, today is a quiet, sleepy little village. But, it did have its wild side when some 4,000 people lived here. That some outsiders were not welcome was seen in many ways. For example, black residents warned carpetbaggers to stay out because "when them bad men in Calvert stomp their foot, their guns jump in their hands." Calvert once had eighteen saloons and hauled whiskey from Kentucky by six trains. Gambling in its salons was wide open. Belle Starr operated a livery stable there. Furnishings in the houses rivaled those of New York.

I had visited Calvert many times and found several unusual subjects for stories when I wrote a column for the *Fort Worth Star-Telegram.* One concerned a black mummy that used to be kept in an aging, creepy funeral home. I once asked the owner about the mummy and where it came from.

The man looked almost as old as the mummy. He smoked cigarettes down to the filter, and his fingers were stained with nicotine.

"Before I talk to you, you'll have to go get permission from the mayor," he said. I went to where he had directed and asked the mayor, an Anglo-American, if it would be all right if I interviewed the black owner of the funeral home.

"Oh, you mean the one with the mummy," he said. "Yeah, that'll be fine."

"Do you need to call him and tell him it's okay?" I asked.

"Naw, just tell him that the mayor said it was okay for him to talk to you," he said. I went back and resumed my interview. The old man fired up another cigarette and talked about the mummy.

"That man, he died here in the 1880s. Was killed while working on some kind of construction job. Only he didn't have no money or any family. So they didn't bury him. They just embalmed him and left him out and he eventually became a mummy and wound up in my funeral home," he said. It was only within the last two years that the deceased had finally been given a proper burial.

Virginia Field Park is a nice city park surrounded by old, stately, southern-style mansions. According to a historical marker, during the Civil War, Company C of the 4th Texas Infantry Regiment of Hood's Texas Brigade once camped here in 1865. But the thing that I found most interesting was the fact that during the reconstruction period from 1868 to 1873, this park was the site for what was called a "sky parlor." That parlor amounted to a room built and mounted on a pole that served as a kind of treehouse/prison for Southern sympathizers. I was never able to get much information about the prison other than it was mainly for women. They got their food from baskets raised to them by ropes and pulleys. They had buckets on the platform that they used for a toilet.

Across from the park is the Calvert Cemetery, started in 1870. One gravestone is shaped like a castle with a steel door. Near the roofline is a single inscription that reads, "Samuel S. Whitemore, born Dec. 25, 1838 and died Dec. 18, 1881." Nothing else to tell who Whitemore might have been to merit such an impressive marker.

Near the cemetery is a building that was originally intended to be the courthouse for Robertson County. However, after it was selected for that honor and after the start of construction of the building, a yellow fever epidemic wiped out many of the local leaders. Before completion of the courthouse, the county seat had been moved to nearby Franklin in 1870. Robert A. Brown, a local merchant and investor, bought the building in 1885 and used it as his residence. It remained a residence until 1966 when it became a museum, which is now closed. A sign says it is being repaired.

More of Calvert's early history can be found in the nineteen historic buildings along its main street. There are several antique shops, the Doll House Museum, and the Katy Strickler Library. It's a town worth visiting. But we had other bridges to see in Robertson County, so we retraced our steps on FM 979 until we came to County Road 259, which is graveled but in good shape. We headed south toward another bridge near another piece of history called Port Sullivan.

CHAPTER THIRTY-ONE

Port Sullivan
and Robertson County Bridges

❖   ❖   ❖

Bridges lead to new cities. Bridges lead to new lives. Sometimes
bridges can return souls to happier times.

Regardless, bridges lead over rivers until time destroys them. But
the music made beneath bridges can live on and on and on. Such it
was with Ely Benningfield's music. His music was like the roots from
the towering pecan trees that grew on the banks of the Brazos River.
One person who was trying to dig up some of those roots said,
"These thangs must go all the way to Chine. They're deeper than the
roots in my jaw teeth."

Maybe they were.

❖   ❖   ❖

A bank of blue-gray clouds gathered in the east. Dust from the gravel
road spiraled onto the windshield as we tried to find the site of Port
Sullivan, where steamships once anchored in the Brazos River. It certainly
seemed like rain was coming. Then the sun broke through the clouds,
creating a scene that looked like fluffed up pillows on a couch. We drove
past banks of Arkansas wild roses with flags of purple blossoms.

I remembered a story I had read in Hyer's book about dogwood and a
Spanish legend told along the Brazos River in the early days of exploring.
That story said that the tears of a woman who had been near the cross when
Christ had been crucified had watered a tiny tree on which white blossoms

grew. From that day on, each flower took on the stigmata of the blood by having a tinge of brownish red that looked like a cross on each petal. Then every year in the spring at the time of Good Friday, the same flower bloomed. As a result, the story said that no politician in the Brazos Valley would announce for public office until the dogwood with its beautiful display of white bloomed in the spring.

We thought we might be lost and considered asking for directions as we drove past two men dressed in overalls and standing near an old house with fading gray paint. Axes and saws lay near stacks of firewood. Several dogs looked at us and began barking as we slowed down. Scenes from the movie *Deliverance* flashed in our minds. We kept driving.

I thought of another story about the roughness of the people and of this land. A man was hunting along the Brazos in this area when an alligator swallowed a young puppy he was training to hunt. The man responded in a burst of anger, killing the gator with an axe. Then he hacked the gator open and retrieved his puppy. That puppy later became a fine hunting dog.

We passed a church building with fading paint. A burned-out mobile home sat near a sign that had a flying eagle painted on it. We came to a mesquite flat bordered by leaning telephone poles. And, there, near the banks of the Brazos, was the marker for Port Sullivan, a one-time trade and educational center in this area.

T. Lindsay Baker has an excellent history of this once-thriving community in his book, *Building the Lone Star.* Baker says that Port Sullivan, one of Texas' best-known steamboat ports, began in 1835 when Augustus W. Sullivan secured title to a tract of land on a high bluff on the west side of the Brazos beside a substantial shoal. "The site in time came to be known as Sullivan's (sic) Bluff," wrote Baker.

In 1851, Rueben Anderson urged Sullivan to lay out a portion of his property as a town site. Sullivan did and in time the new town became the home for many local planters from both Robertson and Milam counties.

"Sullivan and Anderson expected the town to become primarily a river port, but even in good years it was accessible by steamboats only during high water. Through most of the following decade a handful of steamboats actually did call on the port, but it never became a regular port of call," according to Baker.

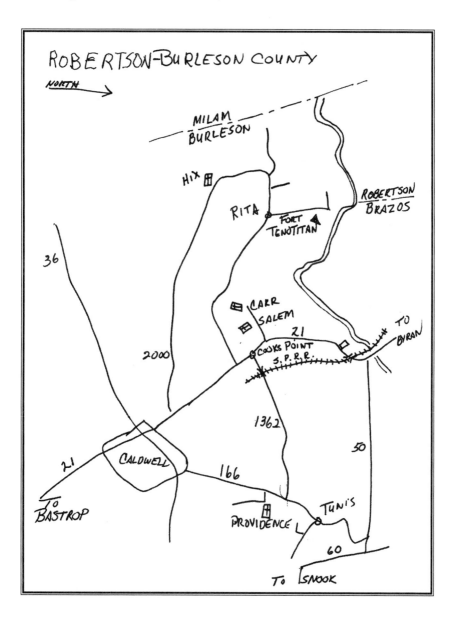

But by 1852, a writer for the *Galveston Weekly Journal* said the town had two hundred residents, four stores, two blacksmith shops, three carpenters' shops, a circular sawmill, and two or three warehouses for goods brought in by the steamboat. He also said the community had weekly mail delivery from Independence, one lawyer, and several doctors.

"In time Methodist, Baptist, and Episcopal churches came to serve Port Sullivan, not to mention the educational facilities provided by the Port Sullivan Male and Female College founded in the 1860s and operated into the 1870s," says Baker.

As time passed, railroads came to the area towns like Hearne and Calvert, bypassing Port Sullivan. By 1880, the population had dropped to 123, less than a tenth of the 1,423 registered a decade earlier. By the 1890s the town had disappeared completely, leaving only scattered building foundations and a cemetery.

"Gosh, it's hard to believe that this place was once that big," said Eddie as we stood and looked into the pastureland behind the historical marker. We could see the waters of the Brazos through the trees. Across the road was a field of corn that had been harvested, leaving shattered stalks sticking from the ground like the rusted ends of nails.

We drove on for about a mile and stopped at an old barn that had pieces of rusting sheet iron hanging from its timbers. I walked to the barn and looked inside. There was an old, two-story log building that had been hidden by the barn. It was like discovering an extra thick nut in chocolate nougat.

The logs had been hand-shaped by an axe, and as I looked at the old slash marks I wondered if this could have once been a part of Port Sullivan. I tried to picture those days as I stood there and breathed in the dust from the hay and listened to crows making their raspy calls outside. You could almost hear the sounds made by the steamboat whistles as they came up the river. Then a jet roared overhead. I was back in the twenty-first century.

A short distance from the Port Sullivan marker is the Highway 485 bridge and evidence of attempts to revive steamboat traffic. The bridge that was number thirty-eight for us is long and fairly new. Just up the river from the bridge are the remains of another huge bridge. Several of its old pillars lie in the river. And just across from them stand the old locks that the U.S. Army Corps of Engineers built between 1910 and 1920. They look like forlorn giants standing near the trees on the river. Conceived as an aid to the navigation of the river, they never were used.

I thought of the money that had been spent to build these huge creations and the hours of work that had been required. I could envision men stripped of their shirts standing in the tall grasses along the riverbanks with thick perspiration pouring from their bodies as they worked. I could hear their cries at night as they fought and scratched the chiggers and ticks that had attached themselves to their bodies. All of this energy had been expended, yet the finished product was never used. I wondered what those workers would think if today they stood where we stood and saw the locks still standing. I am sure they would have felt a bit of pride about the lasting power of their efforts.

Steamboats did once use the Brazos. An excellent history of that period can be found in *Sandbars and Sternwheelers: Steam Navigation on the Brazos*, by Nath Winfield Jr., and Pamela Ashworth Puryear. The writers mention some of the early bridges that played havoc with steamboat trade. One of those was a pile bridge that was thrown across the river and built with a moveable center section that could be pulled aside by a flatboat to permit the passage of river traffic. They said the early days of steamboat traffic were rather chaotic. An early survey of boats on the river found only two small steamers being used between Galveston and Columbia in Brazoria County.

The authors mentioned early bridges like the "trestle of the Austin Tap Line near Chappell Hill, a toll bridge in Austin County, and the crossing of the Galveston, Henderson, and San Antonio Railroad over a bridge at Richmond." But these early bridges were headaches for the passage of the big steamboats because no provisions had been made to allow the boats to pass. In a survey by army engineers in 1874-1875, Captain William Jinks voiced complaints about the bridges. He piloted the *George W. Thomas*—a 168-ton paddle wheeler built in Evansville, Indiana, in 1870—on a regular Brazos run, seldom deviating from his routine of a weekly round trip between Galveston and Columbia. He hauled cotton, sugar, molasses, pecans, hides, lumber, bales of Spanish moss, preserved beef, and whatever else his customers saw fit to pile upon the *Thomas's* decks.

Jinks piloted a steamboat on the Brazos for twenty-five years before quitting. When he was interviewed the old sea captain said, "I'm still ready to take the *Thomas* to Washington if only you (the engineers) would remove from my path three or four of the railroad bridges and a fifteen-year accumulation of snags."

But not only the bridges made steamboat travel difficult. So did the capricious nature of the Brazos. Sometimes its banks would be near over-flowing. Yet in a matter of days the river could drop drastically, revealing sandbars and shallow channels.

That's what happened to the *Hiawatha*, a lavishly appointed boat built in Marietta, Ohio, in 1890. Winfield and Puryear said the boat was furnished with electric lights, twenty-two staterooms, and a saloon one hundred feet long. She could move at fifteen miles an hour while customers sipped mint juleps under stained glass skylights in her red-carpeted grand saloon and a seventeen-piece orchestra played. In addition to the passengers, she could haul fifteen hundred bales of cotton.

The *Hiawatha* sank during one of the Brazos' notorious drops in water level at the town of Columbia. She settled onto a huge oak stump in the river, and attempts to free the ship brought her to the surface. But as Winfield and Puryear said, "The proud *Hiawatha* was a sorry sight. Her once spotless stateroom dripped with river ooze. Her sumptuous furnishings were faded and sodden. Damage to her hull was found to be extensive. They began to strip away her fittings and engines. But, one of the chains snapped and she fell into the river again and no further attempt was ever made to resurface her."

As we gazed at the Brazos on this day, the almost full channel of muddy water upstream was evidence of rain from somewhere. The old paddlewheelers would have loved it. We left for the next bridge in Robertson County, driving past cotton and maize fields that had already been harvested, and in the bottomlands of the Brazos, layered with rich loam that can turn harvests into times of happiness.

Some of the huge blocks of cotton recently pulled from the plants had been left in the fields. They had coverings so the large raindrops that hit our windshield like soft shotgun pellets wouldn't hurt the harvest. We went through Valley Junction and crossed over a train track where a train with a long line of coal cars sat. We turned east on Highway 79-190 and stopped at the historical marker for the long-ago town site of Nashville.

The marker said that the town had been surveyed in the fall of 1835 as the capital of Robertson's Colony. It was named for Nashville, Tennessee, where Sterling C. Robertson and many of his colonists had formerly lived. Nashville was the first home in Texas for George C. Childress, chairman of the committee that drafted the Texas Declaration of Independence. Somebody had expressed displeasure at the wording on the marker by shooting it with a rifle or pistol.

We parked and walked to the bridge, a long structure casting pale shadows on the smooth but muddy river. We walked down the muddy banks and passed wilting bloodweeds, silverleaf, nightshade clover, and the usual trash piled near the bridge by litter rats. I found a piece of old glass sticking from the wet ground and pulled it up. It was faded and thick. I wondered if it might have come from the days of old Nashville. Did it once hold the fruited pleasures like wild plums or peaches picked and pickled and stored inside a glass jar, furnishing a youngster with a stomach howling from hunger with the kind of a taste delight that lingered until he licked the thick syrup from his fingers? Or maybe it had held some of the powerful nectar like homemade whiskey that could be made in a few days with a taste that could be softened by cooking oak chips in a skillet and soaking them for a few days in the jar of liquor.

The late Wallace McPherson of Glen Rose once told me that was the secret to making the taste of that concoction called "white lightning" more acceptable. It carried a punch like a mule kicking you in the stomach. "I even tried cooking mesquite chips a couple of times," he had said. "They weren't as good as the oak, but they did give that homemade fire a better taste."

I looked up at the bottom of the bridge, wondering exactly when it was built and how long it was. As earlier noted, once that information was posted on brass plaques bolted onto the frames of the bridges. I thought of the bullet holes in the Nashville marker and realized probably why plaques are no longer used. Some idiot would only blow holes in them with a high-powered weapon or try to rip the marker off and take it home to put on a wall with other keepsakes like the trophy they won for spitting the farthest in a tobacco-chewing contest.

We walked up the muddy bank and headed for Brazos County and its bridges.

CHAPTER THIRTY-TWO

Brazos County Bridges

❖　　❖　　❖

The years passed. His fingers hardened. Weather marked his face
like stain used to age wood. But still he went to the bridge to play.
And when he touched the harmonica to his mouth, his music lived in
the echoes beneath the bridge.

　　Those times bring back to him many memories. He remembers
the day that they first held hands and listened to the wind strum the
long green blades from the thick clumps of Johnson grass, making
melody for two young lovers.

❖　　❖　　❖

We stayed on Highway 50 as we headed south toward Highway 21 and
the bridges in Brazos County. We went through Mumford and passed where
Steele's Store community once existed. A marker said the settlement could
be traced to 1851 when Henry B. Steele built a general merchandising store
in the vicinity. Originally, the town was called Mudville because of the
frequent Brazos River floods.

But that did not deter Italian immigrants who came to this country
looking for new lives. They arrived by the hundreds from the Italian
provinces of Trapani and Palermo and began settling here in the 1870s. They
established large farms and by the early twentieth century, the Italian community here was one of the largest in the United States.

"I didn't know that but I did know that a lot of Italians came here.
My father was one of those," said Tony Bush, who once lived in these rich

bottomlands and today lives in Beaumont. "My dad still farms and raises cotton. He made three bales to the acre this year . . . that's a helluva crop."

Bush remembers tougher days when he took a hoe and chopped the weeds from the young cotton plants. He laughed. "We didn't have the weed killers that they have today. We were the weed killers." But, he said, it was a good life, and the fairly recent discovery of oil and gas in the bottomlands has made the farming a little easier.

"I remember the bridge on Highway 21. Yeah, I do. It's southwest of Bryan. We used to drive down there and drink beer and think nobody knew what we were doing," he said. "It's quite a place."

We saw he was right when we reached the bridge that was number forty on our list. It has twin traffic lanes going each way. There is an old steel pyramid railroad bridge close by. On this day the river again was muddy from the rains that had left small lakes in nearby cotton fields. We parked and walked to the bottom of the bridge. Suddenly we both jumped at a loud crash.

"What the hell?" yelled Eddie. We looked up. The noise had come from a train that had crossed the bridge and was backing up. We felt kind of childish.

I remembered a story that Charles Poole had earlier told me about the old bridge that had stretched across the river here. He said the bridge was very narrow. "There was barely room for two semi-trucks to go across it without slapping their mirrors against each other," he said. "My granddad had an old pickup that he would drive about thirty miles an hour at top speed. One day we started across that bridge and he got real nervous, thinking we might meet a truck. I said, 'Come on, Grandpa. Give it some gas.' But, he never speeded up. We made it before we met anyone. But let me tell you. I think I was more scared than he was. I like old stuff but I'm glad they've got that new bridge there."

There are two markers near the bridge. One says that this was the route of the Camino Real and the Old San Antonio Road, two famous roads used by the early explorers and pioneers in the early 1700s. Another marker said that this once was the site of Moseley's Ferry.

"It [Moseley's Ferry] was situated where the Old San Antonio Road crossed the Brazos River. Michael Baron began this public ferry about 1846. Travelers, livestock, and freight were transported across the river

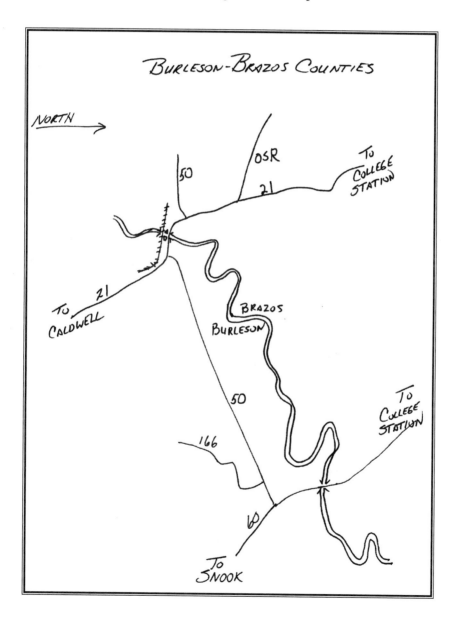

until 1912 when the Houston & Texas Central Railroad (now the Southern Pacific) constructed a railroad bridge at this location. Today a highway bridge spans the Brazos where Moseley's ferry once operated," read the historical marker.

We drove on south on Highway 50 toward the next bridge over Highway 21. We passed the place where the Brazos River levee had been built in an attempt to stop the widespread damage caused by the flooding Brazos. The levee is in Burleson County where residents often found themselves at the mercy of those floods. A historical marker tells about the toll those floods took in 1899 when a thirty-inch rain soaked this area. The floods killed thirty-five people and caused $7 million in damage. Finally, residents asked their county commissioners to build the levees. In July of 1909 voters approved bonds to build an eight-foot levee that extended for thirty miles.

"In December 1913, a storm came that was worse than the 1899 flood. Residents thinking the levee was safe did not leave until the water had risen dangerously. They discovered that the levee had trapped the water and then broke, unleashing a wall of destruction from which there was no escape. Victims rode out the flood in tree tops and on roofs," reads the marker. It said 180 were killed and property damage totaled $8 million.

"That was a lot of dirt to move," said Eddie. We had stopped to look at a gentle swell made by the old levee. "To think, they did that for thirty miles and then it didn't work."

We continued driving toward what is called the Whiskey Bridge. We drove past more cotton fields that had oil and gas pumps scattered among the stripped cotton stalks. Then we came to the Highway 60 bridge. The facilities of Texas A&M University loomed just across the river in the distance to the east. The bridge, a long structure, has concrete columns that look like extended telescopes. When you back up and look at it, it is rather impressive.

"We called it the Whiskey Bridge," said Robert Mausner of College Station. "The reason for that was that they did not sell liquor in Brazos County near the Texas A& M campus back in my younger days. So we had to drive across this bridge and into Burleson County to buy our booze. There was a liquor store waiting for us right where the Burleson County line starts. No telling how much booze was hauled back across this bridge in those days."

On this day, the Brazos looked like dark bourbon, obvious signs of the recent rains. A massive pile of brush had lodged against one of the columns anchored in the river waters. We looked upstream and could see a piling, apparently from an old bridge, sticking up from the bank. We walked under the bridge and realized that it is much larger than it appears when you are driving across it.

Cars and trucks roared overhead making "wham, wham, wham" echoes. From a nearby home a dog barked. We started back to the top. A stiff wind blew from the north and rattled the tall false ragweeds, making them sound like a baby rattling beads stretched across his bed. Or like ice in a glass containing bourbon.

We called it a day and headed for my son Patrick's house in nearby Bryan with our wild stories about the bridges we had seen in his county.

CHAPTER THIRTY-THREE

Washington County Bridge

❖   ❖   ❖

She had become internationally known. One day after she received still another famous award, someone gushed, "What more could you ask for?"

Her answer came quickly.

"To play my harmonica beneath the Brazos Bridge once again," she said.

"Huh?" they asked.

Her eyes flashed a faraway look. "There are sweet melodies that come from simple places. They carry more meaning than recognition from awards such as these. People who have not experienced these have shallow pockets that can never match the depth of the pockets of those who know what I am talking about," she said.

The crowd did not answer her, but obviously they had those shallow pockets of which she talked.

❖   ❖   ❖

We headed for the next bridge on our list, which was in Washington County. The day was brilliant. We drove down Highway 6 and entered Grimes County in which Navasota is located, the town where I worked my first newspaper job.

We stopped in the town for a look at the statue of René-Robert Cavelier Sieur de La Salle. In 1682 this Frenchman explored the Mississippi River to its mouth at the Gulf of Mexico, claiming the territory for France. Two years later, La Salle returned to this country with four ships loaded with colonists.

However, he missed the mouth of the Mississippi by about four hundred miles and landed on the Texas coast. He lost two ships but still established Fort Saint Louis near La Vaca Bay.

Then he and a group of his men began walking toward Canada to try to find French outposts on the Mississippi. "He was treacherously slain by his own men near this spot in March, 1687," reads an inscription on the statue.

We had seen another reminder of LaSalle during a short visit to the facilities of the Nautical Archaeology Program at Texas A&M University. That department has pieced together the hull of the *Belle*, one of the four ships that LaSalle landed on the Texas coast. The *Belle* was discovered covered by mud in Matagorda Bay near the mouth of the Colorado River.

"I wonder if he was buried near the banks of the Brazos?" asked Eddie.

Probably not, because historians think his demise came somewhere near the Trinity River. But nobody really knows where he is buried, one of the archeologists had told us during a visit to Texas A&M. One story about the French explorer—who had the personality of an alligator with a massive toothache—said La Salle was killed by his men, stripped of his clothing, and left lying in a grove of trees.

We left this town and headed west on Highway 105, crossing the Navasota River and reaching Washington County and our next bridge across the Brazos. Huran Delano Burrell, eighty-four, sat on a plastic soft-drink carton near the river. His gray hair peeked out from a cap as he threaded a worm on a fishhook. Shade from the bridge softened his age.

"I was born on this river. Yes, sir. Been fishing it all of my life or since I was old enough to walk. Oh, yeah. I love fishing. And, I love these bridges. They make good places to sit and fish and contemplate about what is going on in the world. Yes sir," he said. "I live up the road in Petersburg. It's just a little settlement. But, it's okay. The old bridge, yes sir, I remember fishing down below it. Mr. Tom Moore had a liquor store just across the river from that bridge. Folks burned up the road over there in Grimes County trying to get to his liquor store. They couldn't buy liquor then in their county so they came to the old bridge and shot across it to buy them some shots. Heh, heh."

He had finished baiting his line, dug his feet into the muddy bank, rocked a couple of times, and raised himself from the plastic carton. He

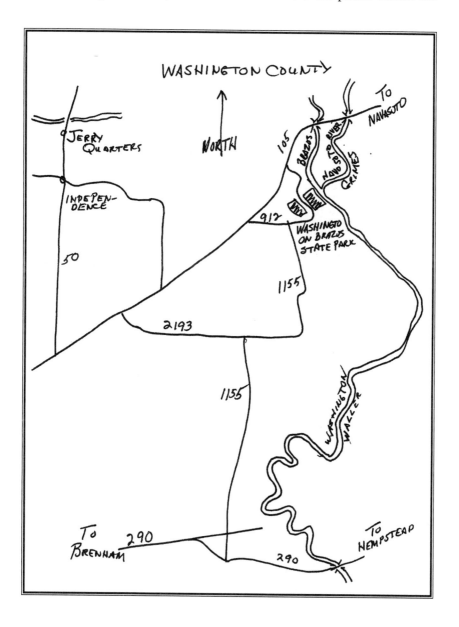

walked toward the river, stopped, and flung his line into the middle of the river.

"You know, sometime in the summer there are so many people down here that you can't even get to the river," he said. He shook his head. "And, some of those people ruin the places along the river. They haul in so much trash that they have built barricades to where you can't get around the bridges anymore. That's a shame, a damn shame."

He lit a cigarette and watched his line. "Doctor told me I am supposed to do a lot of exercising. I told him I do a lot of walking when I am fishing. He said, 'Well, that will be all right. You just keep on fishing.' You know, I wish I had somebody who would go with me to Galveston to fish. My wife used to do that. But she passed last December. So all I got is myself now. I might find somebody else but you've got to be so careful these days. They'll liable to knock you in the head. People ain't like they used to be. Used to, anybody fishing wouldn't think about knocking you in the head."

We told him we were going to Washington-on-the Brazos. "Ha. You ask somebody about Old Man Tom's liquor store. You'll hear some interesting stories, I'll bet," he said.

We drove across the river to Washington-on-the-Brazos. The old H.A. Stolz Groceries and Beer General Store where I ate barbecue sandwiches and drank cool ones on my weekends off from the *Navasota Examiner Review* is now closed. We drove onto the grounds of the 293-acre state park, with well-manicured grounds.

A person could spend a day at this park, hiking and looking at the exhibits like the building that is a reconstruction of Independence Hall. It stands on the original location where the Texas Declaration of Independence was signed and the government of the new nation was formed.

Inside the visitor center are photographs of the early days of Texas. Documents tell some interesting stories of the state in its infancy. William

Bolbert obviously liked the state. He said that "Texas land was so rich if you planted a ten penny nail, you'll have a crop of iron bolts." George Kindall, a journalist of the 1840s, had similar feelings. He described the Texas climate as "so healthy that if a man wants to die here, he must go somewhere else."

There were also words of criticism like the description by a person from England. He said, "I don't see how a man can live as you folks do and be a Christian, for the ticks, the black mud, sand flies, mosquitoes, dry beef, black coffee, sweet potatoes, and the other hard features of your country would ruin me. It is the most perfect purgatory of any place on Earth."

There is no doubt that the early town of Washington-on-the-Brazos was rough. One writer said the town in 1840 had about 350 residents of which fifty to one hundred were described "principally gamblers, horse racers, etc. In almost every other house on the public streets, you see games of all sorts being played both day and night." A British traveler said, "The passion for erecting grog shops superseded the thirst for religious worship."

Tom Scaggs, manager of the state park, a strong and gregarious man with rusty colored hair and a moustache, laughed about those descriptions. "It did take some strong people to live in those days," he said.

We told Scaggs about our mission to look at bridges and what the fisherman had said about the old bridge that people from Grimes County drove over to buy liquor.

"Yes, I have heard about that bridge. It was an old wooden bridge on concrete pillars. I heard that too many trucks got on it and it collapsed. Then the highway department put a temporary ferry there until they could build the new bridge. An interesting thing about the ferry, it was located below both the Navasota and Brazos rivers so you only had to cross the rivers once," he said. "Come on. I'll take you and show you where that old bridge used to be."

As he drove, he told about another park facility called the Barrington Living History Farm. This facility re-creates daily life on an 1850s Brazos

Valley cotton farm through the story of Anson Jones, the last president of the Republic of Texas.

"We have the original Anson Jones house," said Scaggs. He laughed. "That house is probably the most moved house in Washington. We have a team of oxen, chickens, and cows on the farm. Also an old log kitchen. We grow vegetables and show how they are cooked in the fireplaces. That way school kids can smell the cooking and maybe get a taste. It's easier to remember history when a kid can smell and taste it," he said. Then he talked about the Brazos and the fluctuation of its stream. "There's no such thing as a normal depth on the Brazos," he said. "You can see a fifteen-to-twenty foot drop or rise overnight."

We had turned down a gravel road. He stopped, and we crawled from his truck. "That was the old liquor store," he said, pointing at what remains of the store. All that is left are the walls. After looking at those, we walked toward the river. Stepping onto layers of black walnuts that had fallen from nearby trees, we walked past an old hay barn and what had been a cotton gin that has been converted to a hay barn. We passed an old boat with a bottom caved in from rust and went through a forest that had giant poison ivy vines as big as huge cables creeping up the tree trunks. After a few more yards, Scaggs stopped and pulled back some limbs.

"There's one of the columns of the old bridge," he said.

We looked through the branches at the old concrete structure. Poison ivy vines covered it. We walked back to Scaggs' pickup and returned to the park.

"Say, there is a question I would like to ask," said Eddie. "We have noticed on a map of this area from *The Roads of Texas* a place called Jerry's Quarters. We also noticed in the visitor center that Anson Jones had a slave named Jerry and since the site is not too far from here, we wondered, could that be a community named after him? And, do you know exactly where it is?"

"I've never heard of it," said Scaggs. "Let me look at the map."

We showed him the map. He stared at it a moment and then said, "That's got to be in the Independence area. But, I never have heard of it. If you want to find it, I would suggest you go up to Independence and ask somebody." We shook hands and thanked him, deciding that we would go to Independence in search of Jerry's Quarters. It turned out to be a delightful trip.

CHAPTER THIRTY-FOUR

Jerry's Quarters

❖　❖　❖

She began playing again. At first, she was reluctant to fit the sessions into her busy schedule. They made her feel like a child facing her daily chores.

During those first episodes she retrieved the harmonica only after making sure her daughter would not be there. Her music was ragged like the wounds she had stitched while serving her time in the emergency room during her internship. But the music got better.

❖　❖　❖

Independence is a tiny community rich with early Texas history, founded in 1825 and renamed in 1836 to celebrate Texas' independence from Mexico. We got there by following Highway 50 south to 390 and turning east.

Interesting sites include the four masonry columns at the town's Old Baylor Park that commemorates the 1845 site of Mary Hardin-Baylor University at Belton. The site of the male college that became Baylor University in Waco also stands nearby.

The Houston-Lea Family Cemetery, burial site of Margaret Lea, wife of Sam Houston, is on the main street. A marker says that she died of yellow fever during an epidemic in 1867. "The danger of contagion made it impossible to carry her body to Huntsville for burial beside her husband. She lies here with her mother, Mrs. Nancy Lea, near the sites of their last home and the old church they both loved." Another marker says Margaret Lea and her mother were women of "strong character, culture, and staunch devotion to their families and church, each in her own way greatly influenced the career of Sam Houston and the course of Texas History."

Embedded in a rock across the road is the original bell presented by Nancy Lea to the Independence Baptist Church. It reads, "She sleeps within its sound."

As I looked at the marker and waited for Eddie to ask in the museum if anyone knew where Jerry's Quarters was, I thought of the strength of those early Texas women like Lea and her mother. Julien Hyer told of two of those women who lived along the Brazos River in the early days. One was Jane Wilkinson, a Maryland native. She moved to Bolivar Point with her husband Dr. James H. Long. They owned a single cannon that she learned to shoot. Her husband died and soon afterwards, Jane Wilkinson fought off hostile Indian attacks with the cannon. She also birthed a baby on her own. She was a tall woman, and one account says, "She formed a beautiful figure, moving with a grace that is truly and wholly feminine. Her eyes were sparkling, her features regular, her smile, her ease and fluency fascinates people."

One of many suitors wrote a poem for her called "Bonnie Jane." It reads:

To Bonnie Jane, thou are to me
Whatever in both is best.
Thou are the moonbeam in my eye.
The sunbeam in my breast.

She died in 1880 and is buried beside the Brazos River near Richmond. Still another strong woman of those early days was Jane McManus Caznear. She came to Texas in 1832 after her first marriage failed. She knew and contributed to the philosophies of many of the early-day politicians. A relative, Colonel J.R. Lewis of Matagorda, became very angry when she was not invited to an important ball. He sent letters to every one of the members of the invitation committee challenging them to a duel because they had slighted his kinswoman. But his temper cooled down and no duels were fought. As I thought about these early women in Texas and the roles they played in our state's development, Eddie returned from the old Baylor museum.

"They don't know where Jerry's Quarters is. Said they had never heard of it," he said.

"Well, maybe it's a figment of the mapmaker's imagination," I said.

We decided to drive to the Antique Rose Emporium, a delightful local nursery specializing in antique roses. While looking at the hundreds of rose plants there, Eddie asked an attendant if she had heard of Jerry's Quarters.

"No, but let me look at a local map," she said.

She did and there in about the same location as our map noted was Jerry's Quarters.

"You should drive up there and ask somebody. Get on Highway 390 and go west to Highway 50 and then go north. It should be up in that area. It won't be too far from Yegua Creek," she said.

We followed her directions. We came to the spot marked on our map that said this should be the site of Jerry's Quarters. However, no signs stuck in the ground proclaiming this as Jerry's Quarters.

We headed down a gravel road about three miles until we neared Yegua Creek. We saw no signs, so we stopped a rancher driving a pickup.

"Jerry's Quarters, no I've never heard of it," he said.

We headed back for the paved road. "There may not be such a place," I said.

We passed an older-looking man sitting under a tree in a folding chair. "You want to ask him?" asked Eddie.

"Certainly," I said. We stopped and walked up to him.

"Do you know where Jerry's Quarters is?" I asked.

He laughed a deep, raspy chuckle. "You're standing right in it," he said. He laughed again. "Ain't no community by that name but right here my front yard is known as Jerry's Quarters. Has been for years."

He fished a cigarette from a package and lighted it, sucked deeply, and continued. "My name is Robert Moore. I'm related to the man who Jerry's Quarters is named for. He died many years ago. His name was Jerry De Walt," he said. A rooster crowed from a nearby pen. Clothes hung out to dry flapped in the slight cool wind. Moore took more drags from his cigarette. He had gray hair and a workingman's hands.

"Was Jerry once the slave of Anson Jones?" I asked.

"I don't know. I do know he had been a slave. Maybe Anson Jones owned him. But, I don't know. I do know when he got his freedom he came to this community and bought him a little speck of land and lived here," he said.

Then Moore told about serving in World War II. "You know what I did, sir? I have laid in water with a forty-eight-pound pack on my back. Laid there with just my nose sticking out. These young people today say they like to shoot and fight," he said. He snorted in derision. "If they want to shoot and fight, tell them to go over to a place like I was. Yes, sir."

He turned philosophical. "Let me tell you this. I got shot once. But, I didn't get killed. But, I learned something then . . . the power of God," he said. He shook his head. "Some people don't think there is a God. You don't see him. But, he's up there. You see the leaves on a tree and you see the waves in the water. But, you can't see the wind. Think how powerful that wind is. So let me tell you. That wind might be God. Yes sir, that wind has a lot of power so God might be that wind." As he lit another cigarette, I asked him what he knew about the Brazos and its bridges. He shook his head up and down.

"I was born on the Brazos. Lived there as a baby and young man. But, I don't like it. That river can get up as fast as a man taking off his shirt to get some sunshine. And, it is powerful. Yes, sir. I've seen it cover that bridge over there near Washington. Cover it entirely," he said. "But, the bridges over those old angry rivers, I love 'em. Furnish you shade and used to, you could go there and sit and fish and might catch the smell of some wild plums and blackberries growing in the brush along the bank. And when you got done with your fishing, you'd go pick some of them blackberries and get that juice all over your fingers and lick it off as you ate them berries. Yes, sir, those are good memories."

We asked him again about Jerry's Quarters and his obvious love for the location. "Love it? Lordy, yeah, I love it," he said. He smiled. "Let me tell you a story that shows you how much I love Jerry's Quarters. After the war had ended and after we had spent three weeks getting drunk and celebrating and I finally got my discharge, I came straight back home just like a rabbit. Yes, sir. I came home and built me a little nest. Just like a rabbit. Right here in Jerry's Quarters."

We thanked him and left. As we drove toward the pavement we went under some oak trees on each side of the road. They appeared almost like they had grown together, making a beautiful canopy across the road. A breeze from the north stirred the leaves. God was talking.

CHAPTER THIRTY-FIVE

Washington County Area Bridges

❖　❖　❖

Soon she began finding excuses to go home early. She had a long list from which to draw . . . fever, nausea, etc., etc. When she arrived at home and began playing, her mind eased as it flew with the notes to those faraway episodes of pleasure beneath the Brazos River Bridge.

Was he still playing there? she wondered. He couldn't be. So many years have passed. He probably doesn't even play any more.

So she kept playing. And thinking about the musical chamber beneath the bridge.

❖　❖　❖

We began looking for bridges in the Washington County area, and a coming blast of winter highlighted conversations as we drove through Brenham and stopped for gas. We had been blessed with a wonderful day that was more like spring with the temperature near seventy. Yet, the talk was not about the good weather but about the bad weather coming. We told a stout-looking man at a service station about our mission of looking at bridges over the Brazos. He shook his head.

"That's a funny thing to be doing. But boys, let me tell you something. You'd better enjoy looking at them bridges in this good weather because bad weather's a'coming," he said as he pumped gasoline into his pickup truck. "Yes, sir, bad weather's coming and it ain't gonna be good for looking at bridges or anything else except flames from your heating stove."

He sounded like somebody warning a buddy to get ready because the town bully's coming around the corner and he has his buddy's name high on his list of people he's going to fight. So with the man's warning in our minds, we decided to restock our liquor in Brenham, the seat of Washington County where the first Anglo-Americans arrived in 1821.

According to Darwin Spearing in his book *Roadside Geology of Texas*, the Brazos River has entrenched itself in the Pleistocene sandstones called the Willis formation. He said the sandy ridges west of Brenham form the Oakville escarpment, which extends for many miles to the southwest as a recognizable topographic ridge.

Brenham is a delightful town, full of homes and businesses that have been restored and refurbished. It was recognized as a 2002 National Main Street City with attractions like the antique carousel, one of eight that exist in Texas, and the only example of a C.W. Parker Carousel with Herchell-Spillman horses, manufactured in 1910. The Brenham Heritage Museum is housed in the city's former post office, a classical revival structure built in 1915, and the Burton Cotton Gin and Museum is a national Historic Mechanical Engineering Landmark. And, of course, the Blue Bell Creamery that makes the famed Blue Bell Ice Cream has its home here. And, yes, it is the best in the country, said Carol Hutch, owner of the Corner Drug Liquor Store.

"I worked for them for twenty years," she said. She smiled. "I ate enough to qualify as a taste expert. So quote me as saying it is the best ice cream around." She talked about her liquor store that was once a Piggly Wiggly grocery store and then was a drugstore. "Those shelves that they had in the grocery store do come in handy for stocking my liquor," she said.

We told her about our mission to look at all of the bridges over the Brazos River.

"I've got a story for you about the bridge down in Washington-on-the-Brazos," she said. "I lived there as a kid. I can remember that after I got my driver's license, I used to drive my dad over that bridge. But, I have seen it when the river had almost swallowed the bridge and we didn't think about driving across it then."

We laughed and left. Our next stop was Rau's Meat Center, a huge fresh meat market and the kind that my buddy Eddie loves to visit. The smells of fresh sausage were strong. Signs said they slaughter hogs that weigh two hundred pounds for $30. They also make pan sausage for sixty cents a pound, sell fresh sweetbreads for $1.99 a pound, and beef kidney for $1.39. Eddie bought two pounds of sausage and we headed east on Highway 290.

We drove past the old Starlite Drive-In Theater that today is home to an antique auction. We were in country with rolling hills and some picturesque ranches and farms. We stopped in Chappell Hill, a town established in 1847, full of old buildings, including the Providence Baptist Church, built in 1873. The white frame building has a National Register of Historic Places marker given by the U.S. Department of the Interior. It says the church was founded near here in 1842 and the first building was destroyed by a storm.

A historical marker in the town says that this was once the site of Soule University for Boys. It was established in 1855 and chartered in 1856 to replace Rutersville and Wesleyan colleges. The Civil War and a yellow fever epidemic closed the school. Afterwards, Southwestern University succeeded it in 1875.

A few miles east of Chappell Hill we arrived at the next bridge. It's a huge four-lane structure and remarkably clean underneath as far as bridges go. We walked around and looked at the massive concrete pilings and deep scratches into them that had been caused by debris from flooding that had rammed into the sides. The river's color today was a muddy green.

"Good for fishing," said Eddie.

We drove to a nearby meat market that had large gray paintings of hogs on the front. Nearby was a Texas Highway Patrol office. Trooper Brian Frank stood outside. We asked him about the bridge.

"Well, the river does flood in this area. New Year's Creek, which is in this valley, gets up and floods the whole valley. During one of those floods, we went to the river and an old boy was standing out in the middle of it. We wondered what he was standing on and then realized he was standing in the back of his pickup. He had tried to get across that river when it was flooding. He should have known better. He lives here," he said.

We got directions to the ranch of Mike Malinowski, another longtime resident. En route we stopped at a historical marker that says this area was once active for steamboat traffic coming to pick up cotton and sugar grown in these rich bottomlands. These items and others were taken to the markets in New Orleans.

We found the Malinowski ranch close to this marker. Mike and his son, Donald, stood near a shed repairing farm equipment. The father had thick arms and hands. He chewed tobacco as he told about being born and reared in this area.

"I moved away once but came back. When I got back I said I only had one more move in me and that was to the cemetery," he said.

He talked about the old bridge across the Brazos. "It was a nice bridge. Made out of steel and [it] was narrow. When two eighteen-wheelers met on it, you'd see smoke coming from their sides as they rubbed up against each other," he said. He laughed. "When I was just a youngster, me and my brother used to measure the depth of the river's water. One of us had to lean over the railing and the other one would hold onto his feet and we'd drop this tape down into the water to see how deep the river was. We did that twice a day. My dad got $37 a month for us doing it. We did it until one time my momma wanted to know why we were going to the bridge so much, and we told her. She got pretty upset about the danger of us doing that and said we were not going to do that no more. And we didn't."

He said there once was a ferry across the river where the bridge is today. Some of the old cables are still embedded in concrete pillars on the

This modern-looking bridge is located on Highway 159, south of Hempstead, a historic area with roots in the slaveholding territory of the 1820s. A few hundred feet from this concrete-and-steel structure, visitors can see the twisted remains of an old bridge, a fairly common sight at many of the bridges.

bank. Then he told about the old bridge being destroyed before they built the new one.

"They took it down and then blew out all of the pillars," he said.

"They tried to do the same thing to the old railroad bridge, which is just down the river," said Donald Malinowski. "They drilled all of these holes in its columns, put dynamite in them, and set it off. But, after the smoke cleared, the old bridge was still standing. That is one tough old bridge."

We asked directions to the next bridge. The father said to go to Hempstead and then take Highway 159 south and we would find it.

"I hear it is good fishing down there," he said.

We thanked him and headed south.

We reached Hempstead, which lies in a historic area that stretches back to the 1820s. The antebellum area was once slaveholding territory. Today, agriculture is a large part of the economy with many acres of rice and watermelons planted and harvested. We headed south on Highway 159 and drove past cattle grazing on pastures of green grass. We reached the next bridge that almost straddles the borderlines of Waller and Austin counties.

The bridge is a concrete-and-steel structure. The twisted remains of an old bridge can be seen in the river. There are also huge hunks of granite lining the riverbank, placed there in an attempt to prevent erosion. We both recalled the huge ragged gullies eaten into the riverbanks by rain and floods we had seen at other bridges. The granite had prevented this from happening so far.

A young couple sat in a pickup parked beneath the bridge. They were doing more than holding hands. I guess they still use bridges for those purposes.

We walked through huge cocklebur plants. The remains of trash and debris lay high on the bank, testimony that the Brazos does flood in this area. Nearby trees with streaks of yellow and red foliage brightened the area and looked like hand-painted ties. A discarded grocery list with the hand scrawled items of milk, biscuits, and pizza lay near one of the bridge pillars.

I hoped we'd eat better than what those items suggested that family might have. But, before I found out what Master Chef Eddie Lane had planned for our dinner, we had several more bridges to visit.

CHAPTER THIRTY-SIX

Bellville Bridge

One day her daughter confronted her.

*"I've been hiding in the spare bedroom and listening to you play,"
she said. "Your music is beautiful. Those old-time tunes have so
much soul in them. Who are you playing for?"*

*"For him," she said. "For my lover beneath the Brazos River
Bridge. It's a long story."*

"Tell me," said the daughter.

*She did. Afterwards, her daughter said softly, "I was right. Your
music does have soul in it."*

Mysteries like water from a hillside spring seep from many of the
bridges across the Brazos River. We discovered one of those mysteries at the
bridge on FM 529 east of Bellville.

We had gotten there by taking FM 331 south of Hempstead. Passing
through a community named Raccoon Bend, we looked at a vacant old
two-story building with graying shingles that looked like a boardinghouse.
It had red trim and a broken wooden bench on the front porch.

Both of us were curious about the name, Raccoon Bend. So we stopped
at two different houses before we found someone to ask, a youngster who
said he was eighteen. He didn't look his age.

"So do you know where the name came from?" I inquired.

He shook his head and said, "No. Hail, I've only lived here seventeen
years."

We later found out that the community was the scene of a terrible murder some years ago. Four elderly people were found murdered in their home. The crime remains unsolved.

Such a crime is hard to imagine in this country, full of rolling hills and farmhouses with clothes hanging on lines to dry. There are also many abandoned oil pumps in the fields that are a rich, deep color, significant of fertility.

We reached the bridge, a long concrete-and-steel structure. We parked, walked beneath, and found Carmen Stallings and Cindy Preator looking at the bridge and its surroundings.

"There's a dead deer carcass down there," said Preator, of Houston.

We could smell it. There were also swarms of mosquitoes.

"This used to be a good fishing place," said Stallings. "I used to come down here all of the time . . . me and my ex-husband. We had a lot of fun. The river has a strong current so you had to put a heavy anchor on your line to get it to stay in the river. But the fishing was good."

Then she expressed her feelings about the bridge.

"Aw, that bridge. The shade that it gives. To come here when it's really hot and sit down and maybe drink a beer and be cool and listen to the river, well, that is what makes good moments to remember," she said.

We bid good-bye and drove to the other side of the bridge where Henry West (not his real name) lives in a house built on poles. He's a retired Houston policeman and requested that his real name not be used. He's a friendly man with black hair and button brown eyes.

"I've lived here about twenty years," he said. "The bridge . . . let me tell you a couple of things about that bridge. A state highway worker told one to me. He said this was the first bridge in Texas to be built by a continuous pouring of cement. I think what that means is that they poured all of the cement on site and didn't haul it in in those huge chunks."

He lit a cigarette and inhaled deeply. He said he had long been interested in the history of this area.

"I used to have a neighbor who had a book that supposedly had all of the locations where each of the old steamships went down. I wish I had a copy of that. I'm certain that some of them went down around here," he said. "Oh, yeah, something else. Before the bridge was built, they had a ferry here. Let me get a picture and show you."

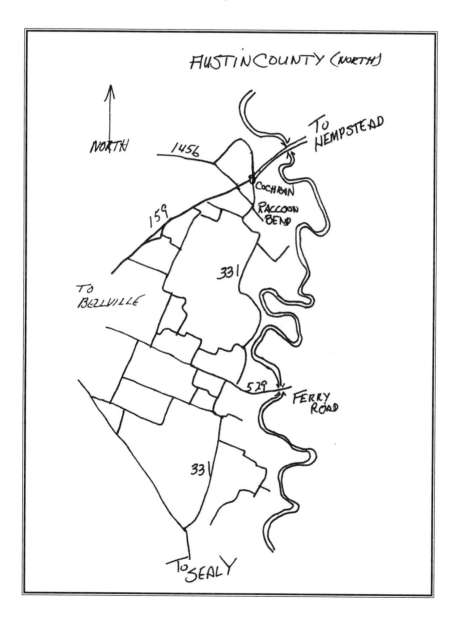

He went into his house and returned with a black-and-white photo of an old ferry. The boat was packed with people and had a Model T parked in the center. A wooden Jon boat was attached to its side.

"That was for safety," said West. He smiled. "Actually, this ferry was owned by Grandpa Larson. This is him." He pointed to a man wearing suspenders and a tall, black hat.

"Now, the mystery of the bridge. A few years ago, a woman drove to one of the little stores around here. She was screaming and wanted someone to call an ambulance. She said her husband was in her car outside and some-body had shot him in the head," he said.

There was no need to call an ambulance. Her husband was dead. The woman told this story . . . she and her husband were about to go across the bridge when a man motioned for them to stop. They did. The man got into the backseat. He pulled a pistol and shot her husband in the head. Then he leaped from the car and tossed the pistol off the bridge.

An intensive search made of the area found no pistol or evidence of the man. Then West changed the subject, saying he would much rather talk about his love of the area.

"I've seen every little creature you can imagine out here . . . things like the walking sticks and the praying mantis. And, one time, I saw a falcon that had been injured. I kept it for a day and then took it to a bird sanctuary. They said it had broken its wing during a dive. But they said they would keep it, so I guess you could say I saved its life," he said.

The sun had become a flag of orange. We knew we had to be leaving, but West kept talking.

"I've found a staff with beaver marks on it. Can you imagine that? I've also seen an alligator beneath that bridge. And, at night you can hear the coyotes howling out here," he said.

The coyotes' lonesome howls and the echoes of the river are a symphony to West at night.

A resident who lives near this bridge on Highway 529 east of Bellville told us that he thinks this is the first bridge in Texas to be built by a continuous pouring of cement, which means all of the cement was poured on site. He also said the bridge was the scene of an unsolved murder, a story typical of many told about the bridges.

"I can hear the river when I am lying in my bed. And when it is up, I have actually heard clumps of the land being eaten away from the bank and falling into the river," he said. "That's like having your own symphony playing for you."

Again he shook his head.

"Let me tell you, it beats living in Houston with all of its noises and crimes. I have never regretted leaving there and coming here," he said. "Plus, I love discovering history of this area. It's packed with interesting stories."

A friend, Linda Brothers, heard some of those stories near the community of Burleigh. There is the Krueger Store, owned and operated by Lucille Krueger-Tefs, eighty-nine, a delightful person who looks like she is sixty. She has worked in the store most of her life. Even though a new store was built in 1961, many of the fixtures are the originals.

Customers, many of whom come for a beer as well as to buy groceries, often tell stories about the area's bridges. Kenneth Uechert, a longtime employee for the highway department, was one of those on the day Linda visited. He related a story about the bridge over Highway 159 as it was being built in the 1950s.

"The bridge fell in and killed five people," he said. "And the old bridge that was replaced by the twin bridges on I-10 was called 'the killer bridge' because it was so narrow and caused so many accidents."

We thought of these stories as we headed for our campground. The sun made a ball of flame in the west but thankfully we were driving east toward Stephen F. Austin State Park.

CHAPTER THIRTY-SEVEN

Bridge at San Felipe

❖   ❖   ❖

He was under the bridge. He was playing, "Give me that Old Time Religion," a song they often had played. He reached the part where the words say, "It was good for Paul and Silas. It was good for Paul and Silas. It was good for Paul and Silas, and it's good enough for you and me."

She answered that with a deep repeat of, "Yes, it's good enough for you and me."

Then he awakened. He stared into the darkness. Nobody was there.

❖   ❖   ❖

Not only does evidence of early Texas history abound in this area, but it is also the site for one of the state's most impressive state parks. At least that is what we thought after camping out two nights at Stephen F. Austin State Park. The Brazos River curls around the 663.3-acre facility and its wonderful camping sites including screen shelters.

The park was named for Stephen F. Austin, known as the father of Texas. Austin brought colonists to nearby San Felipe where the conventions of 1832 and 1833 and the consultation of 1835 were held. Those led to the Texas Declaration of Independence.

Early Texas heroes, including William B. Travis, Sam Houston, David G. Burnet, and Jane Long, often known as the mother of Texas, lived in this town of 819 residents. I thought of these people as I smelled our coffee boiling and bacon sizzling in the frying pan. Early morning fog was still heavy as I looked outside our shelter and saw deer nearby. One buck with a nice rack stared back at us.

We stopped at the park headquarters and asked directions to the bridge from Anne Presley, assistant park manager. She told us and then gave us more facts.

"There used to be a ferry where the bridge is. It operated until the 1940s. Does the river flood here? Oh, yeah. In '94, we had ten to twelve inches of water in this building and about four feet in our clubhouse. Mosquitoes . . . we had clouds of them," she said.

How about the wildlife here?

"We have the deer, which I know you have seen. There are also javelinas and huge numbers of birds," she said.

We drove to nearby San Felipe for a look at the restored buildings and historical markers. There are many firsts registered in this town, including it being the home of the state's first newspaper, *The Texas Gazette*, says the *Texas Almanac*. Also the postal system of Texas started here, as did the Texas Rangers. A historical marker says San Felipe was one of the first Anglo settlements in Texas and its first roads were wagon ruts or beaten trails, marked by notched trees. Near that marker is a bronze statue of Austin. He is sitting, holding what looks like a handful of documents. A few feet from him is a marker in memory of John Bricker, a private in Captain Moseley Baker's Company. Bricker was killed just across the river on April 7, 1836, by a shot from a Mexican cannon. He was buried where he fell.

Highway 1458 passes over the bridge, which is almost in the shadows of these markers. As we walked beneath the bridge, I wondered what our early Texas forefathers would have thought of the debris left here. That included old tires and several long rolls of garden hose.

"Well, we haven't seen any of that before," said Eddie.

The ground, muddy from yesterday's rain, clung to our shoes as we walked to the bank for a glimpse at the river and the other side. The banks and trees on that side were marked by the river's powerful flow that had left the trees in twisted shapes. After looking the bridge over thoroughly, we drove back to San Felipe. We looked at a marker that said we were on the site of Thomas J. Pilgrim's oldest Sunday school and first English school in Texas, opened in 1829. We peered inside the San Felipe Church, established

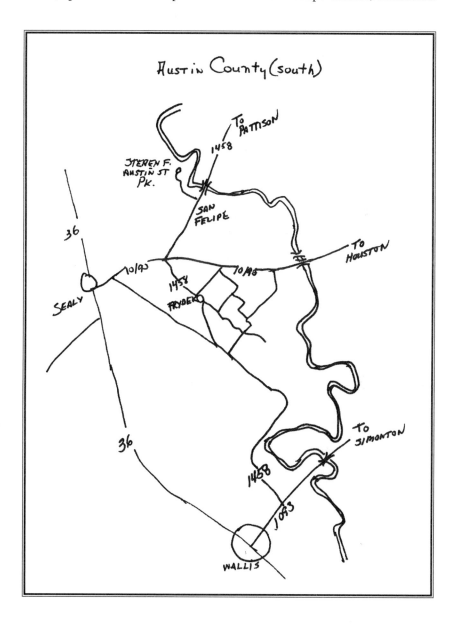

in 1837. It is a skinny, frame building, its narrow, pointed steeple stretching right into the trees.

We went inside the city hall and met Sue L. Porter-Foley, town secretary and a delightful person. Her great-great-grandmother cooked for the Mexican soldiers who fought the Texans during the battle for independence.

"Or maybe it was my great-great-aunt," she said. "Anyway, my family history goes way on back."

However, the local bridge does not go back that far. "Oh, no," she said. "I was raised here and I can remember when there was no bridge . . . just barbed wire across the river. The only way around was to drive to Brookshire. That was about nine miles. Come on and let me show you some photos of that time."

She led us back to the council meeting room. There on the wall were pictures of the San Felipe ferry. A notation said the ferry carried many people, animals, and goods across the Brazos River for a toll and operated from 1823 to 1949. "The ferry was the site of the Atascosa Trail, the route from the United States to Mexico," reads the history. The ferry was packed with people, a wagon, a team, and several other articles. It looked like the pictures made of people leaving the dust bowl during the 1930s and heading for California. "When you get through here, you need to be sure and visit Frydek . . . It's an interesting little ole town not too far from here," she said.

Several other people had already told us that and urged that we visit the tiny community during our trip to this country. So we left San Felipe and headed for Frydek and a visit with a delightfully surprising person.

CHAPTER THIRTY-EIGHT

The Ermis Grocery
and the Brookshire Bridge

❖   ❖   ❖

He continued to go to the bridge to play. Often he would stop
whatever he was doing earlier than he normally quit work, park his
tractor, and head for the bridge. The structure had become his link to
happy times, and he often smiled as he played.

One day as he played, he swore he could hear an answer. He
stopped. He searched the spaces beneath the bridge. There was
nobody there.

He smiled again. No wonder they called him that crazy old man
who plays his mouth harp beneath the bridge.

❖   ❖   ❖

Seventy-five years ago, Ms. Ilvina Ermis read a forecast in a national
magazine that predicted the demise of all small businesses by this time. That
writer did not have knowledge of the strength or durability of people like
Ms. Ermis. She's eighty-eight and still an active worker at the Ermis Grocery
in Frydek, owned by her family for four generations.

She's full of information about the area and told us about some of its
history while waiting on customers in the building that has the kind of overhang sheltering the gasoline pumps in the front that once symbolized what
was then called a filling station. A beautiful rock grotto nearby honors men
from the St. Mary's Parish at Frydek who served in World War II. A list of all
of those men's names, including Edward Gajewski, Stephen Haczniski, Jesse

Rodriques, Rudolph Tydlacka, Joseph Belunek, and William Bogar, is engraved on a bronze plaque. Honeybees swarmed in a bed of native flowers that shadowed the plaque.

"Yes, that is in honor of the boys who served from here," said Ms. Ermis. "There were sixty-five. They all saw action, and yet they all came home safely."

She has gray hair and is short in stature. Her voice is strong as she tells how her grandparents owned and ran the store, then her parents, then she and her husband. "And, today, my son Milton owns it," she said. She smiled. "I just work for him."

Jewel Petersen, a customer, sat at the counter drinking a Coca-Cola and eating a package of potato chips. She has lived here twenty-five years and says Ms. Ermis is like an angel to this community. "I raised my kids here. Sometimes, if I didn't have enough money for food between paychecks, it didn't matter. Ms. Ermis would write me a ticket and at the end of the month I would pay it. Today, if you go to a big store and ask for five cents on the credit, they will arrest you." She told the story about a granddaughter who used to come into the store and come home with a bar of candy. "All she would say is that she got it at Ms. Ermis," she said.

Ms. Ermis laughed. "I remember her. Coming in here with diapers one time. Barely large enough to walk. She apparently had sneaked away. But, I knew her and where she belonged so I closed the store and took her home," she said.

A potential customer came in. His request revealed a kind of ambivalence about credit.

"Do you take MasterCard or American Express?" he asked. "I need to buy some gas."

She shook her head vigorously.

"No, we don't take those things. They are too much trouble," she said.

"So how will I get some gas?" he asked.

"Go to Sealy to some of those big stations," she said.

Petersen smiled at the encounter. "This is an unusual place," she said. "Saturday nights are wonderful here. Everybody comes in and sits around, drinks a few beers and talks about what is going on around here."

The grocery does sell beer. It also sells fresh lunch meat, hardware supplies, and has a huge rack filled with nickel candy like the old Chick Fillets that we bought for a penny when we were youngsters. Ms. Ermis talked of those price changes and other things.

"Used to, a family could farm ten acres and make a living. Not any more. They can farm six hundred acres today and still not make a living," she said.

We listened to her stories and then it was time to go. Eddie asked her if she had any cold drinking water.

"Of course," she said.

She went to a big refrigerator sitting near the front counter, opened it, and removed a two-liter vodka bottle. She filled Eddie's glass with the liquid from the bottle. He had an inquisitive look as she handed him his glass.

"I know what you are thinking. And, no, it's not vodka. But, it does make a good water bottle," she said.

We asked her what she knew about the bridge over I-10 and U.S. Highway 90.

"I can remember when that was a ferry and no bridge," she said. "So, yes, I was glad when they built a bridge there. That certainly helped our business."

She gave us directions to the bridge. As we walked out the door, we heard the deep ring made on the old cash register as she made another sale.

We got on I-10 and headed for Brookshire. We quickly reached the bridge, once known as the old Highway 90 bridge. I looked at a photograph of that bridge. The caption beneath the old iron structure said that it was built in 1940.

"One of the outstanding structures completed by the Texas Highway Department in 1940 was the new bridge across the Brazos River at the county line of Austin and Waller counties on State Highway 73 near the historic town of San Felipe. The structure is 928 feet in length with two main spans of 320 feet each. The contract price was $345,488. The bridge is located on a new shortcut highway between Houston and Columbus. The bridge was replaced with the Interstate 10 bridge in the 1980s."

The old steel railroad bridge is still at the site and is by itself worth a drive for viewing. It has three sections and there are pieces of twisted cable and trees entwined in these. It furnishes a good comparison of bridges of the past and bridges of today, since it sits beside the new four-lane interstate bridge, one of the more massive bridges we had seen.

We walked beneath the concrete-and-steel structure. Somebody had sketched a set of teeth on one side of the bridge. They were smiling.

We walked to the bank of the river, which today looked like a swift swirl of black syrup. I thought of the stories we had heard about how angry the Brazos could become and how evil it was, luring people from the banks into its current that had the power to trap them in spirals of death that would end miles later downriver.

"The river is a lot different in this country than where we first began," said Eddie.

I agreed as we walked back to the car and headed for the next bridge near Simonton in Fort Bend County.

CHAPTER THIRTY-NINE

Fort Bend County Bridges

❖   ❖   ❖

She stayed primed in her constant look for a good story. She was aggressive, good-looking, and a hard worker. Someday she wanted to work for one of the national networks. She knew she would make it. That's why she listened to anyone who might have a good story.

That's how she heard about the crazy old man who played his mouth harp beneath the Brazos bridge. She knew that could be a good story, maybe the one that sent her to the nationals where everybody had those false smiles showing their capped teeth.

❖   ❖   ❖

We had learned never to be surprised at what we found under bridges. The bridge on FM 1093 northwest of Rosenberg in Fort Bend County certainly didn't disappoint us with its collection of debris.

The county was named for the Brazos River bend where some of Stephen F. Austin's colonists settled in 1824. The land became home for many antebellum plantations and that emphasis on agriculture can be seen today in its abundant agribusiness.

We walked beneath this bridge and followed a trail that twisted its way through old tires, pieces of sewer pipe, and chunks of shattered concrete. "This is the trashiest one we've seen," said Eddie. He shook his head. "But, I warned you that the closer we get to the Houston area, the more of this we are going to see."

The bridge is a solid looking concrete-and-steel structure. Within a few yards is a beautiful old iron railroad bridge with massive rivets and steel beams dusted brown with rust. We walked through leaves and mud full of smells of dead fish for a closer look at the railroad bridge.

Huge clots of timber from a recent rise in the river's current were caught on some of the columns. Old cables twisted around the bottom columns. One of the logs had its roots sticking into the air and looked like a large, brown starfish.

As we looked at the railroad bridge, Eddie saw the remains of another bridge sticking out of the river bottom. Light pieces of fog hung on the stream, blotting out some of humanity's wastes, as did towering pecan trees with splashes of fall's brilliant colors.

We drove to a nearby convenience store on which Rex Jarrell worked with two other men. He's a big, friendly, and humorous man. "I may finish this sometime soon," he said. He laughed. "I've only been working on it for about a year. When I open, I'm calling it Big Little Scotty's."

Eddie asked him where he was from since he did not have the Texas accent.

"Toledo," he said.

"Oh, really," said Eddie. "I have a brother who taught school there . . . Skip Lane. He taught history at Whitmer High School."

"Damn. I can't believe this. But he taught me," said Rex.

We all shook our heads about such meetings. Eddie said the odds on such things happening still amazed him. "It's kinda like the Dallas Cowboys going to the Super Bowl next year," he said.

Then we told Jarrell what we were doing.

"That sounds like a lotta fun," he said. He scratched his arm and then said that we should talk to Mary S. Houlihan, editor of the *Brazos Valley News*. "I'll call her for you," he said. He dialed her number on the telephone. "Mary, you need to get down here right away. There are two fellows you need to talk to. Yeah, they got a helluva story that will brighten up the pages of that newspaper you publish.

Houlihan showed up a few minutes later. She is an attractive, friendly person, full of local history.

"I was raised in this area," she said. "The bridge, oh yeah, I remember the bridge. We used to meet there and do the things that teenagers do when they meet at the bridge."

We all laughed.

"When I was a senior, let's see, that would have been 1982, the railroad bridge collapsed and fell into the river. I went down there and saw them actually pulling cars from the river. But, I'll tell you who you need to talk

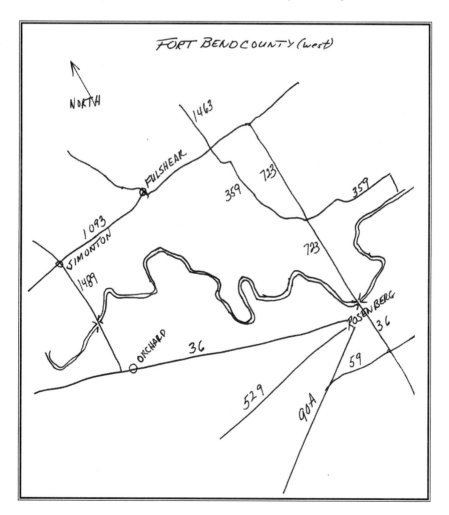

to—Paul Sabrusla. He's been here all of his life. He has a pecan business just up the road."

As we prepared to leave, Rex said, "When you get that book finished, send me some copies so I can sell them at my store."

"Are you certain it [the store] will ever be finished?" asked Houlihan.

We laughed again and drove to Sabrusla's Pecan Company in nearby Simonton. Sabrusla, a man with strong looking fingers and a thick black moustache, operated a pecan sheller in the back of his store. A conveyor belt carried the huge paper-shell pecans through a device that cracked the pecans.

"This has been a disappointing year," he said. "We had the best-looking crop we had seen in years and then all of the rains set in and the pecans just rotted under the trees. We lost about 60 percent of the crop."

Eddie and I ate a couple of the shelled pecans. They were delicious.

"So you want to talk about the bridges. Okay, I'll tell you what I know. I was raised in Hungerford, which is not too far from here. Know how it got its name? Well, let me tell you. They say Henry Ford was coming through the country looking for places to sell his cars. He got hungry and stopped at this place to eat. So they called it Hunger Ford. Get it?"

Then he talked about the bridges.

"When I first came here, they had a one-lane bridge. They took it down and built the concrete bridge," he said. "The old bridge was on the south side of the railroad bridge. But, if you want some good stories, let me tell you about the next bridge you're probably going to. That is the bridge at Orchard."

He said that bridge was also a one-lane bridge. "It wasn't like the bridges in Mexico where if you met somebody coming across, it was whoever has the loudest horn and the most guts goes across first," he said. "The Orchard bridge had a green light and a red light at both ends. So you knew when it was your time to go."

But, as the years passed, the bridge became so rickety that many people would choose to go to Fulcher, a detour of several miles, rather than chance crossing the Orchard bridge. So did he ever go across it when it was in that shape?

"Oh, yeah. But, I held my breath from one end to the other," he said. "They tried to reinforce it with steel runners but eventually they had to build a new one."

He gave us directions to the bridge.

"Be sure and look at the old columns. They're still there," he said.

We drove a few miles south on FM 1489 until we reached the Orchard bridge which was fifty-two on the number of bridges that we had seen. Rain had drenched the area and had started again. We put on our slickers and walked through the mud and grass to look at the new bridge. The pillars from the old bridge loomed from the river and looked out of shape from the rain that now fell in heavy sheets. A thick growth of vines and trees almost hid some of the columns.

As we looked, I remembered something else that Sabrusla had said.

"It may have been rickety, but it still was a lot of fun to look at and to cross," he said.

He certainly was right about the old bridge being fun to look at for a spell. We actually studied it for more than an hour, and both of us wished we could have crossed it before it closed. We shook rain from our slickers and headed for the next bridges at Rosenberg.

CHAPTER FORTY

Fort Bend County Justice

❖　❖　❖

She drove to the small town. She stopped at the local newspaper,
went inside, and met the publisher-editor, a woman who had short
gray hair, a plump build, and a natural smile.

"I've come down here to check out a possible story. It sounds like
a local tale that has grown out of proportion. It's about an old man
who plays his harmonica beneath a bridge here. It's well, like a fairy
story," she said.

"It's true," said the publisher.

She felt the rush inside her like someone does before giving a big
speech. She urged the publisher to tell her about the old man.

"I'll make him famous," she said.

❖　❖　❖

During frontier days justice came hard at some of the bridges over the
Brazos River. One of those instances occurred on the night of April 26, 1869,
at a bridge being built across the Brazos.

"A horse thief was taken from the jail at Richmond and hanged from a
span of the iron bridge being built across the Brazos River," reads a portion
of a chapter entitled, "Vigilantes and Vigilance Committees" in the
Handbook of Texas Online.

But, Fort Bend County, where the Karankawa Indians once roamed
before leaving for Mexico in the 1850s, also was noted for its less severe
justice. A man convicted of stealing cattle learned that. He had been
accused of branding a neighbor's calf with his own mark.

"The trial lasted one day. The man was found guilty and sent to Mexico to work in the mines," reads the story about him in *Texas: The Land of Beginning Again: The Romance of the Brazos*. "But, a new trial was asked for because it was said the man had a wife and five children. So the court reconsidered and gave him a suspended sentence."

As a person drives through the area looking for bridges, it is hard to imagine how large the Brazos River once was. In some excellent literature about the area's history, furnished by the Richmond library, one story said that at one time the Brazos stretched twenty-five miles wide. The river often launched devastating floods. A part of Fort Bend history reads:

> The Brazos River, still one of the state's largest rivers, is no
> longer the size it once was. It now cuts a pleasant path through
> the county, fed by numerous creeks, bayous, and the San Bernard
> River. Magnolia, oak, elm, and pine trees once lined the naturally
> formed river and its streams while grasses provided ample grazing
> for bison, wild cattle, and deer.

During its early days, wild forms of entertainment developed, ranging from horse racing to cockfights to gambling. Horse racing became popular at several sites in the county. One track advertised races for any "nag desirous of contending for the purse of a $500 play or pay entrance fee." Still another racetrack in the community of Fulshear became nationally known for having some of the best racing stock in the nation. That facility was built and operated for nearly thirty years by Churchill Fulshear.

All of that activity, plus the bountiful harvests from the plantations where rice, cotton, and sugar were grown, almost demanded the development of bridges over the Brazos River. A story in the *Herald Coaster* newspaper tells about the building of one of those first bridges. The story said that before 1885, a ferry furnished the only method of crossing the river.

During the year 1885, a wagon bridge across the Brazos was constructed by Fort Bend County, but in 1893 it went down while a herd of cattle was crossing, killing two men and many cattle.

Another wagon bridge was constructed by the county a few hundred feet below the location of the first bridge at a cost of $20,178. This bridge was completed during the year 1894 and remained in service until May 1922 when that structure was swept away by the floodwaters of the Brazos.

Since that time a ferry operated by the county has been the only means of getting across the river at Richmond.

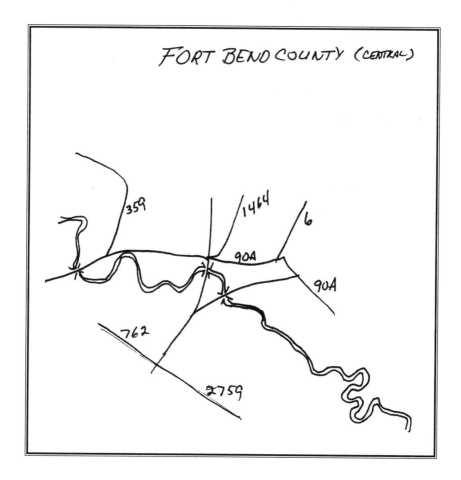

Costs of building a new bridge presented a problem until arrangements were made for the Federal Highway Department to pay half, the state of Texas one-fourth, and the county one-fourth. However, because the county had become involved in a bankruptcy proceeding, some unusual action by the citizens was required. The local newspaper called it patriotic.

"The citizens of the little city of Richmond, realizing the vast importance of the early completion of the bridge, agreed to raise and lend to the county $50,000 and this they did, taking as their only security the assignment from the county of that amount of its claim against the depository. By this patriotic action the early completion of this bridge was made possible and the gratitude of everyone who will use the bridge will no doubt be extended to those citizens," reads the *Herald Coaster* article.

Description of the completed bridge obviously impressed the citizens. They should have been impressed with its floor that weighed about one and a half million pounds. Then there were the forty thousand rivets used to hold the bridge together, the 475 gallons of paint required to paint the structure, and the eighty gallons of lubricating oil used for the roller bearings over the east pier.

"While man proposes and God disposes, yet it is believed that this magnificent structure will serve the public for many generations," read a story's final paragraph about the bridge's opening.

The bridge lasted until July 1988 when it was blown up to make room for a new structure. The old bridge proved tough in its final moments, requiring three separate explosions before it finally tumbled into the river. *Herald Coaster* columnist Fred Hartman described the scene.

"After fifty-three years, Richmond's old Brazos River bridge wasn't going down without a fight. She didn't come close to taking a dive," he said.

He said the event attracted many fans of the bridge.

"I, like many others, drove across the bridge many times on its two narrow lanes, scared to death because I was afraid I was about to scrape the sides when another car was next to me. Aw, what a nostalgic memory," he wrote. "The explosion was quite a spectacle, even an event, as hundreds braved the 90-degree heat to line the river's banks. Some wondered if the bridge was so tough, why was it condemned in the first place. Let's just hope the new bridge is as tough and sturdy as the old one."

Memories abound about the four bridges over the Brazos River in the Rosenberg-Richmond area. We had reached one of these at FM 733 just north of the towns.

"This is the highest bridge we have seen so far," said Eddie.

Clouds thick with rain began a light emptying of their moisture as we walked down banks already soaked from yesterday's rain. We walked through some briars that were tough and thick as cables. The rain had become heavier. We sought cover beneath a huge pecan tree about a hundred feet from the bridge. The rain made its columns look surreal and out of focus.

We stood there among the debris of junk carburetors, pieces of air breathers from car engines, and twisted pieces of steel. The rain hit the tree leaves, making a sound like popping corn. We looked at the river's current—it resembled dark swirls in a milk shake.

"You ready to eat?" I asked Eddie.

"Yeah," he said.

"Well, let's go find Larry's Mexican Restaurant. A friend told me that that was a good place to eat plus he has some interesting stories about one of the bridges downtown," I said.

Another friend had told us about meeting Joan Reese, a docent at the Rosenberg Railroad Museum. She and her husband, Dr. Travis Reese, who has published three books about the area, own some river property in Rosenberg where an old stagecoach relay station and ferry were once located. Dr. Reese said when the stage arrived at the station, male passengers slept on the first floor and women and children on the second.

"The next day they were ferried across the river," he said.

Dr. Reese said it was in Richmond where the Buffalo, Bayou, Brazos, and Colorado Railroad was built up to the river. To transport trains across the river, a pontoon boat was fashioned that swung across the river and connected the tracks. After crossing, the pontoon boat was swung back to enable ships to navigate the river.

"The primary problem with this arrangement was that the train had to get up so much steam to climb the steep grade on the far side of the river, many passengers chose not to take the daredevil ride," said Dr. Reese.

That probably made a heckuva sight, just like Eddie and I made that day as we sprinted through the rain to reach our car and head for Larry's.

CHAPTER FORTY-ONE

Rosenberg-Richmond Bridges

❖   ❖   ❖

She knew she had a prizewinner. She kept going over what the publisher had told her as she drove back to the city. Enthusiasm fired inside her as she entered the TV headquarters and went to her editor's office. He shook his head when he saw her coming.

"Okay, okay. You've got a big story, a really big story. Tell me about it," he said.

After she had told him what she had heard, he said, "I agree. This could be a prizewinner. Go get it, now."

❖   ❖   ❖

Larry's lies beneath a nest of neon signs flashing in loud colors the name, "Larry's Mexican Restaurant." The first bridge built in this area was nearby.

Smells of home-cooked Mexican dishes made the waiting in line for lunch worthwhile. The food was delicious. Larry Guerrero, the owner, laughed and boomed, "It should be. I've been here, cooking good food for forty-two years." He's a solid-looking man with a full head of gray hair combed straight back and a deep, booming voice.

"The bridges . . . certainly I know something about the bridges," he said. "My father used to work on ranches in this country and he used to bring cattle across that old bridge. I've heard many stories about that bridge and about the old ferry that they once used. Here, let me get some photographs and show them to you."

He retrieved a book packed with photographs of the area and the early bridge. One series of pictures made in 1893 showed the county bridge that had collapsed when a herd of cattle was driven across it. Larry gave a quick history of the bridge.

"That was a secondhand bridge," he said. He laughed. "It had been purchased from a company that placed it across the Brazos near Hempstead. Then Waller County condemned it, and it fell into the river. Then it was purchased by Fort Bend County authorities and hauled to Richmond on wagons. Isn't that a good story?"

Then he talked about the Brazos River.

"That river is a mean sonofagun," he said. "Kids go swimming in it and wind up five miles downstream, drowned. Me lose a friend? Oh, heck, yeah. Several times. I have known two guys who got into the river and were never found. One was Manuel Gonzales. He disappeared forty years ago, and they never found nothing. A few years ago, they found some bones and a skull, and I always have wondered if that was Manuel."

He said he often swam in the river when he was a youngster.

"But, we knew how to test it to see if it was safe to swim in," he said. "We'd get some sticks and throw them into the water. If they disappeared all of a sudden, we knew that was a place to avoid. Yes, sir. But, some smart aleck kids that didn't respect or treat that river right, they drowned."

We thanked him and headed for the bridge that is almost within the shadows of his restaurant. He yelled, "You boys be careful of that old river. It's dangerous."

We walked to the bridge on the business part of Highway 99. Houses have been built almost to the banks of the river. Heavy undergrowth hides portions of the bridge columns. Near one of the entrances to the bridge is a crazy-looking sign advertising a fish restaurant. It has a crab or shrimp wearing a helmet.

We could have almost walked to the next bridge, which is also on Highway 99. It is a fairly new bridge named after former Fort Bend County Judge Jodie Stavincha. Apparently it was a well-deserved honor for Stavincha, who died in January 2000. He was a navy veteran of World War II, a Federal Bureau of Investigation agent for twenty-five years, and a longtime civic leader.

"Without a doubt, he's a legend," said Ben Denham, a longtime friend. "He always put the residents of Fort Bend County first. He had an open-door policy for commissioners and residents, too. He came along at a time when the growth of the county was in a boom, and he tackled it and handled it. He left his mark, and his achievements are unsurpassed."

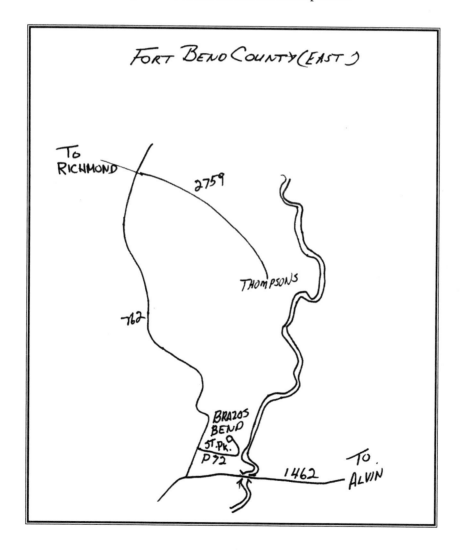

Since the rain had increased to sheets of driving moisture, we looked at the Judge Stavincha Bridge through our windows. We offered it some good words in his memory and then headed for the bridge over Highway 59 and the last one near these two towns.

North of here on Highway 36, the Damon Mound, once a favorite campsite for Karankawa Indians, can be seen, according to Darwin Spearing in *Roadside Geology of Texas*. The mound area, sitting on the coastal plain, has been a fertile ground for archaeologists, yielding such things as arrowheads, pottery, and stone implements from the past.

I thought that today would have been a good day for archaeological digging. At least the soil would have been made soft from the rain, which had slackened when we reached the next bridge over Highway 59. We walked through vines and dead weeds that were six feet tall for a better look. Thick mud stuck to our shoes. The rain began again and chased us under the bridge, which was made of concrete and steel. Deep tracks made by a four-wheel all-terrain vehicle were everywhere. I listened to the cars roaring overhead and looked at the mud on my shoes, which was at least two inches thick.

I tried making notes when a sudden gust of wind blew the rain under the bridge and onto my notebook, smearing the ink. I folded it shut and said, "Eddie, let's go to camp." We left and by the time we reached Stephen F. Austin State Park, the rain had stopped. However, the wetness of the day lay in thick evidence on the floor of our screen shelter. A person could mop without dipping the mop into a bucket of water.

We poured ourselves stiff shots of bourbon and Scotch, sat, and watched the darkness come.

"Jon, did you know, we are about finished with this? I think we only lack four bridges," said Eddie.

"Hard to believe, isn't it," I said. I stared into the coffee cup that held my drink of Scotch. "Well, I guess I've got enough Scotch left to see the rest of the bridges."

Eddie tipped his glass of bourbon toward me.

"Here's to the finale," he said.

Then he began cooking our meal, chicken and broiled vegetables. The humidity made the smell tantalizing. As he cooked, I turned on the radio, sipped my drink, and watched deer wandering around our campground. I flicked the radio dial until I found some Hispanic music.

I thought of my younger days and how I had always loved this music and its people. It was so full of life and made a person want to clap his hands or get up and dance. I thought about something that Larry Guerrero had said.

"Hell, I'm old enough to remember when they called me a Mexcan. And, they called the Czech people Polaks, and the Germans Square Heads." Then came that booming laugh. "So what the hell. We've come forward. They don't call us Mexcans anymore. So, you could say, we've made a bridge. A good bridge."

That was a nice story with which to end this day of bridge searching. Besides, Eddie's chicken and vegetables were ready along with hot tortillas.

CHAPTER FORTY-TWO

Brazoria County Bridges

❖ ❖ ❖

At first they had meant only to interview the man who played his harmonica beneath the Brazos bridge. As she planned what to wear and what would look good on her in the shadows of the bridge, she suddenly thought of a new approach. She went to her editor with the idea.

"Why don't I learn how to play a harmonica? Then I can hide in the brush with the camera crew and when he starts playing, I can answer him."

The editor said he liked the idea. But after she left, he shook his head and thought, "Are we making an emotional bridge that we have no business crossing?"

❖ ❖ ❖

The cold weather predictions came true at 3:00 A.M. that morning. The wind crashed into the trees outside and then rain sounding like somebody was pounding canvas with a cat-o-nine-tails began to fall.

We got up early. Already, rain had blown in on our bedding and floors in the screen shelter. We ate breakfast, fortified ourselves with cups of strong black coffee, broke camp, and headed for the next bridge near Brazos Bend State Park.

"You are really going to like this park," said Eddie. "It has alligators and the Brazos curls around it for miles." I hoped somebody had a campfire going there. In my hurry to pack, I had made a big mistake. I had brought Jane's winter jacket instead of mine. With all of the layers of clothing I had on, I could not button the jacket. "That's the way it is with pioneers," said Eddie. "They have to go tough."

We had just passed a bank with a temperature sign flashing 45 degrees. The wind howled. I knew I was going to have to go tough. We drove down Highway 90 and turned onto FM 762. The rain had slackened to a fine mist but banks of clouds promised this to be one rainy day. A flock of geese passed overhead.

"Know why one line of geese is longer than the other one?" asked Eddie.

"No," I replied thinking I was going to receive a rewarding bit of outdoor wisdom.

"Because it has more geese in it," he said.

We reached Brazos Bend State Park. Signs warned about the dangers of poisonous snakes and alligators. They furnished a list of rules for alligator etiquette. One rule said that if an alligator goes after a fish you have caught, cut the line and let the alligator have the fish. Made sense to me. But, as it turned out, we were not going to see any alligators or poisonous snakes or wild hogs or anything at the park.

"It's closed for deer hunters," said the gate attendant. "Sorry. But this is not a good time for visitors to come in here. The hunters might mistake you for a deer."

I told her we had left our antlers at home. She smiled but still motioned us outside of the park. So we headed for the bridge on FM 1462, about five miles away. We reached it, parked, and walked around the steel-and-concrete structure. A hand-painted message proclaimed, "Irene will love you ever day." The rain had turned the ground into thick mud. Eddie walked up the river and yelled at me.

"Come and see what I found," he said. I went to where he stood. The carcass of a deer lay in a shallow ravine that emptied into the river. "Some hunter must have figured it was an illegal kill and dumped it here," said Eddie.

After looking at the surroundings for a few more minutes, we called Edna and Alvin Fink, two longtime residents who supposedly had knowledge of the area and the bridge.

"Yeah, come on," Fink said. "At least we've got a warm house."

They also had interesting family histories. His grandfather came to this country in 1893 from Russia and settled in nearby Needville.

"Why did they come to this country? Well, they didn't believe in preaching at funerals in Russia. But when somebody died, my grandfather would preach at the funeral. He was warned but he kept preaching. So when the authorities were coming to arrest him and his family, they sneaked out of the country and wound up here," he said.

Then she told about her father who owned eight hundred acres of prime land in this area. "He made his money by trapping raccoons and mink in the area. He would hunt all night and then fix their hides and sell them. He saved the money he made and bought land with it," she said.

They talked about some of their experiences during fifty-four years of marriage and living on a farm. Once he was cutting wood and thought his saw blade had stopped. "But it hadn't and I reached over and it cut my middle finger off," he said.

"He came running in the house with blood dripping everywhere. I wrapped it up," she said.

Another time she heard him screaming. Despite having just had surgery on her knees, she ran outside. He had somehow hit the power lift on his tractor the wrong way, causing a heavy steel shredder to drop on his feet. "I got there, hit the power lift, and it raised the shredder off his feet," she said. "I'll tell you, life has been interesting with him."

Both have a healthy respect for the Brazos River, which flows a short distance from their house. "I worked for the state park in 1992 when we got all of that rain and the Brazos flooded the park. It was under water for two months," he said. "As for the bridge, well that has been a really good thing for us. I think they built it in the mid-1950s. It saves us a lot of time. Before we had that bridge, we had to drive all the way to Richmond to go to West Columbia. That's a lot of miles out of the way."

We thanked them and headed toward Freeport. Because of the aching cold weather, we decided not to camp out that night. "It is not like the pioneers," said Eddie. "But it will be nice cooking inside in this kind of weather."

We reached Freeport with its cluster of chemical and industrial plants. At a supermarket, Eddie went inside to buy groceries, while I sat in the van and saw the darnedest thing. A woman with a baby in her arms walked to the vehicle next to ours. As she leaned inside to put the baby into the car seat, her sweatshirt pulled up. There just above her hips a tattoo stretched across her entire back. That was not so unusual. But, the name in the middle was. It read, "Jon."

"Eddie, you are not going to believe this," I said as he loaded our groceries.

He didn't. But he did laugh about it almost all the way to the cabin we had rented at Quintana Beach County Park. The blast from the heater finally drove the cold shakes from me. Eddie had cooked baked chicken with cheese. We also had tortillas, beans, and salad. The meal, like all of his, was delicious. Afterwards we sipped our drinks and talked about life in general. We listened to the wind howling outside and watched an outdoor thermometer dropping steadily to the lower thirties.

"Thank God that we have enough money for a cabin," I said. "Can you imagine being like those homeless people we saw a few miles back, looking for a place to sleep under that bridge."

"Yeah, that's hard to imagine," said Eddie. He smiled. "Almost as hard to imagine as you seeing a woman with 'Jon' tattooed on her."

We went to bed early and slept well. I dreamed of a bridge with "Jon" written in orange paint across its front. It began flashing like a traffic light. I could hear something crashing down river from the bridge, headed my way. I wakened suddenly. The noise came from the north wind hammering our cabin.

I didn't go back to sleep immediately but lay there thinking of all of the bridges that Eddie and I had looked at and the stories we had heard. A story that my Uncle Ben told me drifted into my thoughts.

Ben, my favorite uncle, lived with his wife, Verge, near the banks of the Colorado and San Saba rivers. He had never gotten caught up in making money. Instead, he made enough so he and Aunt Verge could live what they called a comfortable lifestyle in a frame house with outdoor toilets. They cut their own firewood. Ben caught much of their meat from the nearby rivers. He regularly ran his trotlines and seldom came to the house without a couple of huge catfish hanging from a stringer. He chewed Days Work chewing tobacco and loved telling stories. Naturally, I loved to listen.

One of those involved two brothers named Thalin and Elder. "They were so poor, they didn't even know they were poor," said Ben. "They did know they didn't have as much as others, but they also knew that someday they would make enough money to join those people who lived in fancier houses and had some of the choice land in the county. They spent hours talking about those times and what land they would accumulate and how they would farm it or plant grass on it and raise cattle."

The brothers' favorite place to discuss these future plans was beneath some large pecan trees growing near a bridge over the Colorado River. The brothers would go there and scrape away grass and weeds until they had a large plat of sand. Then they would take sticks and draw in the sand their plans for the future.

"Thalin, someday we'll have this big chunk of bottom land that will go from old man Thurgood's place all the way west, down the river, to where that cattle crossin' is," Elder said one day as they sat on their knees in the sand. He began drawing a long line that represented the river. "We'll have our house right over here, kinda up on this bank so we won't have to worry about floodin' or anythang. We'll build it out of mesquite and cedar logs, and it'll have a smell in it that our ma will just love."

He stopped and gazed at his drawing. Thalin began making marks in the sand.

"Our fields will be here and here," he said. "We'll have those long, curving rows, makin' 'em go up nearly to the river. If it floods, it might hurt our crops but the sand and silt it'll deposit will make it worthwhile."

So their dreams went until one day when Old Man Thurgood caught them.

"Y'all boys know this land is mine and I'm by gawd tired of you comin' in here and stealing my pecans and scraping my grass off and making them doodlin' marks. That kind of thang encourages other people to do it. So I don't want you comin' back in here again. I'm gonna see to it that you don't because I'm fencing this land and putting up some of them no trespassin' signs. They mean you as well as others ain't welcome in here. You can go steal yore pecans somewhere else," he said. He glared at them. The smell of chewing tobacco and sweat steamed from his blue overalls. "Now, y'all git."

They got off the land. They did not return for about four weeks. Then one night as Elder read an old newspaper, he began laughing. "Thalin, I think we got the answer to Old Man Turdgood," he said.

"What is it?" asked Thalin.

"Well, it says here that people are eaten up with thankin' that somebody buried some treasure in here a hunnert or so years ago. They're buying metal detectors and everythang to look for these big stashes of gold," said Elder.

"So?" asked Thalin.

"So, we'll give 'em some clues to look at what they may figure will lead them to the gold," said Elder.

The next week the boys went to the river. They had sharpened their pocketknives and began cutting marks in the bark of trees along the riverbank. They collected some cow's urine in a bottle and poured it on the cuts, to help age them. They made a series of marks that included things like "x"s and "o"s. Their trail of marks led to Old Man Thurgood's place.

Then early one morning, just as the darkness was slipping from the east, they sneaked through the fence on the old man's place. They made marks on several trees. Only these marks were arrows and they pointed down, like they were saying, "Dig here." They made several of these because as Elder said, "We want to make certain those folks have something to make their itch for treasure really strong."

Unfortunately, the boys never knew if their trick worked or not. Shortly after they had carved their last marks in the Thurgood trees, their father decided he had tried to make a living long enough in that part of the country. He accepted a job at a lumber mill in southeastern Oklahoma. The family moved.

But about a year after they left, Old Man Thurgood went to his bottom land one morning and nearly wet on himself. Somebody had torn down his fence and dug a huge hole near one of the pecan trees.

That was only the first of several such acts of digging on his place. Thurgood became so angry that when he began telling people about these acts of depredation occurring on his place, he would forget to spit and suddenly he would shower his listeners with bits of his chewing tobacco. Finally, somebody told him what was causing the digging. People thought a treasure was buried there. Thurgood responded by building a huge sign and erecting it on his fence. It read, "There ain't no buried treasure on this place."

It did no good. One morning he drove to the scene and saw that somebody had torn the sign down, chopped it up and built a campfire with the wood. Right after that, Old Man Thurgood took down his fence. Supposedly the digging stopped. But, people still came there to fish. Said they caught some of the best catfish around right off that riverbank near that bridge on Old Man Thurgood's place.

I smiled as I thought of the end of the story. I had no idea if it were true. But, the way Uncle Ben told it, that really did not matter. I always enjoyed hearing it. I listened to the wind howling outside, sounding like Old Man Thurgood angrily confronting treasure hunters on his land as sleep came to me again.

CHAPTER FORTY-THREE

East Columbia Bridges

❖ ❖ ❖

She bought her harmonica from a pawnshop. She could use its background as part of the story. She also bought a book that gave beginning lessons in harmonica playing. At first she hated the tinny sound coming from the instrument.

"It sounds like somebody's got a string with cans tied to it, stretched between two trees and beating the cans with a spoon," she said.

But, she continued practicing. This story was going to make her famous.

❖ ❖ ❖

The attendants at Quintana Park called us the "bridge searchers" after we told them what we doing in this area. They had also called us a little crazy to be out on a day like this looking at bridges.

I agreed after we had taken a brisk forty-five-minute walk down the beach before we began our drive to East Columbia to look at the bridge over Highway 35 west of Angleton. I looked into our reflections in the car window. The almost freezing temperatures were evident in the phlegm pouring from our noses.

"Well, it is supposed to warm up tomorrow," said Eddie.

We headed to Quintana Beach and its interesting history. The island with six miles of beaches is between the mouth of the old Brazos and the new Brazos. A thriving community existed here as early as 1532. And it was here that Stephen F. Austin landed his boat, the *Lively* in 1832, and laid out the town. Some of those early settlers who became plantation owners found the place so popular that they built homes on the beach. Remarkably, three of those still remain in spite of the poundings dealt to the island by numerous hurricanes.

I thought of some of those hurricanes that I had covered as a reporter. One of them had blown out the walls of a motel room in which I was staying. I remembered some of the sights I had seen after the big winds, like huge flocks of birds covering large chunks of land. They reminded me of the geese we saw this morning on Highway 36, their gray colors looking like light blankets of snow on the black land.

We drove through West Columbia and past Scott's Barbecue that had the state flag of Texas painted so large it covered an entire section of the roof. Then we reached the bridge, a steel-and-concrete structure. Huge piles of trees lay on the bank, a few feet from the Brazos' stream that today looked like spilled cocoa.

The stream flowed fast. The collection of logs and debris around the columns had foam that looked like a calf's slobber as it nurses its mother. The banks had been torn by the awesome power of the water, making ragged creases in them.

I walked beneath the bridge looking at the usual garbage that included a medical book. The rains had softened the pages, which were opened to the definition of bacillary dysentery. It said that bacilli were one of the many divisions of bacteria that had a characteristic rod shape. I thought this was a fitting page to be facing the public amidst all of the garbage left here.

Eddie took a picture, and then we drove to the Bethel Presbyterian Church near the bridge and almost on the banks of the Brazos River. The Rev. James (Jim) Gentner, an outgoing person, greeted us. His church is the third oldest in the state, having been started in 1840. The Methodists once used the current building before it was purchased by the Presbyterians about eighty years ago. He joked about his church being so close to the Brazos, which is noted for its flooding in this area.

"That's why many people moved from here to West Columbia. It's on higher ground," he said.

That reminded me of the lines from the old gospel song that go, "Lord, plant my feet on higher ground." Gentner laughed about that.

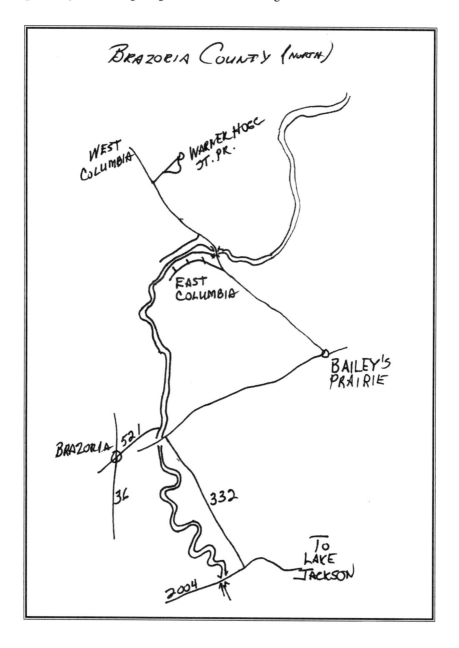

"The bridge was built because of the flooding when the Brazos and the San Bernard merged. The flooding was pretty bad," he said.

So is some of the history about the San Bernard River. Catherine Munson Foster says that in her delightful book, *Ghosts Along the Brazos*. She said the river, which runs through the western portion of Brazoria County, has a long history of smuggling, including the bringing in of slaves to be offered for sale. According to Foster, the slave traders would anchor offshore and then bring the slaves in by the mouth of the Bernard where plantation owners met them.

"The mouth of the San Bernard has the doubtful distinction of being the port of entry in 1840 of the last shipment of slaves brought to the shores of North America. Or so the old timers say," she wrote.

Many of the riverboats stopped at a dock near the church's location. Gentner said the foundation of the dock can still be seen. "And we have a bell from a Louisiana steamboat that used to travel up and down the river. The bell has been placed in our church steeple," he said. "Would you like to hear it?"

We certainly would. We walked from his office to the church, which had old, hand-fashioned, curved wooden seats with beautiful stained glass windows inside the chapel. Gentner pulled the rope leading to the bell, which made a mellow, rich ringing that indeed sounded like the echoes from the old riverboats in movies I had seen.

"Isn't that a wonderful sound?" he asked.

We agreed. Then he told us about finding the history of the church in its minutes that go back as far as the 1840s. In those days, the church was the law and often was called upon to make such decisions. One such case involved two men who had gotten into a serious argument about some land. They threatened to shoot each other.

"The church invited them to come here to discuss the matter. They were instructed to lay their pistols on a table outside. They did and came inside and their differences were worked out without bloodshed," said Gentner.

That reminded me of a story about this area that I read in Julien Hyer's book. It involved the mistreatment of an orphan boy by a farming couple who had adopted him. A neighbor had heard about the couple beating the boy. So he went to the couple's house and called the man outside and whipped him soundly. That resulted in assault and battery charges being filed against the first man. At the trial, his lawyer said, "Our client did what he was commanded to do by the Almighty. What father would not resent this outrage?"

The jury was out for only a few minutes.

"We find the defendant not guilty, and we recommend that he thrash the hell out of the man again," said the foreman.

Gentner laughed at the story. "Justice back in those days had a lot of common sense in it," he said.

We sat for a few more moments in the quiet of the church. Then Gentner gave us directions to some nearby historical markers. "You really should see them. I think you will enjoy them," he said.

We could have walked to the first one. It marked the site of Bell's Landing, founded in 1823 as a Brazos River landing for Josiah H. Bell's plantation where the town site of Marion was laid out in 1824. The name was later changed to East Columbia, and it became an army enlistment point and ferrying dock during the Texas Revolution.

"It was a key river port and trade center during the Republic of Texas Days," reads the marker.

We looked past the marker and could see the river that today was a dark brown color. Some of the old pilings around which the steamships once coiled their lines are still there, almost hidden by grass and vines. Those steamship days were actually ended by the fickleness of the Brazos current in which one day they might find easy portage and yet the next day find their ships stranded on sandbars.

As we gazed at these old pilings, the cold brought tears to our eyes, dimming our vision. We could almost hear the bells of those dear old ships as they rounded the bend and headed for the dock. Some residents have found unusual uses for parts of those old ships. East Columbia residents Olen and Betty Smith, for instance. When Olin began renovating a house built in 1836 that was owned by his wife's sister, he found scraps of material from packing crates and salvage material from the ships that had sunk in the river. He also found that the roof of the house had solid cedar logs with bark still attached.

"There were no sawmills or lumberyards nearby, so the builder apparently used anything available for building materials," he said.

Bonnie and Lloyd Maynard, who have owned the house for the past six years, said research had revealed that Dr. Mason Locke Weems II was the home's original owner. He and his son and grandson served as doctors in East Columbia and used the home's basement as a hospital. Some say this was Texas' first such medical facility.

The Maynards said another early resident of East Columbia who became their friend was Zuleika Weems-Mitchell. She visited the Maynards every Wednesday until her death, always bringing a small bottle of liquor. She remembered one of East Columbia's early bridges having wood planking that made loud explosive sounds when vehicles crossed. Zuleika made a bit of history herself when she won an athletic swimming scholarship to a college, extremely unusual for a woman of that time.

"My favorite way of staying fit was to swim the Brazos every day," she told the Maynards. "That was not a small feat, considering the dangerously strong currents of the river."

Howard Giesler, a resident of the area for sixty-four years, told us several wild stories about the early bridge as well as the Brazos. He said in his early years, he hunted alligators in the Brazos. To attract the gators, he and his brother-in-law would carry an alligator skin to the middle of the bridge and throw it into the river. That practice attracted attention from authorities after a woman mistook one of the skins as a child drowning and called the rescue squad. "I never asked for the skin back," he said. "Just made me a new one."

Giesler said the bridge at East Columbia had a center section that pivoted to allow ships to pass. He said the center section started leaning so badly that the bridge would no longer rotate.

"Finally the state took it down but they left portions of it lying in the river," said Giesler. "One man ripped his boat right down the middle, not knowing about the structure that was barely under the water when the river was low."

Some of those stories can be found in many of the historical markers in the area. One of those that Eddie and I discovered marked the site where Carry Nation, an early-day temperance leader, once operated a hotel. It read:

> During a brief and troubled time in her life, Carry Amelia Moore Nation operated the old Columbia hotel on this site about 1880. She later achieved fame as a hatchet-wielding crusader against the use of alcoholic drink and tobacco. She married David Nation and they acquired seventeen hundred acres of land on the San Bernard River west of here.

I know Miss Carry's ghost would have probably howled even at the thought, but I certainly could have used a shot of those sinful alcoholic beverages to burn away some of the cold I was feeling. Since we had not brought our sinful beverages, we drove on to the next bridge. Carry Nation would have been proud of us.

CHAPTER FORTY-FOUR

Bridge Ghost Stories

❖   ❖   ❖

After one month, she announced she was ready. "I can echo anything he'll play," she said.

She followed the film crew to the Brazos bridge. They arrived long before daybreak and hid in the brush beneath the bridge.

The moon overhead looked like a giant silver dollar. Or a medallion worn by someone's sweetheart.

❖   ❖   ❖

The country we passed en route to the next bridge near Brazoria could well be used for scenes in movies about ghosts, particularly on a day like this one. The rain gave an eerie look to the Spanish moss hanging in strips from the branches.

Ghost stories abound in the area. We read about one of those in a historical marker on Highway 36 north of Brazoria. The marker said the spot was near the site of the Brit Bailey Plantation, established in 1818 by James Briton Bailey. Bailey was a member of Austin's colony. He was tall, fearless, of Irish stock, and noted for his courage, integrity, eccentric behavior, and his love of liquor. He served as captain in the local militia and fought in battles preceding the Texas Revolution.

Prior to his death, he had made an unusual request. He wanted to be buried standing up, facing west, with his gun at his side. That way, he said, "Nobody could look down on me even in death."

Catherine Munson Foster tells about Bailey's ghost in her book, *Ghosts Along the Brazos*. She wrote:

There is a ghostly light that floats across a place called
Bailey's Prairie in southwest Texas, bobs along above the grass,
soars occasionally high into the trees, and often pauses in the
middle of a busy highway, frightening motorists out of their wits.
For more than a hundred years the light has been seen at inter-
vals and though its brilliance has been somewhat dimmed by the
passage of time, it still appears now and then, especially on dark
and rainy nights.

No one has yet come up with a scientific explanation, but old
timers of the area believe, or say they believe, that it is the ghost
of one Brit Bailey walking the prairie that still bears his name,
carrying a lantern, and seeking his long lost jug of whiskey.

The writer was so taken by the Bailey legend that she dedicated her
book to his ghost "with the hope that someday soon he will find his lost jug
and at long last can stand easy in his grave."

Another fascinating story related by Foster concerns Santa Anna, the
Mexican general captured at San Jacinto in the last battle of the Texas
Revolution. The story said he eventually was held at a plantation owned by
the Phelps family in this area. Santa Anna stayed at the plantation for more
than six months before being released in December 1836.

During that period the Mexican army made an attempt to free him. The
plan involved giving guards wine that contained a strong sleeping drug.
Several Mexican soldiers had concealed themselves in some nearby woods.
They had horses to be used in the escape.

The guards drank the wine and soon fell asleep. That's when the
Mexicans began creeping toward the house where General Santa Anna and
other prisoners were held. But, suddenly the barking of dogs shattered the
night's quietness. The would-be rescuers fled.

"Another attempt to free Santa Anna had failed," wrote Foster. "And all because of a pack of dogs. The only thing was, the Phelps' didn't have any dogs. Nor did their neighbors."

Another mystery in this area concerns a legend of phantom music that can be heard. Mrs. T.A. Humphries of Freeport wrote about this in an article in the *Freeport Facts*. The music has been heard near a thick stand of timber called Music Bend.

"A low weird musical sound comes without warning, increases in intensity until it fills the atmosphere, then gradually recedes. Some describe it as the music of violins. Some insist that it comes from the air, and some claim that it is supernatural. It is said that J. Greenville McNeel, who settled on the Gulf Prairie in 1822, was the first of Austin's colonists to hear the phantom music. He immediately went to New York for scientists but after a long investigation, they could find no reasonable explanation for the sound.

"A few years ago two young girls were drowned in the San Bernard and while searching for the bodies, the workers heard the heartbreaking strains of funeral music, as if played on violins. But apparently what they heard coming from the water was weird and ghostly music that they hoped to never hear again," she wrote.

It was easy to understand how those stories got started as we drove through the country with huge trees that had splotches of color like blood splattered from a slaughterhouse. Who knows, maybe that stirring of the moss we could see was caused by Brit Bailey's breath as he slouched his way through the swamp water looking for his whiskey.

CHAPTER FORTY-FIVE

Brazoria's Bridge to Nowhere

❖   ❖   ❖

Beneath bridges is not a good place for city folks to find pleasure.
That was evident by the cursing from the film crew as they waited.

"These @#$% bugs are getting an early breakfast from my legs,"
whispered one.

"What do you expect? We're beneath some @#$% bridge waiting
for some crazy old #$%^," answered another person.

The moon's light began to dim. Would he ever come?

❖   ❖   ❖

The beautiful old steel bridge over Highway 521 near Brazoria has earned the label, "the bridge to nowhere." That sounds like a putdown. It's not, though it did require some effort on our part to learn why the name was applied to the bridge built in 1939 and listed as a Texas Landmark and on the National Register of Historic Places.

We arrived at the three-span steel bridge in the early afternoon. The temperature stood at forty-five degrees. Brisk winds made us feel like we were standing in front of an open door leading to a frozen-food vault. We made our usual walk beneath the bridge and discovered the usual trash, including a couple of new items. One was a pile of what looked to be old pickup tires still on the rims. Near them was a big pile of electrical line. And then I saw a definite first . . . the heads and carcasses of two recently slain wild hogs.

Someone had slashed off the back strap of the animals. I felt a chill as I looked at the huge black heads with eyes that appeared to be staring at me.

I pulled Jane's coat tighter and walked up the bank to a historical marker that gave detailed facts about the bridge. It read:

> The town of Brazoria began in 1828 as a port and trading center in Stephen F. Austin's colony. Partially burned in 1836 during the Texas Revolution, it was rebuilt and served as a county seat until 1897. To escape floods and to enjoy a better life, the townspeople moved to "New Town" near the St. Louis, Brownsville, and Mexico railway in 1912. This town became "old town." The first traffic-bridge built across the Brazos River in this historic region in 1912 provided a vital link between eastern and western Brazoria County. Falling victim to the elements and the lack of maintenance, the wood-decked bridge fell into the river in the 1930s. Built in 1939, during the Great Depression, using local labor, county bond money and funds from the Public Works Administration, this [current] Brazoria bridge sustains the historic transportation route. It was nicknamed "The bridge that goes nowhere" before the soil embankments were built. This 1,124-foot concrete and steel bridge has three Parker-through truss spans. It is supported by concrete filled caisson and concrete piling and approaches composed of 14-concrete supported I beams with steel guard rails. An important example of its style, this Brazoria bridge is a significant part of Brazoria County history.

We looked upriver and could see a single piling that we later learned came from the 1912 bridge. We decided to drive to the local chamber office of this town, which is one of nine cities that compose Brazosport. A slick magazine given out by the Brazosport Chamber office states that the area is where the first Texas port was established and was the site of the Republic of Texas' first capitol.

It is where the group known as Stephen F. Austin's "Old 300" first stepped off the schooner *Lively*. The schooner landed near the mouth of the Brazos River in 1821 bringing men full of hope, courage, and the will to survive. They met the challenge of war that greeted them and achieved the reward that solidified them. After engaging in many hard-fought battles, they defeated General Antonio Lopez de Santa Anna. Texas became a republic. Their hardships and sacrifices were finally rewarded with the signing of the treaties of Velasco, which gave Texas its independence. Stephen F. Austin, a hero and driving force of the Texas Revolution, later died in West Columbia. Austin's body was transported down the Brazos River to Peach Point in present-day Jones Creek and buried with honors at Gulf Prairie Cemetery. In 1910, despite strong family objections, Austin's body was removed from his grave and transported by wagon to Brazoria and placed on a train to Austin, where his final resting place remains today at the State Cemetery.

However, the publication offers no reason of why the bridge here is called "the bridge to nowhere." Two people at the chamber office, Dinah Krause and Cowboy Sarles, had an idea.

"It used to be, the only way you could get to Lake Jackson was to go north and go over that bridge. It was the only way out," she said. "That meant driving many miles out of the way. So maybe that is how it got its name."

Russell Stanger said that before the bridge was built things were even worse. In an interview for the *Freeport Facts* newspaper, he recalled the days when there was no bridge and the effort and time it took to get to Brazoria. As a result, he said, "My own kin folks didn't know me in Brazoria. It was twenty-five miles to Brazoria through West Columbia instead of the three that the bridge provided." Sarles offered this explanation for the name.

"It pretty much goes nowhere," he said.

Krause said there are plans to build a new bridge. There are also plans to keep the old one and turn it into a hiking and walking bridge.

"We certainly don't want it torn down," she said.

We all shook hands and then we headed for the next bridge. En route, I remembered some information the Brazoria library had sent me about the bridge. I looked in a folder and found another story in the *Freeport Facts* that explained why the bridge got the name "the bridge to nowhere."

"The bridge received the nickname soon after it was built in 1939 because the ramp leading to the bridge had not been built," said Margarite Massey Smith, eighty-one, whose father C.W. Massey was a county commissioner at the time. "It was built on time, but there wasn't any money to build the ramps or the roads to the bridge. That is how it got its name."

Marie Beth Jones, chairwoman of the Brazoria County Historical Commission, agreed with those statements. "You couldn't get to it because the approaches weren't built. It was way up above any way you could get on it."

They did have one heckuva celebration to open the bridge. An article from the *Freeport Facts* estimated that "many hundreds had assembled on the bridge to witness this impressive ceremony." The Municipal Band of Houston, with twenty-five members had been invited to play. "This is a professional organization, and one of the best in the whole country. The music was charming," read the article.

The decorations included potted ferns and bouquets of flowers.

In contrast to this gay scene, the old ferry, anchored in the stream below, was draped in black, contrasting its sorrow in having lost its occupation with the joy of the people in having gained something better. But, while the old ferry is relegated to the things that have been but are not now, we must remember it kindly. It has done its work and done it well. It answered the purpose where there was nothing better. We must cherish it in memory as we do the oxcart and the flintlock gun, the scythe, the reaping hook and the spinning wheel. Farewell, noble old craft! You are old and crude and rough, but you have been faithful and that is a virtue.

Then Miss Mary Elease Williamson touched a button that dropped a bottle of champagne onto the bridge.

After reading all of this, Eddie and I decided we should go back for another look at the bridge as well as some of the area around it.

CHAPTER FORTY-SIX

Lake Jackson Bridge

❖   ❖   ❖

*She'd discovered many things about bridges in her research.
They had made the difference in many battles. They had furnished
links to people seeking new homelands. They had become words in
love songs.*

*She thought of these as she waited for the old man to come and
start playing. Then another thought came to her. Was this really
worth a story or was it turning a tender page from someone's life
into a sarcastic joke, like one told in the smoky shadows of a
pool hall?*

The wind howled through the bridge timbers.

❖   ❖   ❖

Frank Booth, who lives near the bridge to nowhere, has long studied
the history of this area. He looks like one of those early-day characters
with his long gray hair and lanky build. When we told him about our
search for stories about the bridges, he had several. His home is on a road
that follows the Brazos River.

"There used to be an old bridge right across the street that was known
as the 'horse bridge,'" he said. "The reason they called it that was because it
could not handle the weight of motor vehicles but it could handle the weight
of horses and wagons."

And he said we were standing near what had been the site of the first
two-story brick house built in Texas. Slaves made those bricks. "Wait just a
minute, and I'll give you something," he said.

As we stood in the wind and looked across the road at the muddy Brazos, he went into his house. He soon returned and handed us two bricks. They were thick and orange.

"I found those. They're all over the place," he said. "They were made by slaves."

He pointed to a historical marker across the street that marked the site of Jane Long's tavern. "I saw a letter that Sam Houston had written in response to somebody who had asked him why he didn't marry Jane Long. Houston had written, 'She wouldn't marry an old drunk like me.'" said Booth.

We walked across the street to read the marker. It said that Jane Herbert Williamson was born in 1798 and died in 1888. In 1812 she married Dr. James Long, a physician and soldier. They were granted land in Austin's colony in 1827 and opened a boardinghouse on this site in 1832.

"The busy port and tavern became a popular center of Anglo political activity here. She hosted a benefit for Austin in 1835 upon his release from a Mexican prison. That was attended by President Sam Houston, and many other famed early Texas pioneers," read the marker.

We stood there and looked at the site. Booth joined us. "In 1839 there were 5,000 people living here," he said. "By 1939 that had dropped to five hundred. The building of that bridge certainly has helped bring the area back."

We thanked him and headed for the bridge over FM 2004 west of Lake Jackson, which got its name from Major Abner Jackson. He established a sugar plantation and orchards along the shores of Lake Jackson during the 1800s.

The bridge is located near the Clemens State Prison. Signs in the area warn about picking up hitchhikers. I would have hated to be hitchhiking on that day. The wind and the mid-forty-degree temperature had dropped the chill factor down below the pleasant level. We looked at the bridge that is a huge arc sitting on large concrete pillars. We could not find any protection from the wind until Eddie noticed a fire built from logs being tended by a couple who were fishing.

"Let's ask them if we can share their fire," said Eddie.

We did and they said, "Certainly." I held my hands over the blaze and then backed up to the heat. It felt wonderful.

The couple talked about fishing. He told about catching a forty-pound blue catfish in this area recently. "Got a five-gallon bucket of meat off of him," the man said.

Then they told about catching gar, a long, skinny fish full of bones, and selling them for $5.

"I don't like them. But some people say they make great gumbo," he said.

I told the woman what we were doing and asked if she knew any stories about this bridge.

"Not really. I know it hasn't been here too long. And, we were certainly glad when they built it. Not only is the fishing pretty good here, but it makes getting to places much easier," she said.

We warmed ourselves some more and then ran to our vehicle. The woman laughed. "Bet you never thought looking at bridges would be this tough," she hollered.

We also laughed and drove onto the highway. We passed an entrance to a large farm or ranch that had huge gates topped by carved figures of playing cards from each suit.

"I think we have been dealt the joker as for having good weather to look at bridges today," I said.

"Do you want to finish this tomorrow?" asked Eddie. "We only have one more."

I thought about that possibility for a few minutes. "Why don't we look at the last one today and then we can head home tomorrow," I said.

Eddie agreed. We headed for Freeport and that last bridge.

CHAPTER FORTY-SEVEN

The Last Bridge

❖ ❖ ❖

Finally, when the sun looked like a red button from a giant's shirt, his music started. It made lonely echoes that filled the spaces beneath the bridge.

She listened. His creations were absolutely wonderful, like sounds made by a spring emptying its life into a remote mountain stream. She lifted her harmonica to her lips. She hesitated. Then she turned to the river and threw the instrument as far as she could. She heard a small splash in the Brazos.

"Come on, let's go," she said.

"Huh? Aren't you gonna play?" asked a cameraperson.

"No," she said. "I will not soil this man's memories. Let's go."

So they left just as he finished his first tune. So much for her national prize. She didn't care.

❖ ❖ ❖

Many people may overlook the historic portions of Freeport when they first enter this city and see the industrial plants with their myriad of pipes punching into the skies. But according to a history of Freeport's early years written by N.C. (Nat) Hickey, this area furnished hunting and fishing for the Karankawa Indians. Later the area became the base for Stephen F. Austin's efforts at colonizing Texas. And prior to the Civil War, it was the site of major plantations making use of the Brazos River for importing and exporting agricultural products.

Freeport's history is tied closely to the nearby city of Velasco that once lay at the mouth of the Brazos River. The hurricane of 1875 changed that, and the city lay dormant until 1891 when Velasco was moved four miles upstream. Then in 1891 the railroad came to this area when the Columbia Tap Rail extended service from Fort Worth to East Columbia. Steamboats worked the Brazos from here to East Columbia. Among those were the *Christine, Edna,* the famed *Hiawatha* and the *Idlewilde,* which pulled barges of sugarcane from the Clemens plantation to warehouses at Velasco. As late as the 1970s, pilings of these warehouses could be seen from the Velasco Memorial Bridge.

In 1925 voters approved a navigation district, which eventually diverted the Brazos River from its downstream course, creating a navigation channel. That also resulted in what today is known as the Old Brazos and the New Brazos.

Jonathan (J.B.) Parker works at the locks operated by the Corps of Engineers on the Intercoastal Waterway that empties into the New Brazos. We talked to him while he opened and closed the locks to allow boats to enter and leave the canal. He lives on Quintana Beach where he once was fire chief. We asked him if he had any unusual stories about bridges over the Brazos. He smiled.

"Yeah, I have a couple about the old bridge. The tides used to cause the bridge, which is a swinging bridge, to raise the middle floats so high vehicles would have a hard time getting across," he said. "I used to bring a fire engine that had a huge pump and try to pump the water from the floats to a level that would allow the vehicles to cross. But, many times a large RV would get hung and they would rip off a muffler or part of the undercarriage in getting off."

We asked him where the bridge over Highway 36 is. He pointed north.

"You can almost see it from here," he said. "Before you look at it, you should go into Freeport and look at the old railroad bridge. It is worth looking at."

We took his advice and headed for downtown Freeport. We soon found the old railroad bridge over the Old Brazos, a rotating bridge. The salt air has aged its parts, including the huge cogs that rotated and swung the bridge to the side to allow ships to pass through. One of the old cogs appeared to be rusted almost in half and sat partially out of the water. The bridge has massive lengths of cables, thick steel rivets, and iron cross members.

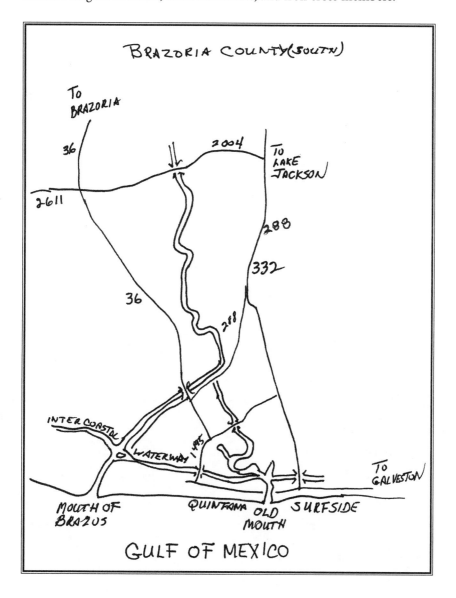

Shrimp boats were tied to docks close by. Gulls looked like they were playing a game of dive-bombing as they climbed high and then dove toward the water, sometimes gliding through the steel braces. Our noses filled with the strong smells of fish and diesel fuel.

After about an hour, we drove to Highways 288 and 36 and headed west. We came to the final bridge on our journey. It turned out to be the largest one we had seen.

We parked and made our last inspection. We found the usual abundance of trash, including a broken commode, soft drink and beer bottles, and old tires. Almost beneath the bridge, a large bird had made tracks that looked like somebody with three prongs tied to their feet had been walking there.

The height of the bridge muted the noise from traffic. A large flock of birds had built their nests under the bridge. Their cries sounded like

bitten-off ends of a tape recording. Nearby, two huge black grackles looked at us and erupted with "chireerp-erp, chireerp-erp" cries.

We walked around kicking at empty beer cans. Eddie picked up a discarded float from a fishing line. I didn't exactly have the feeling I thought I would have when we finally looked at the last bridge. Eddie obviously didn't either.

"Maybe we've been on the road too long," I said.

"Maybe so. I didn't even bring the champagne," said Eddie.

"I didn't either," I said.

"Well, let's go back to the cabin and celebrate the end of all of this," he said.

I agreed. We returned to the cabin and poured two generous drinks into coffee cups. We touched the cups and sipped. Eddie had bourbon and I had Scotch.

This railroad bridge at Freeport swivels so that boats can pass up and down the Brazos.

"Did you enjoy this?" I asked.

"Oh, yeah. I certainly did," said Eddie. "We met some really unusual people and saw a lot of history. Plus, getting to find out how many bridges are over the Brazos and see all of them has long been a goal of mine."

We replenished our drinks and stared outside.

"Did you enjoy this?" Eddie asked.

I pondered the question.

"Yeah, I did. I guess I liked the people we met the most. Also being in places where so much early Texas history took place," I said. "Yeah, I had a good time."

We were silent for a moment.

"I wish I had some deep philosophical statement to make about all of this," I said.

Eddie smiled. "You have. You said you enjoyed it," he said. "But, I have an idea. Why don't we go eat us a good meal somewhere tonight and then end this officially by looking at the mouth of the Brazos tomorrow and then heading home."

"That's a good idea," I said.

We finished our drinks and had a nice dinner in Freeport. We returned to our cabin and I immediately fell asleep. I didn't dream about bridges.

CHAPTER FORTY-EIGHT

Mouth of the Brazos

❖   ❖   ❖

The years passed bringing gray to his hair and a slight bend to his shoulders. Still he went to the bridge to play.

Sometimes he wondered why. Was he looking for more than the good feeling he got when he played? It had been so long, he really didn't know why he came there. Maybe he got some kind of perverse satisfaction, knowing he fulfilled the label people had placed on him . . . that crazy old man who plays beneath the bridge.

Regardless, he kept playing. And, every time he played his favorite, "I'll Fly Away." On this day, he played it last. He thought about shortening the number. He hit the part that went, "I'll fly away, oh glory." He hesitated. From the shadows came the answer.

"I'll fly away, fly away in the morning."

His heart began thundering but he kept playing. The answer kept coming. Finally he looked into the shadows. She stood there, like a piece of beautiful sunshine splitting clouds after a rain. Their notes blended together like the intricate beads of a fine weld, bringing happiness once again beneath the bridge.

Such is an episode from beneath the Brazos bridge. It's a story with a happy ending. Or as the song says, "When I die, hallelujah, bye and bye, I'll fly away."

❖   ❖   ❖

The sun looked like a ball of clay on fire, orange-colored like that clay once used by the slaves to make bricks. We paid for our rooms, and the clerk said, "Well, good-bye bridge searchers. Come back to see us."

We drove past an old house that had once been a famous boarding-house. It was built by the Jarvis family and was one of the original structures that had survived many great storms, including Carla that smashed the Texas coast in September 1961 with wind gusts estimated at 175 miles an hour.

We drove to Bryan Beach. Eddie stopped and pointed.

"There it is, the mouth of the Brazos," he said.

We walked over to Henry Mottu who was fishing.

"Is this the mouth of the Brazos?" I asked.

"Yeah, it is the mouth of the Brazos," he said.

He and Eddie began talking. I listened for a few minutes and then walked along the beach and looked at twisted piles of large trees. I tried to imagine how far they had come before being dumped here. Had some of them come from that country way up north where we had started this trip?

I walked past empty insect repellent cans and large egg cartons that had been torn in half. I passed several more fishermen and looked north toward Freeport. Haze blotted out the city's miniature skyline. But I thought I could see the outline of that last bridge.

I listened to the cries of gulls and the sounds of the roaring Gulf. I looked at more logs, whitened by the pounding of the salt water. Across on the other side sat a huge flock of white pelicans with those mouths that look like large scoops.

A piece of a trotline was tied to a log that had axe and saw cuts on it. I heard the cries of the gulls again. Suddenly an angry fisherman cursing with liberal use of the "F" word interrupted them. I looked to where he was standing. Apparently his line had become entangled so badly, he had had to cut it.

I thought about picking up something to remember all of this by. I looked down at the choices, beer bottles, plastic milk jugs, a plastic surgical glove, and a T-shirt. I said to hell with picking up anything.

I walked back to Eddie and Mottu.

"Hey, he told me you were writing a book about the bridges. So you can use my name. Write this down. I am fishing for black drum. I caught one that weighed about twelve pounds. You getting this down? Put this down, too. He was thirty-six inches long so I couldn't keep him. I can only keep those that are fourteen to thirty inches long. But, hey write this down. Henry Mottu caught a twelve-pound drum and threw it back. Okay?" he said.

He had baited his line and thrown it into the Brazos. "I work for Brown and Root. And, those waves are the actual mouth of the Brazos," he said. "Also, I use fresh dead mullet for bait. It's good. You write that down. It's okay."

I wrote it down. Then I looked at Eddie. "Let's go home," I said.

So the bridge searchers turned north and headed home.

A Word of Thanks

Many people generously helped me find information for this book. Among those I would like to mention are Jeanell Morris, recently retired Hood County Librarian, and her staff, including Carol Hengels and Heather Carmichael; my longtime friend Doc Keen, who furnished a great deal of historical information about bridges when this idea was first talked about; Eddie Lane, who not only came up with the idea of the book but also contributed much research and companionship during our travels; my son, Patrick McConal, who secured many pages of history of the bridges; Linda Brothers, who discovered and furnished the names of several individuals for interviews; and Jane, my lovely and patient wife, who not only made some of these trips with me but also helped edit the manuscript. And, lastly, I would like to thank my good friend Douglas Clarke, who not only edited the final version of the manuscript but boosted my enthusiasm during some rather trying times.

List of Brazos Bridges

Getting a list of the bridges over the Brazos turned out to be almost as hard as driving the length of the river to look at those structures. When Eddie Lane first proposed this idea, he had no idea how many bridges there were across the river. But, he figured, and so did I, that that information would be easily obtained. "Call the BRA (Brazos River Authority)," he said. "I'm certain they will have it."

However, the BRA, although helpful in furnishing information about the river, had no such list. "But, if you get such a list, we certainly would like to have a copy," said a spokesperson for the BRA.

Eventually, I contacted Teresa Scott-Tibbs, information coordinator of the bridge division of the Texas Department of Transportation, who furnished the information. She told me a fact that I had trouble digesting: There are more than 47,000 bridges over Texas rivers and creeks.

The list she supplied me for the Brazos River has a total of seventy-nine bridges. Included in this number are bridges over the Salt Fork of the Brazos, the Clear Fork, and the Little Brazos. The TDT list also counts a bridge that has two passages and four lanes as two bridges. Lane and I counted these as one bridge. These are the reasons that the TDT list total is higher than our list.

But, as Lane noted, "Be sure and point out that we crossed every durned one of these bridges."

Regardless, here's the list of bridges, their location, and some general information about each structure. And Eddie and I have been over every one of them.

COUNTY	HIGHWAY	YEAR BUILT	BRIDGE TYPE	LENGTH FT.	WIDTH FT.
Stonewall	FM-1835	1990	Simple Span Deck Concrete Slab & Girder-Pan Formed	360	31
	FM-1835	1989	Simple Span Deck Concrete Slab & Girder-Pan Formed	440	31
	FM-1263	1967	Simple Span Deck Concrete Slab & Girder-Pan Formed	400	28.3
Brazos	SH 21 WB	1986	Simple Span Deck PS Concrete Girder-Multiple	790	40
	SH 21 EB	1986	Simple Span Deck PS Concrete Girder-Multiple	790	40
	SH 105	1954	Continuous Deck Plate Girder Multiple	1738	29.5
	FM 60	2000	Simple Span Deck PS Concrete Girder-Multiple	659	85
Robertson	FM 979	1956	Simple Span Deck Concrete Slab, Flat	200	25.4
	FM 485	1957	Continuous Deck Plate Girder-Multiple	772	31.5
	FM 485	1941	Simple Span Deck Steel I-Beam	700	29.5
	US 79/ US 190	1949	Continuous Deck Concrete Slab, Flat	650	31.5
Knox	FM 286	2001	Simple Span Deck PS Concrete Girder-Multiple	840	34
	FM 267	2000	Simple Span Deck PS Concrete Girder-Multiple	980	34
	SH 6	1939	Simple Span Through Warren Truss, Parallel Chord	755	29.3
	SH 222	1960	Continuous Deck Steel I-Beam	800	36
Hood	FM 51	2000	Simple Span Deck PS Concrete Girder-Multiple	1724	42
	Loop 426	1968	Simple Span Deck Concrete Slab & Girder-Pan Formed	161	46.2
	Bus 377	1992	Simple Span Deck PS Concrete Girder-Multiple	1138	54
	US 377NB	1986	Simple Span Deck PS Concrete Girder-Multiple	825	52

COUNTY	HIGHWAY	YEAR BUILT	BRIDGE TYPE	LENGTH FT.	WIDTH FT.
Hood *(continued)*	US 377SB	1966	Continuous Deck Plate Girder-Multiple	825	33.1
	SH 144	2002	Simple Span Deck PS Concrete Girder-Multiple	120	67
Palo Pinto	FM 4 (Brazos River Trib)	1998	Simple Span Deck PS Concrete Girder-Multiple	86	32
	US 180	1948	Continuous Deck Plate Girder-Multiple	886	32
	US 281 `	1939	Continuous Through Continuous Truss	1138	28.9
	SH 16	1942	Arch Deck Masonry Arch	433	26.5
	FM 4	1956	Continuous Deck Steel I-Beam	882	29
Parker	IH 20 N	1934	Simple Span Through Parker Truss, Polygonal top Chord	892	27.2
	FM 1189	1962	Continuous Deck Steel I-Beam	859	31.1
	I 20WB	1970	Continuous Deck Plater Girder-Multiple	1280	42.1
	FM 2580	1979	Simple Span Deck PS Concrete Girder-Multiple	757	37.9
	I 20EB	1970	Continuous Deck Plate Girder-Multiple	1280	42.1
Somervell	US 67	1947	Continuous Through Continuous Truss	1197	29.3
	FM 200	2001	Simple Span Deck PS Concrete Girder-Multiple	684	32
Brazoria	FM 521	1939	Simple Span Through Parker Truss, Polygonal top Chord	1124	25.7
	SH 35	1958	Continuous Deck Plate Girder-Multiple	587	31.2
	FM 2004	1988	Simple Span Deck PS Concrete Girder-Multiple	1418	46.1
	FM 1462	1965	Continuous Deck Plate Girder, Var. Depth-Multiple	832	31.2
	FM 1495	1967	Continuous Deck Plate Girder, Var. Depth-Multiple	1820	35
	SH 36 EB	1984	Simple Span Deck PS Concrete Girder-Multiple	3269	41.8
	SH 36 WB	1984	Simple Span Deck PS Concrete Girder-Multiple	3269	42

County	Highway	Year Built	Bridge Type	Length Ft.	Width Ft.
Fort Bend	FM 723	1956	Continuous Deck Plate Girder w/Floor System	683	29.2
	US 59 SB	1971	Continuous Deck Plate Girder-Multiple	1160	43.7
	FM 1489	1967	Continuous Deck Plate Girder-Multiple	770	35.3
	US 59 NB	1971	Continuous Deck Plate Girder-Multiple	1160	43.7
	SH 99	1994	Continuous Deck WS Plate Girder-Multiple	1200	72.8
	US 90A WB	1965	Continuous Deck Plate Girder, Var. Depth-Multiple	942	31.2
	FM 1093	1965	Continuous Deck Plate Girder-Multiple	1337	31.2
	US 90A EB	1989	Continuous Deck WS Plate Girder, Var. Depth-Multiple	1087	44.4
Waller	FM 1458	1972	Continuous Deck Plate Girder-Multiple	1000	36.3
	US 290 EB	1972	Continuous Deck Plate Girder-Multiple	1320	44.2
	US 290 WB	1972	Continuous Deck Plate Girder-Multiple	1320	44.2
	US 290 WB (Brazos Relief)	1963	Simple Span Deck Concrete Slab & Girder-Pan Formed	607	31
	US 290 WB (Brazos Relief)	1963	Simple Span Deck Concrete Slab & Girder-Pan Formed	334	31
	FM 529	1969	Continuous Deck Plate Girder-Multiple	1000	35.3
	US 290 EB (Brazos Relief)	1981	Simple Span Deck Concrete Slab & Girder-Pan Formed	320	40.3
	US 290 WB	1963	Simple Span Deck Concrete Slab & Girder-Pan Formed	121	31
Bosque	FM 1713	1950	Simple Span Deck Plate Girder-Multiple	3054	27.8
	CR 1175 at Brazos Point	Not Available	Not Available	Not Available	Not Available
Falls	SH 7	1950	Simple Span Deck Concrete Slab, Flat	175	46
	FM 712	1976	Continuous Deck PS Concrete Girder-Multiple	700	27.8

County	Highway	Year Built	Bridge Type	Length Ft.	Width Ft.
Falls *(continued)*	SH 7	1962	Continuous Deck Plate Girder, Var. Depth-Multiple	678	33.2
	FM 413	1955	Continuous Deck Plate Girder-Multiple	671	29.2
Hill	SH 174	1950	Continuous Deck Continuous Truss	1295	29.2
McLennan	US 84	1951	Continuous Deck Plate Girder, Var. Depth, Multiple	936	66
	IH 35-NB-SB	1970	Continuous Deck Plate Girder-Multiple	600	61.7
	US 77 BUS SB-NB	1961	Continuous Deck Plate Girder-Multiple	891	44.5
	SH 6 (LP 340)	1984	Simple Span Deck PS Concrete Girder-Multiple	630	42
Baylor	US 183	1937	Simple Span Deck PS Concrete Girder-Multiple	825	80
Young	SH 79	1954	Simple Span Deck Concrete Girder-T Beam	240	32
	FM 1974	1958	Continuous Deck Steel I-Beam	351	27
	FM 1287	1956	Continuous Deck Steel I-Beam	781	29
	FM 209	1962	Continuous Deck Steel I-Beam	721	31
	FM 701	1958	Continuous Deck Steel I-Beam	292	25.3
	FM 701	1958	Continuous Deck Steel I-Beam	291	25.3
	SH 79	1954	Continuous Deck Plate Girder-Multiple	1070	32
	SH 67	1985	Continuous Deck PS Concrete Girder-Multiple	840	46
	US 380	1988	Simple Span Deck PS Concrete Girder-Multiple	1240	46
Austin	SH 159 (Brazos Relief)	1958	Simple Span Deck Concrete Slab & Girder-Pan Formed	152	31.2
	SH 159	Not Available	Not Available	Not Available	Not Available

Interviews

Petersen, Jewel; Frydek

Poole, Charles; Robertson County

Porter-Foley, Sue L; San Felipe

Preator, Cindy; Houston

Presley, Anne; Stephen F. Austin State Park

Reese, Dr. Travis; Rosenberg

Reese, Joan; Rosenberg

Rochelle, Buddy; Palo Pinto County

Sabruska, Paul; Simton

Salvato, Carolo; Wilderville

Sarles, Cowboy; Brazosport

Scaggs, Tom; Washington-on-the-Brazos

Scott-Tubbs, Teresa; Austin

Shaw, John; Lake Whitney

Short, Jerry; Newcastle

Shortes, Sue; Knox City

Sparks, Charlsie; Mineral Wells

Stallings, Carmen; Houston

Sydell, Jeanne; Smith Bend

Tacker, Renee; Wilderville

Taylor, Troy; Granbury

Texas Department of Transportation; Graham

Vechert, Kenneth; Burleigh

Warren, Wilese; Palo Pinto County

Waters, Jana; Falls County

Weinkauf, Dick; Smith Bend

White, Danny; Granbury

White, Gerald; Granbury

Wirt, Lloyd; Glen Rose

Wright, Tom; Lake Whitney

Wydermyer, Alvin; Waco

Yeager, Gene; Young County

Young, Lem; Whitney

Works Consulted

BOOKS AND ARTICLES

T. Lindsay Baker. *Building the Lone Star: An Illustrated Guide to Historic Sites.* College Station: Texas A&M University Press, 1986.

Roger Conger. "The Waco Suspension Bridge." *Texana,* Vol. 1, 3(Summer 1963), 181-224.

Roy Edwards. *History (of) Falls County, Texas.* Marlin, Texas: Compiled and published by the Old Settlers and Veterans Association of Falls County, 1947.

Catherine Munson Foster. *Ghosts Along the Brazos.* Waco, Texas: Texian Press, 1990.

William C. Foster. *Spanish Expeditions into Texas 1689-1768.* Austin: University of Texas Press, 1995.

John Graves. *Goodbye to a River.* 17th edition. New York: Alfred A. Knopf, 2001.

Fred Hartman. "Herald Coaster." *Richmond (Texas) Telegraph,* July 15, 1988.

Kenneth E. Hendrickson Jr. *The Waters of the Brazos: A History of the Brazos River Authority.* Waco, Texas: Texian Press, 1981.

Verne Huser. *Rivers of Texas.* College Station: Texas A&M University Press, 2000.

Julien Capers Hyer. *The Land of Beginning Again: The Romance of the Brazos.* Waco, Texas: Texian Press, 1970.

History of Marlin. Marlin, Texas: Marlin Chamber of Commerce, 2002.

Joachim McGraw, John W. Clark Jr., and Elizabeth A. Robbins, eds. *A Texas Legacy: The Old San Antonio Road and The Camino Reales: A Tricentennial History, 1691-1991,* Austin: Texas State Department of Highways and Public Transportation, 1991.

Father Jeremy Myers. *A Century of Faith.* Sherman, Texas: n.p., 1996.

Kate Nowak. *Painted Post Crossroads.* Gordon, Texas: n.p., Octrober 2002.

The Roads of Texas. Fredericksburg, Texas: Shearer Publishing, 1988.

Willard Robinson. *Texas Public Buildings of the 19th Century.* Published for the Amon Carter Museum of Western Art. Austin, TX: University of Texas Press, 1974.

Lucia St. Clair Robson. *Ride the Wind.* New York: Ballantine, 1985.

Darwin Spearing. *Roadside Geology of Texas.* Missoula, Montana: Mountain Press Publishing Co., 1991.

Harold Taft, and Ron Godbey. *Texas Weather.* Oklahoma City: England and May, 1975.

Texas Almanac. Dallas: *Dallas Morning News,* 2004-2005.

Thomas E. Turner. "Waco Suspension Bridge." *Texas Parade,* November 1964.

"Waco, Texas." *The Developer.* Vol. 10, 9(August 1903).

Sally Wasowski with Andy Wasowski. *Native Texas Plants: Landscaping Region by Region.* Houston: Gulf Publishing Co., 1991.

J.W. Williams. *Old Texas Trails.* Austin: Eakin Press, 1979.

Nath Winfield Jr., and Pamela Ashworth Puryear. *Sandbars and Sternwheelers: Steam Navigation on the Brazos.* College Station: Texas A&M University Press, 1976.

NEWSPAPERS CONSULTED

Dallas Morning News, Dallas, Texas, January 1933.

Fort Worth Star-Telegram, Fort Worth, Texas, July 1960.

Freeport Facts, Freeport, Texas, June 1927; August 8, 2002; September 23, 1938.

Galveston Weekly Journal, Galveston, Texas, November 1852.

Glen Rose Reporter, Glen Rose, Texas, January 9, 1945.

Marlin Democrat, Marlin, Texas, May 10-16, 1922.

Texas Gazette, published 1829-1832.

Waco News Tribune, Waco, Texas, May 16, 1952; December 18, 1969; November 21, 1974; May 23, 1983.

MISCELLANEOUS SOURCES

Gazetteer of Streams of Texas. Washington, D.C.: U.S. Department of Interior, 1919.

Handbook of Texas Online, http://www.tsha.utexas.edu/handbook/online/.

The National Register of Historic Places. Washington, D.C.: U.S. Department of Interior, December 1972.